Edward Ramsay

Reminiscences of Scottish life and character

Edward Ramsay

Reminiscences of Scottish life and character

ISBN/EAN: 9783741103094

Manufactured in Europe, USA, Canada, Australia, Japa

Cover: Foto ©ninafisch / pixelio.de

Manufactured and distributed by brebook publishing software
(www.brebook.com)

Edward Ramsay

Reminiscences of Scottish life and character

REMINISCENCES

OF

SCOTTISH LIFE AND CHARACTER

BY

E. B. RAMSAY, M.A., LL.D., F.R.S.E.

DEAN OF EDINBURGH

THE TWENTY-FIRST EDITION

EDINBURGH

EDMONSTON AND DOUGLAS

1872

CONTENTS.

CHAPTER VI.

PREFACE TO TWENTY-FIRST EDITION.

I AM desirous of explaining the circumstances under which another edition of the "Reminiscences of Scottish Life and Character" has been so soon brought before the public. It is a *bona fide* new edition, and really is the twenty-first edition of the work. It has not, however, grown out of the *last* edition, but from the edition which went before, namely the 19th. The 20th edition had been got up with more expense, as to paper, type, and embellishment, than any of those which had gone before. It was, in fact, to borrow an expression of French bibliopoles, *un edition de luxe.* The *price* was, of course, proportionally higher, and now the publishers are desirous of meeting the requirement for a *cheaper* edition. This has caused the 21st edition to be printed from the 19th, rather than from the 20th edition. One of the first uses I would make of this new edition is to correct an error into which we had fallen in copying the account of a Highland toast given to us by the respected minister of Moulin, at page 70. The printer has, by mistake, inserted a word that has no existence in the Gaelic language. The text reads—

"Lud ris! Lud ris! You again! you again!"

It should be

Sud ris! Sud ris! Yon again! yon again!

that is—"yon cheer again."

The demand for copies of this work on "Scottish Reminiscences," and of which the subjects are necessarily of a limited and local character—a demand which has taken place during the course of little more than fifteen years since its first publication—proves, I think, the correctness of the idea upon which it was first undertaken—viz. that it should depict a phase of national manners which was fast passing away, and thus, in however humble a department, contribute something to the materials of history, by exhibiting social customs and habits of thought which at a particular era were characteristic of a race. It may perhaps be very fairly said that the Reminiscences came out at a time specially suitable to rescue these features of national life and character from oblivion. They had *begun* to fade away, and many had, to the present generation, become obsolete. To give an example of the precarious duration of social habits, and of those circumstances which give rise to anecdotes such as I have recorded in the following pages.—At page 128 is an account of the pains taken by Lord Gardenstone to extend and improve his rising village of Laurencekirk; amongst other devices he had brought down, as settlers, a variety of artificers and workmen from England. With these he had introduced a *hatter* from Newcastle; but on taking him to church next day after his arrival, the poor man saw that he might decamp without loss of time, as he could not expect much success in his calling at Laurencekirk; in fact, he found Lord Gardenstone's and his own the only hats in the kirk—the men all wore then the flat Lowland bonnet. But how quickly times change! My excellent friend Mr. Gibbon of Johnstone, Lord Gardenstone's own place, which is near Laurencekirk, tells me that at the present time *one* solitary Lowland bonnet lingers in the parish.

I wish my readers always to bear in mind that these Reminiscences are meant to bear upon the changes which would include just such a revolution as this in the bonnet practice of Laurencekirk. There is no pretension to any researches of *antiquarian* character; they are in fact Reminiscences which come almost within personal recognition. A kind friend gave me anecdotes of the past in her hundredth year. In early life I was myself consigned to the care of my granduncle, Sir Alexander Ramsay, residing in Yorkshire, and he was born in 1715; so that I can go pretty far back on my own experience, and have thus become cognisant of many changes which might be expected as a consequence of such experience.

Dr. Gregory (of immortal mixture memory) used to tell a story of an old Highland chieftain, intended to show how such Celtic potentates were once held to be superior to all the usual considerations which affected ordinary mortals. The doctor, after due examination, had, in his usual decided and blunt manner, pronounced the liver of a Highlander to be at fault, and to be the cause of his ill-health. His patient, who could not but consider this as taking a great liberty with a Highland chieftain, roared out —"And what business is it of yours whether I have a liver or not?"

An amusing application of the Scottish territorial denominative system to the locality of London was narrated to me by a friend who witnessed it. A Scottish gentleman, who had never been in the metropolis, arrived fresh from the Highlands, and met a small party at the house of a London friend. A person was present of most agreeable manners, who delighted the Scotchman exceedingly. He heard the company frequently referring to this gentleman's residence in Piccadilly, to his house in Piccadilly, and so on. When addressed by the gentleman, he commenced his reply, anxious to pay him all due respect—"Indeed, Piccadilly," etc. He supposed Piccadilly must be his own territorial locality. Another instance of mistake, arising out of Scottish ignorance of London ways, was made by a North Briton on his first visit to the great city. He arrived at a hotel in Fleet Street, where many of the country coaches then put up. On the following morning he supposed that such a crowd as he encountered could only proceed from some "occasion,"* and must pass off in due time. Accord-

* A term used for dispensation of the Lord's Supper.

ingly, a friend from Scotland found him standing in a doorway, as if waiting for some one. His countryman asked him what made him stand there? to which he answered—"Ou, I was just stan'ing till the kirk had scaled." The ordinary appearance of his native borough made the crowd of Fleet Street suggest to him the idea of a church crowd passing out to their several homes, called in Scotland a "kirk scaling." A London street object called forth a similar simple remark from a Scotchman. He had come to London on his way to India, and for a few days had time to amuse himself by sight-seeing before his departure. He had been much struck with the appearance of the mounted sentinels at the Horse Guards, Whitehall, and bore them in remembrance during his Eastern sojourn. On his return, after a period of thirty years, on passing the Horse Guards, he looked up to one, and seeing him, as he thought, unchanged as to horse, position, and accoutrements, he exclaimed—"Od, friend, ye hae had a lang spell on't sin' I left," supposing him the identical sentinel he had seen before he sailed.

It is interesting to preserve national peculiarities which are thus passing away from us. One great pleasure I have had in their collection, and that is the numerous and sympathetic communications I have received from Scotchmen, I may literally say from Scotchmen *in all quarters of the world;* sometimes communicating very good examples of Scottish humour, and always expressing their great pleasure in reading, when in distant lands and foreign scenes, anecdotes which reminded them of Scotland, and of their ain days of "auld langsyne."

There is no mistaking the national attachment so strong in the Scottish character. Men return after long absence, in this respect, unchanged; whilst absent, however long a time, Scotchmen never forget their Scottish home. In all varieties of lands and climates their hearts ever turn towards the "land o' cakes and brither Scots." Scottish festivals are kept with Scottish feelings on "Greenland's icy mountains" or "India's coral strand." I received an amusing account of an ebullition of this patriotic feeling from my noble friend the late Marquis of Lothian, who met with it when travelling in India. He happened to arrive at a station upon the eve of St. Andrew's Day, and received an invitation to join a Scottish dinner-party in commemoration of old Scotland. There was a great deal of Scottish enthusiasm. There were *seven* sheep-heads (singed) down the table; and Lord Lothian told me that after dinner he sang with great applause "The Laird o' Cockpen."

Without disturbing the order of the materials as they are arranged in the body of the work, I would record here several anecdotes which bear upon the general subject which we have before us—viz. the illustration of Scottish manners and habits.

The quiet, dry, matter-of-fact with which Scotchmen of a particular class deal with the most solemn subjects, not intending any irreverence, supplies some curious subjects for such a work as the present. Anecdotes by which it is illustrated, although having sometimes an appearance of familiarity and even of irreverence, were never, I believe, at all intended to express a want of respect towards sacred things, although occasionally they may seem to go pretty near the wind. I am assured that the genuineness of the following anecdote is unquestionable, as my informant received it from the person to whom it occurred. A popular Anglican Nonconformist minister was residing with a family in Glasgow, while on a visit to that city, whither he had gone on a deputation from the Wesleyan Missionary Society. After dinner, in reply to an invitation to partake of some fine fruit, he mentioned to the family a curious circumstance concerning himself (which he had also mentioned repeatedly to my correspondent)—viz. that he had never in his life tasted an apple, pear, grape, or indeed any kind of green fruit. This fact seemed to evoke considerable surprise from the company, but a cautious Scotchman, of a practical matter-of-fact turn of mind, and who had listened with much unconcern, drily remarked: "It's a peety but ye had been in Paradise, and there micht na hae been ony faa." I have spoken (p. 23) of the cool matter-of-fact manner in which the awful questions connected with the funerals of friends are often approached by Scottish people, without the least intention or purpose of being irreverent or unfeeling. By the kindness of Mr. Lyon, I am enabled to give an authentic anecdote of a curious character, illustrative of this habit of mind; and I cannot do better than give it in his own words:—"An old tenant of my late father, George Lyon of Wester Ogil, many years ago, when on his deathbed, and his end near at hand, his wife thus addressed him: 'Willie, Willie, as lang as ye can speak, tell us are ye for your burial baps round or *square?*' Willie, having responded to this inquiry, was next asked if the *murners* were to have *glooes* (gloves) or mittens, the former being articles with fingers, the latter having only a thumb-piece; and Willie, having also answered this question, was allowed to depart in peace."

There could not be a better example of this familiar handling, without meaning offence, than one which has just been sent to me by a kind correspondent. I give her own words. "Happening to call on a poor neighbour, I asked after the children of a person who lived close by. She replied, 'They're no hame yet—gaed awa to the English Kirk to get *a clap o' the heid.*' It was the day of *confirmation* for St. Paul's. This definition of the 'outward and visible sign' would look rather odd in the Catechism. But the poor woman said it from no disrespect; it was merely her way of answering my question." A kind correspondent sends me an illustration of this quaint matter-of-fact view of a question as affecting the sentiments or the feelings. He tells me he knew an old lady who was a stout large woman, and who with this state of body had many ailments, which she bore cheerfully and patiently. When asked one day by a friend, "How she was keeping," she replied, "Ou, just meddling; there's *ower muckle o' me* to be a' weel at ae time." No Englishwoman would have given such an answer. The same class of character is very strongly marked in a story which used to be told by the late Mr. Constable, who was very fond of Scottish humour. He used to visit an old lady who was much attenuated by long illness, and on going up stairs one tremendously hot afternoon, the daughter was driving away the flies, which were very troublesome, and was saying, "These flies will eat up a' that remains o' my puir mither." The old lady opened her eyes, and the last words she spoke were, "What's left's guid eneuch for them."

Of the wise and shrewd judgment of the Scottish character, as bearing upon religious pretensions, I have an apt example from my friend Dr. Norman Macleod. During one of the late revivals in Scotland, a small farmer went about preaching with much fluency and zeal the doctrine of a "full assurance" of faith, and expressed his belief of it for himself in such extravagant terms as few men would venture upon who were humble and cautious against presumption. The preacher, being personally rather remarkable as a man of greedy and selfish views in life, excited some suspicion in the breast of an old sagacious countryman, a neighbour of Dr. Macleod, who asked what *he* thought of John as a preacher, and of his doctrine? Scratching his head, as if in some doubt, he replied, "I'm no verra sure o' Jock. I never ken't a man *sae sure o' Heaven and sae sweert** *to be gaing taet*." He showed his sagacity, for John was soon after in prison for theft.

Another story by Dr. Macleod gives a good idea of the Scottish matter-of-fact view of things being brought to bear upon a religious question without meaning to be profane or irreverent.

* Slow, reluctant.

He was on a Highland loch when a storm came on which threatened serious consequences. Dr. Macleod, himself a large powerful man, was accompanied by a clerical friend of diminutive size and small appearance, who began to speak seriously to the boatmen of their danger, and proposed that all present should join in prayer. "Na, na," said the chief boatman, "let the *little* ane gang to pray, but first the big ane maun tak an oar."

Illustrative of the same spirit was the reply of a Scotchman of the genuine old school to a relative of mine—"Boatie" of Deeside, of whom I have spoken, p. 72. He had been nearly lost in a squall, and saved after great exertion, and was told by my aunt that he should be grateful to Providence for his safety. The man, not meaning to be at all ungrateful, but viewing his preservation in the purely hard matter-of-fact light, quietly answered, "Weel, weel, Mrs. Russell; Providence here or Providence there, an I hadna worked sair mysell I had been drouned."

Old Mr. Downie, the parish minister of Banchory, was noted in my earliest days for his quiet, pithy remarks on men and things as they came before him. His reply to his son, of whose social position he had no very exalted opinion, was of this class. Young Downie had come to visit his father from the West Indies, and told him that on his return he was to be married to a lady whose high qualities and position he spoke of in extravagant terms. He assured his father that she was "quite young, was very rich, and very beautiful." "Aweel, Jemmy," said the old man, very quietly and very slily, "I'm thinking there maun be some *faut.*"

I think about as cool a Scottish "aside" as I know, was that of the old dealer who, when exhorting his son to practise honesty in his dealings, on the ground of its being the "best policy," quietly added, "*I hae tried baith.*"

But nothing could better illustrate this quiet pawky style for which our countrymen have been distinguished, than the old story of the piper and the wolves. A Scottish piper was passing through a deep forest. In the evening he sat down to take his supper. He had hardly begun, when a number of hungry wolves, prowling about for food, collected round him. In self-defence, the poor man began to throw pieces of his victuals to them, which they greedily devoured. When he had disposed of all, in a fit of despair he took his pipes and began to play. The unusual sound terrified the wolves, which, one and all, took to their heels and scampered off in every direction. On observing which, Sandy quietly remarked, "Od, an I'd kenned ye liket the pipes sae weel, I'd a gien ye a spring *afore* supper."

I can give a very shrewd observation, which will also serve as, "Aberdonice," an example of true Scottish phraseology. The anecdote which introduces it my correspondent thinks must belong to Laurencekirk or to Glenbervie. In the course of the week after the Sunday on which several elders had been set apart for the service of the parish, a knot of the parishioners had assembled at what was in all parishes a great place of resort for idle gossiping—the smiddy or blacksmith's workshop. The qualifications of the new elders were severely criticised. One of the speakers emphatically laid down that the minister should not have been satisfied, and had in fact made a most unfortunate choice. He was thus answered by another parish oracle—perhaps the schoolmaster, perhaps a weaver :—"Fat better culd the man dee nir he's dune ?—he bud tae big's dyke wi' the feal at fit o't." He meant there was no choice of material—he could only take what offered.

This imperturbable mode of looking at the events of life can, in fact, only be illustrated by familiar records of what has been said and done on ordinary occasions. The *most* cautious answer certainly on record is that of the Scotchman who, being asked if he could play the fiddle, warily answered, "He couldna say, for he had never tried." But take other cases better authenticated. For example : One tremendously hot day, during the old stage-coach system, I was going down to Portobello, when the coachman drew up to take in a gentleman who had hailed him on the road. He was evidently an Englishman—a fat man, and in a perfect state of "thaw and dissolution" from the heat and dust. He wiped himself, and exclaimed, as a remark addressed to the company generally, "D—d hot it is !" No one said anything for a time, till a voice from the corner drily remarked, "I dinna doubt, sir, but it may." The caution of the speaker against committing himself unreservedly to any proposition, however plausible, was quite delicious.

The following is a good specimen of the same humour:—A minister had been preaching against covetousness and the love of money, and had frequently repeated how "love of money was the root of all evil." Two old bodies walking home from church—one said, "An wasna the minister strang upo' the money?" "Nae doubt," said the other, rather hesitatingly; and added, "ay, but it's grand to hae the wee bit siller in your haund when ye gang an errand."

A more determined objection to giving a categorical answer occurred, as I have been assured, in regard to a more profound question than the degree of heat on a hot day. A party travelling on a railway got into a deep discussion on theological questions. Like Milton's spirits in Pandemonium, they had

"Reason'd high
Of providence, fore-knowledge, will, and fate—
Fix'd fate, free-will, fore-knowledge absolute—
And found no end, in wand'ring mazes lost."

A plain Scotchman present seemed much interested in these matters, and having expressed himself as not satisfied with the explanations which had been elicited in the course of discussion on a particular point regarding predestination, one of the party said to him that he had observed a minister in the adjoining compartment, and that when the train stopped at the next station a few minutes he could go and ask *his* opinion. The good man accordingly availed himself of the opportunity, and went to get hold of the minister who was, he had been informed, in the train. He returned in time to resume his own place, and when they had started again, the gentleman who had advised him, finding him not much disposed to voluntary communication, asked if he had seen the minister. "O, ay," he said," he had seen him." "And did you propose the question to him?" "O, ay." "And what did he say?" "O, he just said he didna ken, and what was mair, he didna *care!*"

I have still another specimen of this national, cool, and deliberative view of a question, which seems characteristic of the temperament of our good countrymen. Some time back, when it was not uncommon for challenges to be given and accepted for insults, or supposed insults, an English gentleman was entertaining a party at Inverness with an account of the wonders he had seen and the deeds he had performed in India, from whence he had lately arrived. He enlarged particularly upon the size of the tigers he had met with at different times in his travels, and, by way of corroborating his statements, assured the company that he had shot one himself considerably above forty feet long. A Scottish gentleman present, who thought that these narratives rather exceeded a traveller's allowed privileges, coolly said that no doubt those were very remarkable tigers; but that he could assure the gentleman there were in that northern part of the country some wonderful animals, and as an example he cited the existence of a skate-fish captured off Thurso, which exceeded half-an-acre in extent. The Englishman saw this was intended as a sarcasm against his own story; so he left the room in indignation, and sent his friend to demand satisfaction or an apology from the gentleman who had, he thought, insulted him. The narrator of the skate story coolly replied, "Weel, sir, gin yer freend will tak' a few feet aff the length o' his tiger, we'll see what can be dune about the breadth o' the skate." He was too cautious to commit himself to a rash or decided course of conduct. When the tiger was shortened he would take into consideration a reduction of superficial area in his skate.

A kind correspondent has sent me about as good a specimen of dry Scottish quiet humour as I know. A certain Aberdeenshire laird, who kept a very good poultry-yard, could not command a fresh egg for his breakfast, and felt much aggrieved by the want. One day, however, he met his grieve's wife with a nice basket, and very suspiciously going towards the market; on passing and speaking a word, he discovered the basket was full of beautiful white eggs. Next time he talked with his grieve, he said to him, "James, I like you very well, and I think you serve me faithfully, but I cannot say I admire your wife." To which the cool reply was, "Oh, 'deed, sir, I'm no surprised at that, for I dinna muckle admire her mysel'." The laird could say no more.

There is something very amusing in the idea of what may be called the "fitness of things," in regard to snuff-taking, which occurred to an honest Highlander, a genuine lover of sneeshin. At the door of the Blair-Athole Hotel he observed standing a magnificent man in full tartans, and noticed with much admiration the wide dimensions of his nostrils in a fine up-turned nose. He accosted him, and, as his most complimentary act, offered him his mull for a pinch. The stranger drew up, and rather haughtily said: "I never take snuff." "Oh," said the other, "that's a peety, for there's grand *accommodation!*"

I don't know a better example of the sly sarcasm than the following answer of a Scottish servant to the violent command of his enraged master. A well-known coarse and abusive Scottish law functionary, when driving out of his grounds, was shaken by his carriage coming in contact with a large stone at the gate. He was very angry, and ordered the gatekeeper to have it removed before his return. On driving home, however, he encountered another severe shock by the wheels coming in contact with the very same stone, which remained in the very same place. Still more irritated than before, in his usual coarse language he called the gatekeeper, and roared out: "You rascal, if you don't send that beastly stone to h—, I'll break your head." "Well," said the man quietly, and without meaning anything irreverent, "aiblins gin it were sent to heevan *it wad be mair out of your Lordship's way.*"

In the body of the Reminiscences various examples are given of the quiet self-sufficiency of domestics of the Scottish type. I heard of a boy making a very cool and determined exit from the house into which he had very lately been introduced. He had been told that he should be dismissed if he broke any of the china that was under his charge. On the morning of a great dinner-party he was entrusted (rather rashly) with a great load of plates, which he was to carry up-stairs from the kitchen to the dining-room, and which were piled up, and rested upon his two hands. In going up-stairs his foot slipped, and the plates were broken to atoms. He at once went up to the drawing-room, put his head in at the door, and shouted : "The plates are a' smashed, and I'm awa."

I have received the four following admirable anecdotes, illustrative of dry Scottish pawky humour, both lay and clerical, from an esteemed minister of the Scottish Church, the Rev. W. Mearns of Kineff. I have concluded that it would be best for me to record them nearly in the same words as his own kind communication of them.—An aged minister of the old school, Rev. Patrick Stewart, one Sunday took to the pulpit a sermon without observing that the first leaf or two were so worn and eaten away that he couldn't decipher or announce the text. He was not a man, however, to be embarrassed or taken aback by a matter of this sort, but at once intimated the state of matters to the congregation,—"My brethren, I find that the mice have made free with the beginning of my sermon, so that I cannot tell you whaur the text is; but we'll just begin whaur the mice have left aff, and we'll find out the text as we go along."

In the year 1843, shortly after the Disruption, a parish minister had left the manse and removed to about a mile's distance. His pony got loose one day, and galloped down the road in the direction of the old glebe. The minister's man in charge ran after the pony in a great fuss, and when passing a large farm-steading on the way, cried out to the farmer, who was sauntering about, but did not know what had taken place—"Oh, sir, did *ye* see the minister's shault?" "No, no," was the answer,—"but what's happened?" "Ou, sir, fat do ye think! the minister's shault's *got lowse* frae his tether, an I'm frichtened he's ta'en the road doun to the auld glebe." "Weel-a-wicht!"—was the shrewd clever rejoinder of the farmer, who was a keen supporter of the old parish church, "I wad *na* wonder at *that*. An' I'se warrant, gin the minister was gettin' *lowse* frae *his* tether, he wad jist tak the same road."

An old clerical friend upon Speyside, a confirmed old bachelor, on going up to the pulpit one Sunday to preach, found, after giving out the psalm, that he had forgotten his sermon. He accordingly stood up in the pulpit, stopped the singing which had commenced, and thus accosted his faithful domestic:—"Annie; I say, Annie, *we've* committed a mistak the day. Ye maun jist gang your waa's hame, and ye'll get my sermon oot o' my breek-pouch, an' we'll sing to the praise o' the Lord till ye come back again." Annie, of course, at once executed her important mission, and brought the sermon out of "the breek-pouch," and the service, so far as we heard, was completed without further interruption.

The same minister had also a very faithful "*minister's man*" who had been in his service for many years, and was engaged, at the time we speak of, to be married to the younger of the minister's two female servants.

Johnnie went up-stairs one evening to arrange details with the old gentleman, who immediately said to him,—"Ou, Johnnie man, is this you? Fat's this you're come aboot the nicht? Sit doun an' tell me."

"Weel, sir, I jist cam to tell you that I'm gaun to be married, an' I wint to settle fat day'll be convenient for you."

"Vera weel, Johnnie man, but wha is't that you're takin'?"

"Ou," says Johnnie, "I'm no gaun far for a wife, for I'm jist takin' the lassie doun in your kitchen, an' we're gaun to be proclaimed upo' *Sabbath;* an' we'll gie you as little trouble as we can, an' jist come up the stairs ony evenin' convenient for you, sir, an' get it a' dune here by yoursel, sir."

"Weel, weel, Johnnie, I sall be *rale gled* to settle some nicht neist week wi' you baith. An' I'm rale happy to hear a' this, for," added the good old bachelor, at this time above *fourscore* years old, "in *my* opinion, Johnnie, marriage is a *vera harmless amusement.*"

By the kindness of Dr. Begg, I have a most amusing anecdote to illustrate how deeply long-tried associations were mixed up with the habits of life in the older generation. A junior minister having to assist at a church in a remote part of Aberdeenshire, the parochial minister (one of the old school) promised his young friend a good glass of whisky-toddy after all was over, adding slily and very significantly, "and gude *smuggled* whusky." His southron guest thought it incumbent to say, "Ah, minister, that's wrong, is it not? you know it is contrary to Act of Parliament." The old Aberdonian could not so easily give up his fine whisky, so he quietly said, "Oh, Acts o' Parliament lose their breath before they get to Aberdeenshire."

The Scottish clergy, from having mixed so little with life, were often men of simple habits and of very childlike notions. The opinions and feelings which they expressed were often of a cast, which, amongst persons of more experience, would appear to be not always quite consistent with the clerical character. In them it arose from their having nothing *conventional* about them. Thus I have heard of an old bachelor clergyman whose landlady declared he used to express an opinion of his dinner by the grace which he made to follow. When he had had a good dinner which pleased him, and a good glass of beer with it, he poured forth the grace, "For the riches of thy bounty and its blessings we offer our thanks." When he had had poor fare and poor beer, his grace was, "We thank thee for the least of these thy mercies."

I recollect my friend, the late Mr. Ogilvy of Tannadice, who had much of the dry quaint humour which we speak of, making use of an expression which was often used in that part of the country fifty or sixty years ago, without any idea of irreverence towards a subject of the most awful consideration. I had asked him if a neighbour of his were still alive whom I had remembered as a very old man. His quiet answer was —"Alive! Hout, ay. I'm thinking Jemmy means to live and blaw the last trumpet!"

My dear friend, the late Rev. Dr. John Hunter, told me an exquisite anecdote illustrative of the pawky Scotch view, taken by a Scottish minister, of domestic matters. One of the ministers of Edinburgh, a man of dry humour, had a daughter who had for some time passed the period of youth and of beauty. She had become an Episcopalian, an event which the Doctor accepted with much good-nature, and he was asking her one day if she did not intend to be confirmed. "Well," she said, "I don't know. I understand Mr. Craig always kisses the candidates whom he prepares, and I could not stand that." "Indeed, Jeanie," said the Doctor slily, "gin Edward Craig *were* to gie ye a kiss, I dinna think ye would be muckle the waur."

At page 13 is an answer given to a traveller, who admired the number of churches in a town through which they were travelling, as sure indication of an abundant prevalence of religious feeling. The answer implied that curstness (or crabbedness) of man's nature, that the spirit of party, or, in short, other motives than piety, *might* cause churches to be built. This sentiment was stated in what, I should hope, is a most extravagant form, at a meeting of ploughmen, of which I read an account, lately held at Ratho, upon quite a different question from church-building. One of the speakers commenced his address by stating that he had heard his "mither" give forth the sentiment: "*The mair kirks the mair sin.*"

Many anecdotes characteristic of the Scottish peasant often turn upon words and ideas connected with Holy Scripture. This is not to be considered as in any sense profane or irreverent; but it arises from the Bible being to the peasantry of an older generation their library—their only book. We have constant indications of this almost exclusive familiarity with Scripture ideas. At the late ceremonial in the north, when the Archbishop of Canterbury laid the foundation of a Bishop's Church at Inverness, a number of persons, amid the general interest and kindly feeling displayed by the inhabitants, were viewing the procession from a hill as it passed along. When the clergy, to the number of sixty, came on, an old woman, who was watching the whole scene with some jealousy, exclaimed, at sight of the surplices, "There they go, the *whited* sepulchres!" I received another anecdote illustrative of the same remark from an esteemed minister of the Free Church: I mean of the hold which Scripture expressions have upon the minds of our Scottish peasantry. One of his flock was a sick nervous woman, who hardly ever left the house. But one fine afternoon, when she was left alone, she fancied she would like to get a little air in the field adjoining the house. Accordingly she put on a bonnet and wrapped herself in a huge red shawl. Creeping along the dyke-side, some cattle were attracted towards her, and first one and then another gathered round, and she took shelter in the ditch till she was relieved by some one coming up to her rescue. She afterwards described her feelings to her minister in strong language, adding, "And eh, sir! when I lay by the dyke, and the beasts round a' glowering at me, I thocht what Dauvid maun hae felt when he said—'Many bulls have compassed me; strong bulls of Bashan have beset me round.'"

With the plainness and pungency of the old-fashioned Scottish language there was sometimes a coarseness of expression, which, although commonly repeated in the Scottish drawing-room of last century, could not now be tolerated. An example of a very plain and downright address of a laird has been recorded in the annals of "Forfarshire Lairdship." He had married one of the Misses Guthrie, who had a strong feeling towards the Presbyterian faith in which she had been brought up, although her husband was one of the zealous old school of Episcopalians. The young wife had invited her old friend, the parish minister, to tea, and had given him a splendid "*four hours.*" Ere the table was cleared the laird came in unexpectedly, and thus expressed his indignation, not very delicately, at what he considered an unwarrantable exercise of hospitality at his cost—"Helen Guthrie, ye'll no think to save yer ain saul at the expense of my meal-girnel!"

The answer of an old woman under examination by the minister to the question from the Shorter Catechism—"What are the *decrees* of God?" could not have been surpassed by the General Assembly of the Kirk, or even the Synod of Dort—"Indeed, sir, He kens that best Himsell." We have an answer analogous to that, though not so pungent, in a catechumen of the late Dr. Johnston of Leith. She answered his own question, patting him on the shoulder—"'Deed, just tell it yersell, *bonny* doctor (he was a very handsome man); naebody can tell it better."

To pass from the answers of "persons come to years of discretion"—I have, at pages 25 and 165, given examples of peculiar traits of character set forth in the answers of mere *children*, and no doubt a most amusing collection might be made of very juvenile "Scottish Reminiscences." One of these is now a very old story, and has long been current amongst us:—A little boy who attended a day-school in the neighbourhood, when he came home in the evening was always asked how he stood in his own class. The invariable answer made was, "I'm second dux," which means in Scottish academical language second from the top of the class. As his habits of application at home did not quite bear out the claim to so distinguished a literary position at school, one of the family ventured to ask what was the number in the class to which he was attached. After some hesitation he was obliged to admit: "Ou, there's jist me and *anither* lass." It was a very *practical* answer of the little girl, when asked the meaning of "darkness," as it occurred in Scripture reading—"Ou, just steek your een." The same examiner asked the class what was the "pestilence that walketh in darkness?" After consideration a little boy answered—"Ou, it's just *bugs*."

I did not anticipate when I introduced this answer, which I received from my nephew Sir Alexander Ramsay, that it would call forth a comment so interesting as one which I have received from Dr. Barber of

Ulverston. He sends me an extract from Matthew's *Translation of the Bible*, which he received from Rev. L. R. Ayre, who possesses a copy of date 1553, from which it appears that Psalm xci. 5 was thus translated by Matthew, who adopted his translation from Coverdale and Tyndale :—" So that thou shalt not need to be afrayed for any bugge by nyght, nor for the arrow that flyeth by day." * Dr. Barber ingeniously remarks —" Is it possible the little boy's mother had one of these old Bibles, or is it merely a coincidence ?"

I have said before, and I would repeat the remark again and again, that the object of this work is *not* to string together mere funny stories, or to collect amusing anecdotes. We have seen such collections, in which many of the anecdotes are mere Joe Millers translated into Scotch. The purport of these pages has been throughout to illustrate Scottish life and character, by bringing forward those modes and forms of expression by which alone our national peculiarities can be familiarly illustrated and explained. Besides Scottish replies and expressions which are most characteristic—and in fact unique for dry humour, for quaint and exquisite wit—I have (pages 87 and 135) entered upon the question of dialect and proverbs. There can be no doubt there is a force and beauty in our Scottish *phraseology*, as well as a quaint humour, considered merely *as* phraseology, peculiar to itself. I

* The truth is, in old English usage "bug" signifies a spectre or anything that is frightful. Thus in Henry VI., 3d part, act v. sc. ii.—" For Warwick was a *bug* that feared us all."

have already (page 88) spoken of the phrase "Auld lang-syne," and of other words, which may be compared in their Anglican and Scottish form. Take the familiar term common to many singing-birds. The English word linnet does not, to my mind, convey so much of simple beauty and of pastoral ideas as belong to our Scottish word LINTIE.

I recollect hearing the Rev. Dr. Norman Macleod give a most interesting account of his visit to Canada. In the course of his eloquent narrative he mentioned a conversation he had with a Scottish emigrant, who in general terms spoke favourably and gratefully of his position in his adopted country. But he could not help making this exception when he thought of the "banks and braes o' bonny Doon"—"But oh, sir," he said, "there are nae *linties* i' the wuds." How touching the words in his own dialect! The North American woods, although full of birds of beautiful plumage, it is well known, have no singing-birds.

A worthy Scottish Episcopal minister one day met a townsman, a breeder and dealer in singing-birds. The man told him he had just had a child born in his family, and asked him if he would baptize it. He thought the minister could not resist the offer of a bird. "Eh, Maister Shaw," he said, "if ye'll jist do it, I hae a fine lintie the now, and if ye'll do it I'll gie ye the lintie." He quite thought that this would settle the matter!

By these remarks I mean to express the feeling that the word *lintie* conveys to my mind more of tenderness and endearment towards the little songster than linnet. And this leads me to a remark (which I do not remember to have met with) that Scottish dialects are peculiarly rich in such terms of endearment, more so than the pure Anglican. Without at all pretending to exhaust the subject, I may cite the following as examples of the class of terms I speak of. Take the names for parents—"Daddie" and Minnie;" names for children, "My wee bit lady" or "laddie," "My wee bit lamb;" of a general nature, "My ain kind dearie." "Dawtie," especially used to young people, described by Jamieson a darling or favourite, one who is *dawted*—*i.e.* fondled or caressed. My "joe" expresses affection with familiarity, evidently derived from *joy*, an easy transition—as "My joe, Janet;" "John Anderson, my joe, John." Of this character is Burns's address to a wife, "My winsome"—*i.e.* charming, engaging—"wee thing;" also to a wife, "My winsome marrow"—the latter word signifying a dear companion, one of a pair closely allied to each other; also the address of Rob the Ranter to Maggie Lauder, "My bonnie bird." Now, we would remark, upon this abundant nomenclature of kindly expressions in the Scottish dialect, that it assumes an interesting position as taken in connection with the Scottish Life and *Character*, and as a set-off against a frequent short and *grumpy* manner. It indicates how often there must be a current of tenderness and affection in the Scottish heart, which is so frequently represented to be, like its climate, "stern and wild." There could not be such *terms* were the feelings they express unknown. I believe it often happens that in the Scottish character there is a vein of deep and kindly feeling lying hid under a short and hard and somewhat stern manner. Hence has arisen the Scottish saying which is applicable to such cases—"His girn's waur than his bite:" his disposition is of a softer nature than his words and manner would often lead you to suppose.

There are two admirable articles in *Blackwood's Magazine*, in the numbers for November and December 1870, upon this subject. The writer abundantly vindicates the point and humour of the Scottish tongue. Who can resist, for example, the epithet applied by Meg Merrilees to an unsuccessful probationer for admission to the ministry:—"a sticket stibler"? Take the sufficiency of Holy Scripture as a pledge for any one's salvation:—"There's eneuch between the brods o' the Testament to save the biggest sinner i' the warld." I heard an old Scottish Episcopalian thus pithily describe the hasty and irreverent manner of a young Englishman:—"He ribbled aff the prayers like a man at the heid o' a regiment." A large family of young children has been termed "a great sma' family." It was a delicious dry rejoinder to the question—"Are you Mr. so and so?" "It's a' that's to be had for him." I have heard an old Scottish gentleman direct his servant to mend the fire by saying, "I think, Dauvid, we wadna be the waur o' some coals."

The stories of humorous encounters between ministers and their hearers are numerous, and are pretty plentifully scattered through our pages. Some of them I had from ministers themselves, and though often seasoned with dry and caustic humour, they never indicate appearance of bitterness or ill-feeling between the parties. As an example, a clergyman thought his people were making rather an unconscionable objection to his using a MS. in delivering his sermon. They urged, "What gars ye tak up your bit papers to the pu'pit?" He replied, that it was best, for really he could not remember his sermon, and must have his paper. "Weel, weel, minister, then dinna expect that *we* can remember them."

Some of these encounters arise out of the old question of sleeping in church (pp. 27, etc.) For example—"I see, James, that you tak a bit nap in the kirk," said a minister to one of his people; "can ye no tak a mull with you? and when you become heavy an extra pinch would keep you up." "Maybe it wad," said James, "but pit you the sneeshin intil your sermon, minister, and maybe that'll serve the same purpose."

Of the many *betheral* stories, which are now passing fast away, I may add one to those at p. 208, as bearing upon the self-importance which once used to characterise the betheral family. One of them being asked to name some one whom he thought he could recommend as suitable for that office in a certain neighbouring parish, answered with great solemnity—"If it had been a *minister* now ye had asked me to recommend, I could hae gien you some help. But to recommend a betheral is a different matter, and needs to be weel considered."

Mr. Turnbull of Dundee kindly sends me an excellent anecdote of the "Bethrel" type (pages 201, 206-11), which illustrates the *esprit de corps* of the bethrelian mind. The late Dr. Robertson of Glasgow had, while in the parish of Mains, a quaint old church attendant of the name of Walter Nicoll, commonly called "Watty Nuckle," whom he invited to come and visit him after he had been removed to Glasgow. Watty accordingly ventured on the (to him) terrible journey, and was received by the Doctor with great kindness. The Doctor, amongst other sights, took him to see the Cathedral Church, and showed him all through it, and after they were coming away the Doctor asked Watty what he thought of it, and if it was not better than the Mains Church. Watty shook his head, and said, "Aweel, sir, you see she's bigger; but she has nae laft, and she's sair fashed wi' thae pillars."

On the same subject of beadle peculiarities, I have received from Mrs. Mearns of Kineff Manse an exquisitely characteristic illustration of beadle *professional* habits being made to bear upon the tender passion:—A certain beadle had fancied the manse housemaid, but at a loss for an opportunity to declare himself, one day—a Sunday—when his duties were ended, he looked sheepish, and said, "Mary, wad *ye* tak a turn, Mary?" He led her to the churchyard, and pointing with his finger, got out, "My fowk lie there, Mary; wad ye like to lie there?" The *grave* hint was taken, and she became his wife, but does not yet lie *there*.

Mention is made (pp. 126-127) of John Clerk, who

was known as a Scotch Judge under the title of Lord Eldin. He was a man remarkable at the bar and on the bench for his dry, sarcastic, and (I might add) *caustic* humour, of which many authentic examples might be noted besides those referred to in the body of the work. His defence of a young friend, who was an advocate, and had incurred the displeasure of the Judges, has often been repeated. Mr. Clerk had been called upon to offer his apologies for disrespect, or implied disrespect, in his manner of addressing the Bench. The advocate had given great offence by expressing his "*astonishment*" at something which had emanated from their Lordships, implying by it his disapproval. He got Lord Eldin, who was connected with him, to make an apology for him. But Clerk could not resist his humorous vein by very equivocally adding, "My client has expressed his astonishment, my Lords, at what he had met with here; if my young friend had known this court as long as I have, he would have been *astonished at nothing*."

A kind, though anonymous correspondent, has sent me a characteristic anecdote, which has strong internal evidence of being genuine. When Clerk was raised to the bench he presented his credentials to the Court, and, according to custom, was received by the presiding Judge—who, on this occasion, in a somewhat sarcastic tone, referred to the delay which had taken place in his reaching a position for which he had so long been qualified, and to which he must have long aspired. He hinted at the long absence of the Whig party from political power as the cause of this delay, which offended Clerk; and he paid it off by intimating in his pithy and bitter tone, which he could so well assume, that it was not of so much consequence—"Now ye see, my Lord, I didna get just sae soon doited as some o' your Lordships did."

Under this head I should like to introduce a characteristic little Scottish scene, which my cousin, the late Sir Thomas Burnett of Leys, used to describe with great humour. Sir Thomas had a tenant on his estate, a very shrewd clever man, whom he was sometimes in the habit of consulting about country matters. On one occasion he came over to Crathes Castle, and asked to see Sir Thomas. He was accordingly ushered in, accompanied by a young man of very simple appearance, who gazed about the room in a stupid vacant manner. The old man began by saying that he understood there was a farm on the estate to be let, and that he knew a very fine young man whom he wished to recommend as tenant. He said he had plenty of *siller*, and had studied farming on the most approved principles—sheep-farming in the Highlands, cattle-farming in the Lowlands, and so forth, and, in short, was a model farmer. When he had finished his statement, Sir Thomas, looking very significantly at his companion, addressed the old man (as he was usually addressed in the county by the name of his farm)—"Well, Drummy, and is this your friend whom you propose for the farm?" to which Drummy replied, "Oh fie, na. Hout! that is a kind o' a *Feel*, a friend (*i.e.* a relation) of the wife's, and I just brought him over wi' me to show him the place."

One very interesting feature belonging to Scottish life and social habits is, to a certain extent, becoming with many a matter of reminiscence and of the past—I mean *Poetry in the Scottish dialect.* It is becoming a matter of history, in so far as we find that it has for some time ceased to be cultivated with much ardour or to attract much popularity. In fact, since the time of Burns, it has been losing its hold on the public mind. It is a remarkable fact, that neither Scott nor Wilson, both admirers of Burns, both copious writers of poetry themselves, both also so distinguished as writers of Scottish *prose,* should have written any poetry strictly in the form of pure Scottish dialect. "Jock of Hazeldean" I hardly admit to be an exception. It is not Scottish. If, indeed, Sir Walter wrote the scrap of the beautiful ballad in the "Antiquary"—

> Now, haud your tongue, baith wife and carle,
> And listen, great and sma',
> And I will sing of Glenallan's Earl,
> That fought at the red Harlaw"—

one cannot but regret that he had not written more of the same. Campbell, a poet and a Scotchman, has not attempted it. In short, we do not find poetry in the Scottish dialect at all *kept up* in Scotland. It is every year becoming more a matter of research and reminiscence. Nothing new is added to the old stock, and indeed it is surprising to see the ignorance and want of interest displayed by many young persons in this department of literature. How few read the works of Allan Ramsay, once so popular, and still so full of pastoral imagery? There are occasionally new editions of the *Gentle Shepherd*, but I suspect for a limited class of readers. I am assured the boys of the High School, Academy, etc., do not care even for Burns. As poetry in the Scottish dialect is thus slipping away from the public Scottish mind, I thought it very suitable to a work of this character upon "Scottish Reminiscences" to supply a list of modern *Scottish dialect writers.* This I am able to provide by the kindness of our distinguished antiquary, Mr. David Laing—the fulness and correctness of whose acquirements are only equalled by his readiness and courtesy in communicating his information to others:—

Scottish Poets of the Last Century.

Allan Ramsay. B. 1686. D. 1757. His *Gentle Shepherd*, completed in 1725, and his *Collected Poems* in 1721-1728.

It cannot be said there was any want of successors, however obscure, following in the same track. Those chiefly deserving of notice were—

Alexander Ross of Lochlee. B. 1700. D. 1783. *The Fortunate Shepherdess.*

Robert Fergusson. B. 1750. D. 1774. *Leith Races, Caller Oysters*, etc.

Rev. John Skinner. B. 1721. D. 1807. *Tullochgorum.*

Robert Burns. B. 1759. D. 1796.

Alexander, Fourth Duke of Gordon. B. 1743. D. 1827. *Cauld Kail in Aberdeen.*

Alexander Wilson of Paisley, who latterly distinguished himself as an American ornithologist. B. 1766. D. 1813. *Watty and Meg.*

Hector Macneill. B. 1746. D. 1818. *Will and Jean.*

Robert Tannahill. B. 1774. D. 1810. *Songs.*

James Hogg. B. 1772. D. 1835.

Allan Cunningham. B. 1784. D. 1842.

We must firmly believe, however, that obsolete as the dialect of Scotland may become, and its words and expressions a matter of tradition and of reminiscence with many, still there are Scottish lines, and broad Scottish lines, which can never cease to hold their place in the affections and the admiration of innumerable hearts whom they have charmed. Can the choice and popular Scottish verses, endeared to us by so many kindly associations of the past, and by so many beauties and poetical graces of their own, ever lose their attractions for a Scottish heart? Can the charm ever die of such strains as "Ye Banks and Braes o' Bonny Doon," by Robert Burns; "I'm wearin' awa, Jean," by Lady Nairne; "Young Jamie lo'ed me weel," by Lady A. Lindsay; "Tullochgorum," by Rev. J. Skinner of Langside; "Roy's Wife," by Mrs. Grant of Laggan; "Farewell to Lochaber," by Allan Ramsay, etc. etc.?

I think one subsidiary cause for permanency in the

popularity still belonging to particular Scottish *songs* has proceeded from their association with Scottish *music.* The melodies of Scotland can never die. In the best of these compositions there is a pathos and a feeling which must preserve them, however simple in their construction, from being vulgar or commonplace. Mendelssohn did not disdain taking Scottish airs as themes for the exercise of his profound science and his exquisite taste. It must, I think, be admitted that singing of Scottish songs in the perfection of their style—at once pathetic, graceful, and characteristic—is not so often met with as to remove all apprehension that ere long they may become matters only of reminiscence. Many accomplished musicians often neglect entirely the cultivation of their native melodies, under the idea of their being inconsistent with the elegance and science of high-class music. They commit a mistake. When judiciously and tastefully performed, it is a charming style of music, and will always give pleasure to the intelligent hearer. I have heard two young friends, who have attained great skill in scientific and elaborate compositions, execute the simple song of "Low down in the Broom," with an effect I shall not easily forget. Who that has heard the Countess of Essex, when Miss Stephens, sing "Auld Robin Gray," can ever lose the impression of her heart-touching notes? In the case of "Auld Robin Gray," the song composed by Lady Anne Lindsay, although very beautiful in itself, has been, I think, a good deal indebted to the air for its great and continued popularity. The history of that tender and appropriate melody is somewhat curious and not generally known. The author was *not* a Scotchman. It was composed by the Rev. Mr. Leves, rector of Wrington in Somersetshire, either early in this century or just at the close of the last. Mr. Leves was fond of music, and composed several songs, but none ever gained any notice except his "Auld Robin Gray," the popularity of which has been marvellous. I knew the family when I lived in Somersetshire, and had met them in Bath. Mr. Leves composed the air for his daughter, Miss Bessy Leves, who was a pretty girl and a pretty singer.

I cannot but deeply regret to think that I should in these pages have any ground for classing Scottish poetry and Scottish airs amongst "Reminiscences." It is a department of literature where, of course, there must be *selection*, but I am convinced it will repay a careful cultivation. I would recommend, as a copious and judicious selection of Scottish *tunes*, "The Scottish Minstrel," by R. A. Smith (Purdie, Edinburgh). There are the *words*, also, of a vast number of Scottish songs, but the account of their *authorship* is very defective. Then, again, for the fine Scottish ballads of an older period, we have two admirable collections—one by Mr. R. Chambers, and one by the late Professor Aytoun. For Scottish dialect songs of the more modern type, a copious collection will be found (exclusive of Burns and Allan Ramsay) in small volumes published by David Robertson, Glasgow, at intervals from 1832 to 1853, under the title of *Whistlebinkie*.

But there are more than lines of Scottish poetry

which may become matter of reminiscence, and more than Scottish melodies which may be forgotten. There are strains of Scottish PSALMODY which may have lost their charm and their hold with Scottish people. That such psalmody, of a peculiar Scottish class and character, *has* existed, no one can doubt who has knowledge or recollection of past days. In the glens and retired passes, where those who fled from persecution met together—on the moors and heaths, where men suffering for their faith took refuge—in the humble worship of the cottar's fireside, airs of sacred Scottish melody were heard to "beet"* the heavenward flame, in lays of the "sweet Psalmist of Israel." These psalm-tunes are in their way as peculiar as the song-tunes we have referred to. Nothing can be more touching than the description by Burns of the domestic psalmody of his father's cottage. Mr. R. Chambers, in his Life of Burns, informs us that the poet, during his father's infirmity and after his death, had himself conducted the family worship. He looked back in after-life upon those innocent and happy days, ere he had encountered the temptations of the world, and ere he had fallen before the solicitations of guilty passion. How beautifully does he describe the characteristic features of this portion of the cottar's worship! He enumerates the psalm-tunes usually made use of on such occasions, and discriminates the character of each :—

"They chant their artless notes in simple guise ;
They tune their hearts, by far the noblest aim :

* Fan.

> Perhaps DUNDEE's wild warbling measures rise,
> Or plaintive MARTYRS, worthy of the name,
> Or noble ELGIN beets the heavenward flame."

In proof of such psalmody being quite national, I have been told that many of these tunes were composed by artizans, such as builders, joiners, blacksmiths, etc.

Several of the psalm-tunes more peculiar to Scotland are no doubt of an early date. In Ravenscroft's *Psalms,* published with the music in four parts in 1621, he gives the names of seven as purely Scottish—*King's, Duke's, Abbey, Dunfermline, Dundee, Glasgow, Martyrs.* I was used to hear such psalmody in my early days in the parish church of Fettercairn, where we always attended during summer. It had all the simple characteristics described by Burns, and there was a heartiness and energy too in the congregation when, as he expresses it, they used to "skirl up the Bangor," of which the effects still hang in my recollection. It may be said these Scottish tunes are rude and unscientific, but the effect was striking, as I recall it through the vista of threescore years and ten. Great advances, no doubt, have been made in Scotland in congregational psalmody; choirs have been organised with great effect by choir-masters of musical taste and skill. But I hope the spirit of piety, which in past times once accompanied the old Scottish psalm, whether sung in the church or at home, has not departed with the music. Its better emotions are not, I hope, to become a "Reminiscence."

There is a very interesting Reminiscence, and one of a sacred character also, with which I would now conclude. When I joined the Scottish Episcopal Church, nearly fifty years ago, it was quite customary for members of our communion to ask for the blessing of their Bishop, and to ask it especially on any remarkable event in their life, as marriage, loss of friends, leaving home, returning home, etc.; and it was the custom amongst the old Scottish Episcopalians to give the blessing in a peculiar form, which had become venerable from its traditionary application by our bishops. I have myself received it from my bishop, the late good Bishop Walker, and have heard him pronounce it on others. But whether the custom of asking the bishop's blessing be past or not, the form I speak of has become a Reminiscence, and I feel assured is not known even by some of our own bishops. I shall give it to my readers as I received it from the family of the late Bishop Walker of Edinburgh :—

> "God Almighty bless thee with his Holy Spirit;
> Guard thee in thy going out and coming in;
> Keep thee ever in his faith and fear;
> Free from Sin, and safe from Danger."

It is quite evident that those who have in Scotland come to an advanced age, must have found some things to have been really changed about them, and some things on which great alterations have already taken place. There are others, however, which yet may be in a transition state; and others in which, although changes are threatened, it cannot yet be said that the changes are begun. We have been led to a consideration of impending alterations as likely to take place by the recent appearance of two very remarkable and very interesting papers on subjects closely connected with great social Scottish questions, where a revolution of opinion may be expected. There are two articles in *Recess Studies*, a volume edited by our distinguished Principal, Sir Alexander Grant. One essay is by Sir Alexander himself, upon the "Endowed Hospitals of Scotland;" the other by Rev. Dr. Wallace of the Greyfriars, upon "Church Tendencies in Scotland." It would be quite irrelevant for me to enlarge here upon the merits of those articles. No one could study them attentively without being impressed with the ability and power displayed in them by the authors, their grasp of the subjects, and their fair impartial judgment on the points which are so skilfully discussed. One conclusion seems quite obvious.—Men's views upon many important social and religious questions are undergoing great change. It is a curious and an interesting subject both to mark what are past and to anticipate what are to come. But I would hope that we have all learned to view such changes under a more serious national aspect than a mere question of amusement or speculation. The Christian, when he looks around him on society, must observe many things which, as a patriot, he wishes might be permanent, and he marks many things which, as a patriot, he wishes were obliterated. What he desires should be enduring in his countrymen is, that abiding attributes of Scottish character should be associated amongst all men with truth and virtue—

with honour and kindly feelings—with temperance and self-denial—with divine faith and love—with generosity and benevolence. On the other hand, he desires that what may become questions of tradition, and, in regard to his own land, REMINISCENCES of Scottish life, shall be—cowardice and folly, deceit and fraud, the low and selfish motives to action which make men traitors to their God and hateful to their fellow-men.

On this ground every observer of human life may make the question of his Reminiscences serve his own personal improvement. We all know how the characters of various persons, as they pass away, are always spoken of, and freely discussed, by those who survive them. Men recall the eccentric, and are amused with their eccentricities. They admire the wise and dignified of the past. There are some recollected only to be detested for their vices—some to be pitied for their weaknesses and follies—some to be scorned for their mean and selfish conduct. But there are others whose memory is embalmed in tears of grateful remembrance. There are those whose generosity and whose kindness, whose winning sympathy and noble disinterested virtues, have called forth a blessing. Might it not, therefore, be good for all of us to ask ourselves how *we* are likely to be spoken of when the grave has closed our intercourse with friends whom we leave behind? The thought might, at any rate, be useful as an additional motive for men's kind and honourable and generous conduct to each other. And then the inquiry would come home to each one in some such form as this—"Within the circle of my family and friends—within the hearts of those who have known me, and were connected with me in all social relations—what will be the estimate formed of me when I am gone? What will be the spontaneous impression produced by our past intercourses in life? Will the thought of me furnish the memory of those who survive me with recollections of the past that will be fond and pleasing?" In one word, let each one ask himself (I speak to countrymen), "Will *my* name be associated with gentle and happy 'REMINISCENCES OF SCOTTISH LIFE AND CHARACTER?'"

I have a strong desire, before closing this preface, to introduce to my readers the beautiful Latin lines which my honoured and learned friend the Bishop of St. Andrews addressed to me on the publication of the 20th edition of this work. The pleasure which every scholar must derive from the classical beauty of their composition will, I hope, compensate for any appearance of vanity in their introduction.

Ad virum venerabilem, optimum, dilectissimum, EDUARDUM B. RAMSAY, LL.D., Edinburgi Decanum, accepto ejus libro, cui titulus "Reminiscences of Scottish Life and Character," vicesimum jam lautiusque et amplius edito.

EDITIO accessit vicesima! plaudite, quicquid
  Scotia festivi fert lepidique ferax!
Non vixit frustrà, qui frontem utcunque severam
  Noverit innocuis explicuisse jocis:
Non frustrà *vixit*, qui tot monumenta Priorum
  Salsa piâ vetuit sedulitate *mori*:
Non frustrà *vixit* qui quali nos sit amore

Vivendum, exemplo præcipiensque docet.
Nec merces te indigna manet : Juvenesque senesque
Gaudebunt nomen concelebrare tuum ;
Condiet appositum dum fercula nostra salinum,
Præbebitque suas mensa secunda nuces ;
Dum stantis rhedæ aurigam tua pagina fallet,
Contentum in sella tædia longa pati !
Quid, quod et ipsa sibi devinctum Scotia nutrix
Te perget gremio grata fovere senem ;
Officiumque pium simili pietate rependens,
Sæcula nulla sinet *non* meminisse* Tui.

The following elegant and ingenious poetical translation has been kindly supplied by my esteemed friend, Very Rev. A. P. Stanley, D.D., Dean of Westminster :—

HAIL, twentieth edition ! from Orkney to Tweed
Let the wits of all Scotland come running to read.
Not in vain hath he lived, who by innocent mirth
Hath lightened the frowns and the furrows of earth :
Not in vain hath he *lived*, who will never let die
The humours of good times, for ever gone by :
Not in vain hath he lived, who hath laboured to give
In himself the best proof how by love we may live.
Rejoice, my dear Dean, thy reward to behold
In united rejoicing of young and of old ;
Remembered, so long as our boards shall not lack
A bright grain of salt, or a hard nut to crack ;
So long as the cabman aloft on his seat
Broods deep o'er thy page as he waits in the street !
Yea, Scotland herself, with affectionate care,
Shall nurse an old age so beloved and so rare ;
And still gratefully seek in her heart to enshrine
One more *Reminiscence*, and that shall be Thine.

* Alluditur ad titulum libri, "Reminiscences," etc.

EDINBURGH, 23 AINSLIE PLACE,
January 1872.

REMINISCENCES

OF

SCOTTISH LIFE AND CHARACTER.

CHAPTER THE FIRST.

INTRODUCTORY.

MANY things connected with our Scottish manners of former times are fast becoming obsolete, and we seem at present to be placed in a juncture when some Scottish traditions are in danger of being lost entirely. Being impressed with this truth, I made my own "Reminiscences of Scottish Life and Character" the subject of a lecture, which was delivered as one of the series given at Ulbster Hall in 1857 by different contributors, some of whom were amongst the most distinguished of our citizens. The idea met with so much approval, that the lecture was published. Since that time the materials have been growing under my hand, and I received many contributions on the subject, which were soon embodied in a second edition. The public interest continued, and brought forth many flattering and pleasing communications from various quarters; and I would here express how deeply I have been gratified by the sympathy with which my humble endeavours to exhibit a phase of Scottish social life have been received.

I still think that it forms a most interesting chapter of our *domestic national* annals. In fact, if it were not presumption, I might be inclined to consider myself a fellow-labourer with Mr. Robert Chambers ; as in a very humble degree, and in a very limited sphere, this little volume takes a portion of the same field of illustration which he has selected. I should consider myself to have done well if I shall direct any of my readers to his able volumes. Whosoever wishes to know what this country really was in times past, and to learn, with a precision beyond what is supplied by the narratives of history, the details of the ordinary current of our social, civil, and national life, must carefully study the "Domestic Annals of Scotland." Never before were a nation's domestic features so thoroughly portrayed. Of those features the specimens of quaint Scottish humour still remembered are unlike anything else, but they are fast becoming obsolete, and my motive for this publication has been an endeavour to preserve marks of the past which would of themselves soon become obliterated, and to supply the rising generation with pictures of social life, faded and indistinct to their eyes, but the strong lines of which an older race still remember. By thus coming forward at a favourable moment, no doubt many beautiful specimens of SCOTTISH MINSTRELSY have in this manner been preserved from oblivion by the timely exertions of Bishop Percy, Ritson, Walter Scott, and Professor Aytoun. Lord Macaulay, in his preface to "The Lays of Ancient Rome," shows very powerfully the tendency in all that lingers in the memory to become obsolete, and he does not hesitate to say that "Sir Walter Scott was but *just in time* to save the precious relics of the minstrelsy of the Border."

My esteemed friend, Lord Neaves, who, it is well known, combines, with his great legal knowledge and high literary acquirements, a keen sense of the humorous, has sometimes pleasantly complained of my drawing so many of my specimens of Scottish humour from sayings and doings of Scottish ministers. There can be no doubt that the older school of our national clergy supply some most amusing anecdotes. They were a shrewd and observant race. They lived amongst their own people from year to year, and understood the Scottish type of character. Their retired habits and familiar intercourse with their parishioners gave rise to many quaint and racy communications. They were excellent men, well suited to their pastoral work, and did much good amongst their congregations; for it should be always remembered that a national church requires a sympathy and resemblance between the pastors and the flocks. Both will be found to change together. Nothing could be further from my mind in recording these stories, than the idea of casting ridicule upon such an order of men. My own feelings as a Scotchman, with all their ancestral associations, lead me to cherish their memory with pride and deep interest. I may appeal also to the fact that many contributions to this volume are voluntary offerings from distinguished clergymen of the Church of Scotland, as well as of the Free Church and of other Presbyterian communities. Indeed, no persons enjoy these stories more than ministers themselves. I recollect many years ago travelling to Perth in the old stage-coach days, and enjoying the society of a Scottish clergyman, who was a most amusing companion, and full of stories, the quaint humour of which accorded with his own disposition. When we had come through Glen Farg, my companion pointed out that we were in the parish of Dron. With much humour he introduced an anecdote of a brother minister not of a brilliant order of mind, who had terminated in this place a course of appointments in the Church, the names of which, at least, were of an ominous character for a person of unimaginative temperament. The worthy man had been brought up at the school of *Dunse*; had been made assistant at *Dull*, a parish near Aberfeldy, in the Presbytery of Weem; and had here ended his days and his clerical career as minister of *Dron*.

Sir Walter Scott, in the dedication to the King (George the Fourth) of his collected edition of the Waverley Novels, with much complacency records the fact that "the perusal of them has been supposed, in some instances, to have succeeded in amusing hours of relaxation, or relieving those of languor, pain, or anxiety." No doubt it is a source of allowable satisfaction to an author to think that he has in any degree, even the lowest and the most humble, contributed to the innocent recreation of a world where care and sorrow so generally prevail. The work of preparing these Reminiscences has sometimes succeeded in drawing off the mind of the author from sad and painful recollections of his own domestic trials, and he may perhaps be permitted to state, that in several cases he has received assurance that his pages have beguiled an hour of languor and debility ; that they have in distant lands recalled many pleasant associations with the past, and have given a permanent and agreeable impression of a pleasantry and humour exclusively and essentially of a Scottish type and character.

I wish it to be distinctly understood that these desultory records were never intended to treat of the changes which have taken place amongst us during the last half century, in literature or philosophy, in laws, commerce, manufactures, or in the deeper phases of our national character. I treat of changes and of transitions which lie rather upon the surface of social life. In fact, I speak of what, to a great degree, I can verify from my own experience—what I have not seen and known in my own person I generally narrate from the *direct* testimony of others. I can myself go back in memory for sixty years ; and therefore these observations, trivial and superficial as they may be, I might name, in imitation of my distinguished great-great-great-uncle, Bishop Burnett, and call them "Memoirs of my own time," or, more correctly, to follow a recent example of collected reminiscences (that of the late lamented Lord Cockburn), "Memorials of my Time." I have recorded the following remarks in the way of an *experiment*, hoping that it might form a precedent or example for others to take up the question of changes amongst us, and for those to state results of their observation who have had more experience than mine (as I was only an occasional visitor to my own country from the age of eight to the age of thirty), who have more opportunities of judging, and who are possessed of far better powers of description. As Lord Cockburn has observed, "A change has been going on for a long time."—"The feelings and habits which had prevailed at the Union, and which had left so many picturesque peculiarities on the Scottish character, could not survive the enlarged intercourse with England and the world." Much of this change had of course taken place before any of the present generation can remember. Much has been done in my own recollection, and now there remain only comparatively the slighter shades of difference to be assimilated, and soon there will be little to notice. Now, a subject like this can only be illustrated by a copious application of anecdotes which must show the features of the past. And let me premise that I make use of anecdotes not for the purpose of telling a good story, but solely in the way of *illustration*. I am quite certain that there was an originality, a dry and humorous mode of viewing persons and events quite *peculiar* to the older Scottish characters. And I am equally certain, that their peculiar humour can only be exhibited in examples. I have just been supplied, by two much valued and kind friends, with anecdotes highly illustrative of what I have endeavoured to record; from Mr. Erskine of Linlathan I have received the following: —Mr. Erskine recollects an old housekeeper at Airth who belonged to this class of character. A speech of this Mrs. Henderson was preserved in the family as having been made by her at the time of the execution of Louis XVI. in 1793. She was noticing the violent emotion exhibited by Mr. Bruce of Kinnaird, the Abyssinian traveller, at the sad event which had just taken place, and added, in the following quaint and caustic terms, "There's Kinnaird greeting as if there was nae a saunt on earth but himsel' and the king o' France." How utterly unlike anything that would be said on such an occasion by an English person in the same position in life!

The other anecdote (which has just been sent by a kind correspondent from Aberdeenshire) I introduce here as a pure sample of the Scottish humour we are speaking of. It seems to me to possess more than the ordinary amount of those racy qualities which so often distinguished the older class of Scottish parish functionaries. The story is recorded as having been told by the late Rev. Alexander Allardice, minister of Forgue in Aberdeenshire, who possessed an unusual vein of dry caustic humour, and who told stories of that description in a most relishable way.

A neighbouring minister was to assist Mr. Allardice, and arrived at the manse on Saturday, where he was to sleep, and take the duty on Sunday following. He was a conceited youth—a frothy declamatory preacher—and, as a stranger, anxious to make a great sensation in the country. After dinner, he strolled out into the churchyard, and encountered John the beddal and parish oracle engaged in digging a grave—and much of a humorist in his way—moreover, a formidable critic of the theological soundness of the neighbouring ministers. Our young divine, having been very recently *placed*, supposed himself to be personally unknown to the Forgue functionary. Accordingly he began to pump Beddal John as to the opinion held of the brethren around who had assisted at Forgue. To query after query John gave out his unvarying oracular response, "Na, sir, we dinna like him; he's nae soun'"—and "we dinna like him eather; *he's* nae soun'," clenching every decision with the "yerk" of a spadeful of earth on the grave's brink. At last the reverend pumper having exhausted the circle of his brethren of the Presbytery, and secretly gratified, no doubt, with this summary and unqualified testimony against them, anxious to hear what was thought in the country side about himself, where he rather flattered himself he was creating a sensation, and trusting to his incognito (though John was perfectly aware who his colloquist was), ventured to ask, "Well, now, the parish of —— has got a famous preacher, the Rev. Mr. ——, what do you think of *him*? is *he* 'soun'?" "'Od, sir," replied John, with a sly twinkle, and resting for a moment on his spade, "I hinna heard him mysel'; but folk that hae, say *he's* A' *soun'*." John recommenced digging with redoubled diligence, and exit the reverend querist, feeling, we may fancy, rather small.

If my anecdotes should occasionally excite amusement or even laughter, there is no harm done; but let it be remembered this is not the *object*. The object, as I say, is to illustrate the sort of quaint humour we are losing. In short, whatever tends to illustrate changes—to mark times that are gone—I have not hesitated to use.

We have now, therefore, to deal with common events and with changes which, though in themselves really deep and important, often appear to the observer to affect only what is external; and as we must have a classification or arrangement of the topics on which changes are to be marked, I would propose to record some Reminiscences on the following subjects:

On Religious Feelings and Religious Observances.

On Scottish Conviviality of the past.

On the Old Scottish Domestic Servant.

On the Humour and Peculiarities of the Scottish Language, including Scottish Proverbs.

On Scottish Stories of Wit and Humour

CHAPTER THE SECOND.

ON RELIGIOUS FEELINGS AND RELIGIOUS OBSERVANCES.

On this subject we would speak with deference. We have no intention of entering, in this volume, upon those great questions which are connected with certain church movements amongst us, or with national peculiarities of faith and discipline. It is impossible, however, to overlook entirely the fact of a gradual relaxation which has gone on for some years, of the sterner features of the Calvinistic school of theology—at any rate, of keeping its theoretic peculiarities more in the background. What we have to notice, in these pages, are changes in the feelings with regard to religion and religious observances, which have appeared upon the *exterior* of society—the changes which belong to outward habits rather than to internal feelings. Of such changes many have taken place within my own experience. Scotland has ever borne the character of a moral and religious country; and the mass of the people are a more church-going race than the masses of English population. I am not at all prepared to say that in the middle and lower ranks of life, our countrymen have undergone much change in regard to religious observances. But there can be no question that amongst the upper classes there are manifestations connected with religion now, which some years ago were not thought of. The attendance of *men* on public worship is of itself an example of the change we speak of. I am afraid that when Walter Scott described Monkbarns as being with difficulty "hounded out" to hear the sermons of good Mr. Blattergowl, he wrote from a knowledge of the habits of church-going then generally prevalent amongst Scottish lairds. The late Bishop Sandford told me that when he first came to Edinburgh—I suppose fifty years ago—few gentlemen attended church—very few indeed were seen at the communion—so much so that it was a matter of conversation when a male communicant, not an aged man, was observed at the table for the first time. Sydney Smith, when preaching in Edinburgh some forty years ago, seeing how almost exclusively congregations were made up of ladies, took for his text the verse from the Psalms, "Oh that men would therefore praise the Lord;" and with that touch of the facetious which marked everything he did, laid the emphasis on the word "men." Looking round the congregation and saying, "Oh that *men* would therefore praise the Lord," implying that he used the word, not to describe the human species generally, but the male individuals as distinguished from the female portion. In regard to attendance by young men, both at church and communion, a marked change has taken place in my own experience. In fact, there is an attention excited towards church subjects, which, thirty years ago, would have been hardly credited. Nor is it only in connection with churches and church services that these changes have been brought forth, but an interest has been raised on the subject from Bible societies, missionary associations at home and abroad, schools and reformatory institutions, most of which, as regard active operation, have grown up during fifty years.

Nor should I omit to mention, what I trust may be considered as a change belonging to religious feeling, viz., that conversation is now conducted without that accompaniment of those absurd and unmeaning oaths which were once considered an essential embellishment of polite discourse. I distinctly recollect an elderly gentleman, when describing the opinion of a refined and polished female upon a particular point, putting into her mouth an unmistakeable round oath as the natural language in which people's sentiments and opinions would be ordinarily conveyed. This is a change wrought in men's feelings, which all must hail with great pleasure. Putting out of sight for a moment the sin of such a practice, and the bad influence it must have had upon all emotions of reverence for the name and attributes of the Divine Being, and the natural effect of profane swearing, to "harden a' within," we might marvel at the utter folly and incongruity of making swearing accompany every expression of anger or surprise, or of using oaths as mere expletives in common discourse. A quaint anecdote, descriptive of such senseless ebullition, I have from a friend who mentioned the names of parties concerned :—A late Duke of Athole had invited a well-known character, a writer of Perth, to come up and meet him at Dunkeld for the transaction of some business. The Duke mentioned the day and hour when he should receive the man of law, who accordingly came punctually at the appointed time and place. But the Duke had forgotten the appointment, and gone to the hill, from which he could not return for some hours. A Highlander present described the Perth writer's indignation, and his mode of showing it by a most elaborate course of swearing. "But whom did he swear at?" was the inquiry made of the narrator, who replied, "Oh, he didna sweer at ony thing particular, but juist stude in ta middle of ta road and swoor at lairge." I have from a friend also an anecdote which shows how entirely at one period the practice of swearing had become familiar even to female ears when mixed up with the intercourse of social life. A sister had been speaking of her brother as much addicted to this habit—"Our John sweers awfu', and we try to correct him; but," she added in a candid and apologetic tone, "nae doubt it *is* a great set aff to conversation." There was something of rather an *admiring* character in the description of an outbreak of swearing by a Deeside body. He had been before the meeting of Justices for some offence against the excise laws, and had been promised some assistance and countenance by my cousin, the laird of Finzean, who was unfortunately addicted to the practice in question. The poor fellow had not got off so well as he had expected, and on giving an account of what took place to a friend, he was asked, " But did not Finzean speak for you ?" " Na," he replied, " he didna say muckle ; but oh, he damned bonny !"

This is the place to notice a change which has taken place in regard to some questions of taste in the building and embellishing of Scottish places of worship. Some years back there was a great jealousy of ornament in connection with churches and church services, and, in fact, all such embellishments were considered as marks of a departure from the simplicity of old Scottish worship,—they were distinctive of Episcopacy as opposed to the severer modes of Presbyterianism. The late Sir William Forbes used to give an account of a conversation, indicative of this feeling, which he had overheard between an Edinburgh inhabitant and his friend from the country. They were passing St. John's, which had just been finished, and the countryman asked, " Whatna kirk was that ? " " Oh," said the townsman, " that is an English chapel," meaning Episcopalian. " Ay," said his friend, " there'll be a walth o' *images* there." But, if unable to sympathize with architectural church ornament and embellishment, how much less could they sympathize with the performance of divine service, which included such musical accompaniments as intoning, chanting, and anthems ? On the first introduction of Tractarianism into Scotland, the full choir service had been established in an Episcopal church, where a noble family had adopted those views, and carried them out regardless of expense. The lady who had been instrumental in getting up these musical services was very anxious that a favourite female servant of the family—a Presbyterian of the old school—should have an opportunity of hearing them ; accordingly, she very kindly took her down to church in the carriage, and on returning asked her what she thought of the music, etc.; "Ou, it's verra bonny, verra bonny; but oh, my lady, it's an awfu' way of spending the Sabbath." The good woman could only look upon the whole thing as a musical performance. The organ was a great mark of distinction between Episcopalian and Presbyterian places of worship. I have heard of an old lady describing an Episcopalian clergyman, without any idea of disrespect, in these terms:—"Oh, he is a whistle-kirk minister." From an Australian correspondent I have an account of the difference between an Episcopal minister and a Presbyterian minister, as remarked by an old Scottish lady of his acquaintance. Being asked in what the difference was supposed to consist, after some consideration she replied, "Weel, ye see, the Presbyterian minister wears his sark under his coat, the Episcopal minister wears his sark aboon his coat." Of late years, however, a spirit of greater tolerance of such things has been growing up amongst us,—a greater tolerance, I suspect, even of organs and liturgies. In fact, we may say a new era has begun in Scotland as to church architecture and church ornaments. The use of stained glass in churches—forming memorial windows for the departed,* a free use of crosses as architectural ornaments, and restoration of ancient edifices, indicate a revolution of feeling regarding this question. Beautiful and expensive churches are rising everywhere, in connection with various denominations. It is not long since the building or repairing a new church, or the repairing and adapting an old church, implied in Scotland simply a production of the greatest possible degree of ugliness and bad taste at the least possible expense, and certainly never included any notion of ornament

* Distinguished examples of these are to be found in the New Greyfriars' Church, Edinburgh, and in the Cathedral of Glasgow; to say nothing of the beautiful specimens in St. John's Episcopal Church, Edinburgh.

in the details. Now, large sums are expended on places of worship without reference to creed. First-rate architects are employed. Fine Gothic structures are produced. The rebuilding of the Greyfriars' Church, the restoration of South Leith Church and of Glasgow Cathedral, the very bold experiment of adopting a style little known amongst us, the pure Lombard, in a church for Dr. W. L. Alexander, on George IV. Bridge, Edinburgh ; the really splendid Free Churches, St. Mary's, in Albany Street, and the Barclay Church, Bruntsfield, and many similar cases, mark the spirit of the times regarding the application of what is beautiful in art to the service of religion. One might hope that changes such as these in the feelings, tastes, and associations, would have a beneficial effect in bringing the worshippers themselves into a more genial spirit of forbearance with each other. A friend of mine used to tell a story of an honest builder's views of church differences, which was very amusing, and quaintly professional. An English gentleman, who had arrived in a Scottish country town, was walking about to examine the various objects which presented themselves, and observed two rather handsome places of worship in course of erection nearly opposite to each other. He addressed a person, who happened to be the contractor for the chapels, and asked, "What was the difference between these two places of worship which were springing up so close to each other?"—meaning, of course, the difference of the theological tenets of the two congregations. The contractor, who thought only of architectural differences, innocently replied, "There may be a difference of sax feet in length, but there's no aboon a few inches in the breadth." Would that all our religious differences could be brought within so narrow a compass!

The variety of churches in a certain county of Scotland once called forth a sly remark upon our national tendencies to religious division and theological disputation. An English gentleman sitting on the box, and observing the great number of places of worship in the aforesaid borough, remarked to the coachman that there must be a great deal of religious feeling in a town which produced so many houses of God. "Na," said the man quietly, "it's no religion, it's *curstness*," *i.e.*, crabbedness, insinuating that acerbity of temper, as well as zeal, was occasionally the cause of congregations being multiplied.

It might be a curious question to consider how far motives founded on mere taste or sentiment may have operated in creating an interest towards religion, and in making it a more prominent and popular question than it was in the early portion of the present century. There are in this country two causes which have combined in producing these effects :—1st. The great disruption which took place in the Church of Scotland no doubt called forth an attention to the subject which stirred up the public, and made religion at any rate a topic of deep interest for discussion and partizanship. Men's minds were not *allowed* to remain in the torpid condition of a past generation. 2d. The æsthetic movement in religion, which some years since was made in England, has of course, had its influence in Scotland, and many who showed little concern about religion, whilst it was merely a question of doctrines, of precepts, and of worship, threw themselves keenly into the question when it became associated with ceremonial, and music, and high art. New ecclesiastical associations have been presented to Scottish tastes and feelings. With some minds, attachment to the church is attachment to her Gregorian tones, jewelled chalices, lighted candles, embroidered altar-cloths, silver crosses, processions, copes, albs, and chasubles. But from whatever cause it proceeds, a great change has taken place in the general interest excited towards ecclesiastical questions. Religion now has numerous associations with the ordinary current of human life. In times past it was kept more as a thing apart. There was a false delicacy which made people shrink from encountering appellations that were usually bestowed upon those who made a more prominent religious profession than the world at large.

A great change has taken place in this respect with persons of *all* shades of religious opinions. With an increased attention to the *externals* of religion, we believe that in many points the heart has been more exercised also. Take, as an example, the practice of family prayer. Many excellent and pious households of the former generation would not venture upon the observance, I am afraid, because they were in dread of the sneer. There was a foolish application of the terms "Methodist," "saints," "over-righteous," where the practice was observed. It was to take up a rather decided position in the neighbourhood; and I can testify, that less than fifty years ago, a family would have been marked and talked of for a usage of which now throughout the country the *exception* is rather the unusual circumstance. A little anecdote from recollections in my own family will furnish a good illustration of a state of feeling on this point now happily unknown. In a northern town of the east coast, where the earliest recollections of my life go back, there was usually a detachment of a regiment, who were kindly received and welcomed to the society, which in the winter months was very full and very gay. There was the usual measure of dining, dancing, supping, card-playing, and gossipping, which prevailed in country towns at the time. The officers were of course an object of much interest to the natives, and their habits were much discussed. A friend was staying in the family who partook a good deal of the Athenian temperament, viz., delight in hearing and telling some new thing. On one occasion she burst forth in great excitement with the intelligence that "Sir Nathaniel Duckinfield, the officer in command of the detachment, had family prayers *every* morning!" A very near and dear relative of mine, knowing the tendency of the lady to gossip, pulled her up with the exclamation: "How can you repeat such things, Miss Ogilvy; nothing in the world but the ill-natured stories of Montrose!" The remark was made quite innocently and unconsciously of the bitter satire it conveyed upon the feeling of the place. The "ill-nature" of these stories was true enough, because ill-nature was the motive of those who raised them; not because it is an ill-natured thing of itself to say of a family that they have household worship, but the ill-nature consisted in their intending to throw out a sneer and a sarcasm upon a subject where all such reflections are unbecoming and indecorous. It is one of the best proofs of change of habits and associations on this matter, that the anecdote, exquisite as it is for our purpose, will hardly be understood by many of our young friends, or, at least, happily has lost much of its force and pungency.

These remarks apply perhaps more especially to the state of religious feeling amongst the upper classes of society. Though I am not aware of so much change in the religious habits of the Scottish peasantry, still the elders have yielded much from the sternness of David Deans; and upon the whole view of the question there have been many and great changes in the Scottish people during the last sixty years. It could hardly be otherwise, when we consider the increased facilities of communication between the two countries—a facility which extends to the introduction of English books upon religious subjects. The most popular and engaging works connected with the Church of England have now a free circulation in Scotland; and it is impossible that such productions as the "Christian Year," for example, and many others—whether for good or bad is not now the question—should not produce their effects upon minds trained in the strictest school of Calvinistic theology. I should be disposed to *extend* the boundaries of this division, and to include under "Religious Feelings and Religious Observances" many anecdotes which belong perhaps rather indirectly than directly to the subject. Thus it has struck me that on a subject closely allied with religious feelings a great change has taken place in Scotland during a period of less than fifty years—I mean the attention paid to cemeteries as depositories of the mortal remains of those who have departed. In my early days I never recollect seeing any efforts made for the embellishment and adornment of our churchyards; if tolerably secured by fences, enough had been done. The English and Welsh practices of planting flowers, keeping the turf smooth and dressed over the graves of friends, were quite unknown. Indeed, I suspect such attention fifty years ago would have been thought by the sterner Presbyterians as somewhat savouring of superstition. The account given by Sir W. Scott, in "Guy Mannering," of an Edinburgh burial-place, was universally applicable to Scottish sepulchres.* A very different state of matters has grown up within the last few years. Cemeteries and churchyards are now as carefully ornamented in Scotland as in England. Shrubs, flowers, smooth turf, and neatly-kept gravel walks, are a pleasing accompaniment to head-stones, crosses, and varied forms of monumental memorials, in freestone, marble, and granite. Nay, more than these, not unfrequently we see an imitation of French sentiment, in wreaths of "everlasting" placed over graves as emblems of immortality; and in one of our Edinburgh cemeteries, I have seen these enclosed in glass cases, to preserve them from the effects of wind and rain.

In consequence of neglect, the unprotected state of churchyards was evident from the number of stories in circulation connected with the circumstance of timid and excited passengers going amongst the tombs of the village. The following, amongst others, has been communicated.

* "This was a square enclosure in the Greyfriars' Churchyard, guarded on one side by a veteran angel without a nose, and having only one wing, who had the merit of having maintained his post for a century, while his comrade cherub, who had stood sentinel on the corresponding pedestal, lay a broken trunk, among the hemlock, burdock, and nettles which grew in gigantic luxuriance around the walls of the mausoleum."

The *locale* of the story is unknown, but it is told of a weaver who, after enjoying his potations, pursued his way home through the churchyard, his vision and walking somewhat impaired. As he proceeded, he diverged from the path, and unexpectedly stumbled into a partially made grave. Stunned for a while, he lay in wonder at his descent, and after some time he got out, but he had not proceeded much farther when a similar calamity befell him. At this second fall, he was heard, in a tone of wonder and surprise, to utter the following exclamation, referring to what he considered the untenanted graves : "Ay ! ir ye a' up an' awa ?"

The kindly feelings and interest of the pastoral relation always formed a very pleasing intercourse between minister and people. I have received from an anonymous correspondent an anecdote illustrative of this happy connection, for which he vouches as authentic :—

John Brown, Burgher minister at Whitburn (son of the commentator, and father of the late Rev. Dr. John Brown of Edinburgh, and grandfather of the present accomplished M.D. of the same name, author of "Rab and his Friends," etc.), in the early part of the century was travelling on a small sheltie * to attend the summer sacrament at Haddington. Between Musselburgh and Tranent he overtook one of his own people. "What are ye daein' here, Janet, and whaur ye gaun in this warm weather ?" "Deed, sir," quo Janet, "I'm gaun to Haddington *for the occasion*,† an' expeck to hear ye preach this efternoon." "Very weel, Janet, but whaur ye gaun to sleep ?" "I dinna ken, sir, but Providence is aye kind, an'll provide a bed." On Mr. Brown jogged, but kindly thought of his humble follower ; accordingly, after service in the afternoon, before pronouncing the blessing, he said from the pulpit, "Whaur's the auld wifie that followed me frae Whitburn ?" "Here I'm, sir," uttered a shrill voice from a back seat. "Aweel,"

* A Shetland pony. † The Lord's Supper.

said Mr. Brown, "I have fand ye a bed; ye're to sleep wi' Johnnie Fife's lass."

There was at all times amongst the older Scottish peasantry a bold assertion of their religious opinions, and strong expression of their feelings. The spirit of the Covenanters lingered amongst the aged people whom I remember, but which time has considerably softened down. We have some recent authentic instances of this readiness in Scotchmen to bear testimony to their principles:—

A friend has informed me that the late Lord Rutherfurd often told with much interest of a rebuke which he received from a shepherd, near Bonaly, amongst the Pentlands. He had entered into conversation with him, and was complaining bitterly of the weather, which prevented him enjoying his visit to the country, and said hastily and unguardedly, "What a d——d mist!" and then expressed his wonder how or for what purpose there should have been such a thing created as east wind. The shepherd, a tall, grim figure, turned sharp round upon him. "What ails ye at the mist, sir? it weets the sod, it slockens the yowes, and"—adding with much solemnity—"it's God's wull;" and turned away with lofty indignation. Lord Rutherfurd used to repeat this with much candour as a fine specimen of a rebuke from a sincere and simple mind.

There was something very striking in the homely, quaint, and severe expressions on religious subjects which marked the old-fashioned piety of persons shadowed forth in Sir Walter Scott's Davie Deans. We may add to the rebuke of the shepherd of Bonaly, of Lord Rutherfurd's remark about the east wind, his answer to Lord Cockburn, the proprietor of Bonaly. He was sitting on the hill-side with the shepherd, and observing the sheep reposing in the coldest situation, he observed to him, "John, if I were a sheep, I would lie on the other side of the hill." The shepherd answered, "Ay, my lord, but if ye had been a sheep ye would hae had mair sense."

Of such men as this shepherd were formed the elders

—a class of men who were marked by strong features of character, and who, in former times, bore a distinguished part in all church matters.

The old Scottish elder was in fact quite as different in character from the modern elder, as the old Scottish minister was from the modern pastor. These good men were not disposed to hide their lights, and perhaps sometimes encroached a little upon the office of the minister. A clergyman had been remarking to one of his elders that he was unfortunately invited to two funerals on one day, and that they were fixed for the same hour. "Weel, sir," answered the elder, "if ye'll tak the tane I'll tak the tither."

Some of the elders were great humorists and originals in their way. An elder of the kirk at Muthill used to manifest his humour and originality by his mode of collecting the alms. As he went round with the ladle, he reminded such members of the congregation as seemed backward in their duty, by giving them a poke with the "brod," and making, in an audible whisper, such remarks as these—"Wife at the braid mailin, mind the puir;" "Lass wi' the braw plaid, mind the puir," etc., a mode of collecting which marks rather a bygone state of things. But on no question was the old Scottish disciplinarian, whether elder or not, more sure to raise his testimony than on anything connected with a desecration of the Sabbath. In this spirit was the rebuke given to an eminent geologist, when visiting in the Highlands:—The professor was walking on the hills one Sunday morning, and partly from the effect of habit, and partly from not adverting to the very strict notions of Sabbath desecration entertained in Ross-shire, had his pocket hammer in hand, and was thoughtlessly breaking the specimens of minerals he picked up by the way. Under these circumstances, he was met by an old man steadily pursuing his way to his church. For some time the patriarch observed the movements of the geologist, and at length, going up to him, quietly said, "Sir, ye're breaking something there forbye the stanes!"

The same feeling under a more fastidious form was exhibited to a traveller by a Scottish peasant:—An English artist travelling professionally through Scotland had occasion to remain over Sunday in a small town in the north. To while away the time, he walked out a short way in the environs, where the picturesque ruin of a castle met his eye. He asked a countryman who was passing to be so good as tell him the name of the castle. The reply was somewhat startling—"It's no the day to be speering sic things!"

A manifestation of even still greater strictness, on the subject of Sabbath desecration, I have received from a relative of the family in which it occurred. About fifty years ago the Hon. Mrs. Stewart lived in Heriot Row, who had a cook, Jeannie by name, a paragon of excellence. One Sunday morning when her daughter (afterwards Lady Elton) went into the kitchen, she was surprised to find a new jack (recently ordered, and which was constructed on the principle of going constantly without winding up) wholly paralyzed and useless. Miss Stewart naturally inquired what accident had happened to the new jack, as it had stopped. The mystery was soon solved by Jeannie indignantly exclaiming that "she was nae gaeing to hae the fule thing clocking and rinning about in *her* kitchen a' the blessed Sabbath day."

There sometimes appears to have been in our countrymen an undue preponderance of zeal for Sabbath observance as compared with the importance attached to *other* religious duties, and especially as compared with the virtue of sobriety. The following dialogue between Mr. M—— of Glasgow, the celebrated artist, and an old highland acquaintance whom he had met with unexpectedly, will illustrate the contrast between the severity of judgment passed upon treating the Sabbath with levity and the lighter censure attached to indulgence in whisky. Mr. M—— begins. "Donald, what brought you here?" "Ou, weel, sir, it was a baad place yon; they were baad folk—but they're a God-fearin' set o' folk here !" "Well, Donald," said Mr. M., "I'm glad to hear it." "On ay, sir, 'deed are they ; an' I'll gie ye an instance o't. Last Sabbath, just as the kirk was skailin', there was a drover chield frae Dumfries comin' along the road whustlin', an' lookin' *as happy* as if it was ta muddle o' the week ; weel, sir, oor laads is a God-fearin' set o' laads, an' they were just comin' oot o' the kirk—'od they yokit upon him, an' a'most killed him !" Mr. M., to whom their zeal seemed scarcely sufficiently well directed to merit his approbation, then asked Donald whether it had been drunkenness that induced the depravity of his former neighbours ? "Weel, weel, sir," said Donald, with some hesitation, "*may*-be ; I'll no say but it micht." "Depend upon it," said Mr. M., it's a bad thing whisky." "Weel, weel, sir," replied Donald, "I'll no say but it *may* ;" adding in a very decided tone—"speeciallie *baad* whusky !"

I do not know any anecdote which illustrates in a more striking and natural manner the strong feeling which exists in the Scottish mind on this subject. At a certain time, the hares in the neighbourhood of a Scottish burgh had, from the inclemency of the season or from some other cause, become emboldened more than usual to approach the dwelling-places of men ; so much so that on one Sunday morning a hare was seen skipping along the street as the people were going to church. An old man, spying puss in this unusual position, significantly remarked, "Ay, yon beast kens weel it is the Sabbath-day ;" taking it for granted that no one in the place would be found audacious enough to hurt the animal on a Sunday.

Lady Macneil supplies an excellent pendant to Miss Stewart's story about the jack going on the Sunday. Her henwife had got some Dorking fowls, and on Lady M. asking if they were laying many eggs, she replied, with great earnestness, "Indeed, my leddy, they lay every day, no' excepting the blessed Sabbath."

There were, however, old persons at that time who

were not quite so orthodox on the point of Sabbath observance ; and of these a lady residing in Dumfries was known often to employ her wet Sundays in arranging her wardrobe. " Preserve us !" she said on one occasion, " anither gude Sunday ! I dinna ken whan I'll get thae drawers redd up."

In connection with the awful subject of death and all its concomitants, it has been often remarked, that the older generation of Scottish people used to view the circumstances belonging to the decease of their nearest and dearest friends with a coolness which does not at first sight seem consistent with their deep and sincere religious impressions. Amongst the peasantry, this was sometimes manifested in an extraordinary and startling manner. I do not believe that those persons had less affection for their friends than a corresponding class in England, but they had less awe of the concomitants of death, and approached them with more familiarity. For example, I remember long ago at Fasque, my sister-in-law visiting a worthy and attached old couple, of whom the husband, Charles Duncan, who had been gardener at Fasque for above thirty years, was evidently dying. He was sitting on a common deal chair, and on my sister proposing to send down for his use an old arm-chair, which she recollected was laid up in a garret, his wife exclaimed against such a needless trouble. " Hout, my lady, what would he be duin' wi' an arm-chair ; he's just deein' fast awa ?" I have two anecdotes, illustrative of the same state of feeling, from a lady of ancient Scottish family accustomed to visit her poor dependants on the property, and to notice their ways. She was calling at a decent cottage, and found the occupant busy carefully ironing out some linens. The lady remarked, " Those are fine linens you have got there, Janet." " Troth, mem," was the reply, " they're just the gudeman's *deed* claes, and there are nane better i' the parish." On another occasion, when visiting an excellent woman, to condole with her on the death of her nephew, with whom she had lived, and whose loss must have been severely felt by her, she remarked, "What a nice white cap you have got, Margaret." "Indeed, mem, ay, sae it is; for ye see the gude lad's winding-sheet was ower lang, and I cut aff as muckle as made twa bonny mutches (caps).

There certainly was a quaint and familiar manner in which sacred and solemn subjects were referred to by the older Scottish race, who did not mean to be irreverent, but who no doubt appeared so to a more refined but not really a more religious generation.

It seems to me that this plainness of speech arose in part from the *sincerity* of their belief in all the circumstances of another condition of being. They spoke of things hereafter as positive certainties, and viewed things invisible through the same medium as they viewed things present. The following is illustrative of such a state of mind, and I am assured of its perfect authenticity and literal correctness :—"Joe M'Pherson and his wife lived in Inverness. They had two sons, who helped their father in his trade of a smith. They were industrious and careful, but not successful. The old man had bought a house, leaving a large part of the price unpaid. It was the ambition of his life to pay off that debt, but it was too much for him, and he died in the struggle. His sons kept on the business with the old industry, and with better fortune. At last their old mother fell sick, and told her sons she was dying, as in truth she was. The elder son said to her, 'Mother, you'll soon be with my father; no doubt you'll have much to tell him; but dinna forget this, mother, mind ye, tell him *the house is freed.* He'll be glad to hear that.'"

A similar feeling is manifest in the following conversation, which, I am assured, is authentic :—At Hawick, the people used to wear wooden clogs, which make a *clanking* noise on the pavement. A dying old woman had some friends by her bed-side, who said to her, "Weel, Jenny, ye are gaun to heeven, an' gin you should see our folk, ye can tell them that we're a' weel." To which Jenny replied, "Weel, gin I should see them I'se tell them, but you manna expect that I am to gang clank clanking through heeven looking for your folk."

But of all stories of this class, I think the following death-bed conversation between a Scottish husband and wife is about the richest specimen of a dry Scottish matter-of-fact view of a very serious question:—An old shoemaker in Glasgow was sitting by the bed-side of his wife, who was dying. She took him by the hand. "Weel, John, we're gawin to part. I hae been a gude wife to you, John." "Oh, just middling, just middling, Jenny," said John, not disposed to commit himself. "John," says she, "ye maun promise to bury me in the auld kirk-yard at Stra'von, beside my mither. I couldna rest in peace among unco folk, in the dirt and smoke o' Glasgow." "Weel, weel, Jenny, my woman," said John soothingly, "we'll just pit you in the Gorbals *first*, and gin ye dinna lie quiet, we'll try you sine in Stra'von."

The same unimaginative and matter-of-fact view of things connected with the other world extended to a very youthful age, as in the case of a little boy who, when told of heaven, put the question, "An' will faather be there?" His instructress answered, "of course, she hoped he would be there;" to which he sturdily at once replied, "then I'll no gang."

We might apply these remarks in some measure to the Scottish pulpit ministrations of an older school, in which a minuteness of detail and a quaintness of expression were quite common, but which could not now be tolerated. I have two specimens of such antiquated language, supplied by correspondents, and I am assured they are both genuine.

The first is given on the authority of a St. Andrews professor, who is stated to be a great authority in such narratives.

In one of our northern counties, a rural district had its harvest operations affected by continuous rains. The crops being much laid, wind was desired in order to restore them to a condition fit for the sickle. A minister, in his Sabbath services, expressed their wants in prayer as follows :—"O Lord, we pray thee to send us wind, no a rantin' tantin' tearin' wind, but a noohin' (noughin ?) soughin' winnin' wind." More expressive words than these could not be found in any language.

The other story relates to a portion of the Presbyterian service on sacramental occasions, called "fencing the tables," *i.e.*, prohibiting the approach of those who were unworthy to receive.

This fencing of the tables was performed in the following effective manner by an old divine, whose flock transgressed the third commandment, not in a gross and loose manner, but in its minor details : "I debar all those who use such minced oaths as faith ! troth ! losh ! gosh ! and lovanendie !"

These men often showed a quiet vein of humour in their prayers, as in the case of the old minister of the Canongate who always prayed, previous to the meeting of the General Assembly, that the Assembly might be so guided as "*no to do ony harm.*"

A circumstance connected with Scottish church discipline has undergone a great change in my time—I mean the public censure from the pulpit, in the time of divine service, of offenders previously convicted before the minister and his kirk-session. This was performed by the guilty person standing up before the congregation on a raised platform, called the *cutty stool,* and receiving a rebuke. I never saw it done, but have heard in my part of the country of the discipline being enforced occasionally. Indeed, I recollect an instance where the rebuke was thus administered and received under circumstances of a touching character, and which made it partake of the moral sublime. The daughter of the minister had herself committed an offence against moral purity, such as usually called forth this church censure. The minister peremptorily refused to make her an exception to his ordinary practice. His child stood up in the congregation, and received, from her agonized father, a rebuke similar to that administered to other members of his congregation for a like offence. The spirit of the age became unfavourable to the practice. The rebuke on the cutty stool, like the penance in a white sheet in England, went out of use, and the circumstance is now a matter of "reminiscence." I have received some communications on the subject, which bear upon this point; and I subjoin the following remarks from a kind correspondent, a clergyman, to whom I am largely indebted, as indicating the great change which has taken place in this matter.

"Church discipline," he writes, "was much more vigorously enforced in olden time than it is now. A certain couple having been guilty of illicit intercourse, and also within the forbidden degrees of consanguinity, appeared before the Presbytery of Lanark, and made confession in sackcloth. They were ordered to return to their own session, and to stand at the kirk-door, barefoot and barelegged, from the second bell to the last, and thereafter in the public place of repentance; and, at direction of the session, thereafter to go through the whole kirks of the presbytery, and to satisfy them in like manner. If such penance were now enforced for like offences, we believe the registration books of many parishes in Scotland would become more creditable in certain particulars than they unfortunately are at the present time."

But there was a less formidable ecclesiastical censure occasionally given by the minister from the pulpit against lesser misdemeanours, which took place under his own eye, such as levity of conduct or *sleeping* in church. A most amusing specimen of such censure was once inflicted by the minister upon his own wife for an offence not in our day visited with so heavy a penalty. The clergyman had observed one of his flock asleep during his sermon He paused, and called him to order. "Jeems Robson, ye are sleepin' ; I insist on your wauking when God's word is preached to ye." "Weel, sir, you may look at your ain seat, and ye'll see a sleeper forbye me," answered Jeems, pointing to the clergyman's lady in the minister's pew. "Then, Jeems," said the minister, "when ye see my wife asleep again, haud up your hand." By and by the arm was stretched out, and sure enough the fair lady was caught in the act. Her husband solemnly called upon her to stand up and receive the censure due to her offence. He thus addressed her :—"Mrs. B., a' body kens that when I got ye for my wife, I got nae beauty ; yer frien's ken that I got nae siller ; and if I dinna get God's grace, I shall hae a puir bargain indeed."

The quaint and original humour of the old Scottish minister came out occasionally in the more private services of his vocation as well as in church. As the whole service, whether for baptisms or marriages, is supplied by the clergyman officiating, there is more scope for scenes between the parties present than at similar ministrations by a prescribed form. Thus, a late minister of Caithness, when examining a member of his flock, who was a butcher, in reference to the baptism of his child, found him so deficient in what he considered the needful theological knowledge, that he said to him, "Ah, Sandy, I doubt ye're no fit to haud up the bairn." Sandy, conceiving that reference was made not to spiritual but to physical incapacity, answered indignantly, "Hout, minister, I could haud him up an he were a twa-year-auld stirk."* A late humorous old minister, near Peebles, who had strong feelings on the subject of matrimonial happiness, thus prefaced the ceremony by an address to the parties who came to him :—"My friends, marriage is a blessing to a few, a curse to many, and a great uncertainty to all. Do ye venture ?" After a pause, he repeated with great emphasis, "Do ye venture ?" No objection being made to the venture, he then said, "Let's proceed."

* Bullock.

The old Scottish hearers were very particular on the subject of their minister's preaching old sermons; and to repeat a discourse which they could recollect was always made a subject of animadversion by those who heard it. A beadle, who was a good deal of a wit in his way, gave a sly hit in his pretended defence of his minister on the question. As they were proceeding from church, the minister observed the beadle had been laughing as if he had triumphed over some of the parishioners with whom he had been in conversation. On asking the cause of this, he received for answer, "Dod, sir, they were saying ye had preached an auld sermon to-day, but I tackled them, for I tauld them it was no an auld sermon, for the minister had preached it no sax months syne."

I remember the minister of Banchory, Mr. Gregory, availed himself of the feelings of his people on this subject for the purpose of accomplishing a particular object. During the building of the new church, the service had to be performed in a schoolroom, which did not nearly hold the congregation. The object was to get part of the parish to attend in the morning, and part in the afternoon. Mr. Gregory prevented those who had attended in the morning from returning in the afternoon by just giving them, as he said, "cauld kail het again."

It is somewhat remarkable, however, that notwithstanding this feeling in the matter of a repetition of old sermons, there was amongst a large class of Scottish preachers of a former day such a sameness of subject as really sometimes made it difficult to distinguish the discourse of one Sunday from amongst others. These were entirely doctrinal, and however they might commence, after the opening or introduction, hearers were certain to find the preacher falling gradually into the old channel. The fall of man in Adam, his restoration in Christ, justification by faith, and the terms of the new covenant, formed the staple of each sermon, and without which it was not in fact reckoned complete as an orthodox exposition of Christian doctrine.

Without omitting the essentials of Christian instruction, preachers now take a wider view of illustrating and explaining the gospel scheme of salvation and regeneration, without constant recurrence to the elemental and fundamental principles of the faith. From my friend Dr. Cook of Haddington (who it is well known has a copious stock of old Scotch traditionary anecdotes) I have an admirable illustration of this state of things as regards pulpit instruction.

"Much of the preaching of the Scotch clergy," Dr. Cook observes, "in the last century was almost exclusively doctrinal—the fall: the nature, the extent, and the application of the remedy. In the hands of able men, no doubt, there might be much variety of exposition, but with weaker or indolent men, preaching extempore, or without notes, it too often ended in a weekly repetition of what had been already said. An old elder of mine, whose recollection might reach back from sixty to seventy years, said to me one day, 'Now-a-days, people make a work if a minister preach the same sermon over again in the course of two or three years. When I was a boy, we would have wondered if old Mr. W—— had preached anything else than what we heard the Sunday before.' My old friend used to tell of a clergyman who had held forth on the broken covenant till his people longed for a change. The elders waited on him to intimate their wish. They were examined on their knowledge of the subject, found deficient, rebuked, and dismissed, but after a little while they returned to the charge, and the minister gave in. Next Lord's day he read a large portion of the history of Joseph and his brethren, as the subject of a lecture. He paraphrased it greatly, no doubt, to the detriment of the original, but much to the satisfaction of his people, for it was something new. He finished the paraphrase, 'and now,' says he, 'my friends, we shall proceed to draw some lessons and inferences; and 1*st*, you will observe that the sacks of Joseph's brethren were *ripit*, and in them was found the cup; so your sacks will be ripit at the day of judgment, and the first thing found in them will be the broken covenant;' and having gained this advantage, the sermon went off into the usual strain, and embodied the usual heads of elementary dogmatic theology."

In connection with this topic, I have a communication from a correspondent, who remarks—The story about the minister and his favourite theme, "the broken covenant," reminds me of one respecting another minister whose staple topics of discourse were "Justification, Adoption, and Sanctification." Into every sermon he preached, he managed, by hook or by crook, to force these three heads, so that his general method of handling every text was not so much *expositio*, as *impositio*. He was preaching on these words—"Is Ephraim my dear son? Is he a pleasant child?" and he soon brought the question into the usual formula by adding Ephraim was a pleasant child—first, because he was a justified child; second, because he was an adopted child; and third, because he was a sanctified child.

It should be remembered, however, that the Scottish peasantry themselves—I mean those of the older school—delighted in expositions of *doctrinal* subjects, and in fact were extremely jealous of any minister who departed from their high standard of orthodox divinity, by selecting subjects which involved discussions of strictly moral or *practical* questions. It was condemned under the epithet of *legal* preaching; in other words, it was supposed to preach the law as independent of the gospel. A worthy old clergyman having, upon the occasion of a communion Monday, taken a text of such a character, was thus commented on by an ancient dame of the congregation, who was previously acquainted with his style of discourse:—"If there's an ill text in a' the Bible, that creetur's aye sure to tak it."

The great change—the great improvement, I would say—which has taken place during the last half century in the feelings and practical relations of religion with social life is, that it has become more diffused through all ranks and all characters. Before that period many good sort of people were afraid of making their religious views very prominent, and were always separated from those who did. Persons who made a profession at all beyond the low standard generally adopted in society were marked out as objects of fear or of distrust. The anecdote at page 15 regarding the practice of family prayer fully proves this. Now religious people and religion itself are not kept aloof from the ordinary current of men's thoughts and actions. There is no such marked line as used to be drawn round persons who make a decided profession of religion. Christian men and women have stepped over the line, and, without compromising their Christian principle, are not necessarily either morose, uncharitable, or exclusive. The effects of the old separation were injurious to men's minds. Religion was with many associated with puritanism, with cant, and unfitness for the world. The difference is marked also in the style of sermons prevalent at the two periods. There were sermons of two descriptions—viz., sermons by "*moderate*" clergy, of a purely moral or practical character; and sermons purely doctrinal, from those who were known as "evangelical" ministers. Hence arose an impression, and not unnaturally, on many minds, that an almost exclusive reference to doctrinal subjects, and a dread of upholding the law, and of enforcing its more minute details, were not favourable to the cause of moral rectitude and practical holiness of life. This was hinted in a sly way by a young member of the kirk to his father, a minister of the severe and high Calvinistic school. Old Dr. Lockhart of Glasgow was lamenting one day, in the presence of his son John, the fate of a man who had been found guilty of immoral practices, and the more so that he was one of his own elders. "Well, father," remarked his son, "you see what you've driven him to." In our best Scottish preaching at the present day, no such distinction is visible.

The same feeling came forth with much point and humour on an occasion referred to in "Carlyle's Memoirs." In a company where John Home and David Hume were present, much wonder was expressed what *could* have induced a clerk belonging to Sir William Forbes' bank to abscond, and embezzle £900. "I know what it was," said Home to the historian, "for when he was taken there was found in his pocket a volume of your philosophical works and Boston's 'Fourfold State'"—a hit, 1st, at the infidel, whose principles would have undermined Christianity; and 2d, a hit at the Church, which he was compelled to leave on account of his having written the tragedy of Douglas.

I can myself recollect an obsolete ecclesiastical custom, and which was always practised in the church of Fettercairn during my boyish days—viz., that of the minister bowing to the heritors in succession who occupied the front gallery seats; and I am assured that this bowing from the pulpit to the principal heritor or heritors after the blessing had been pronounced was very common in rural parishes till about forty years ago, and perhaps till a still later period. And when heritors chanced to be pretty equally matched, there was sometimes an unpleasant contest as to who was entitled to the precedence in having the *first* bow. A case of this kind once occurred in the parish of Lanark, which was carried so far as to be laid before the Presbytery; but they, not considering themselves "competent judges of the points of honour and precedency among gentlemen, and to prevent all inconveniency in these matters in the future, appointed the minister to forbear bowing to the lairds at all from the pulpit for the time to come;" and they also appointed four of their number "to wait upon the gentlemen to deal with them, for bringing them to condescend to submit hereunto, for the success of the gospel, and the peace of the parish."

In connection with this subject, we may mention a ready and complimentary reply once made by the late

Reverend Dr. Wightman of Kirkmahoe, on being rallied for his neglecting this usual act of courtesy one Sabbath in his own church. The heritor who was entitled to and always received this token of respect, was P. Miller, Esquire, proprietor of Dalswinton. One Sabbath the Dalswinton pew contained a bevy of ladies, but no gentlemen, and the Doctor—perhaps because he was a bachelor and felt a delicacy in the circumstances—omitted the usual salaam in their direction. A few days after, meeting Miss Miller, who was widely famed for her beauty, and who afterwards became Countess of Mar, she rallied him, in presence of her companions, for not bowing to her from the pulpit on the previous Sunday, and requested an explanation; when the good Doctor immediately replied—"I beg your pardon, Miss Miller, but you surely know that angel-worship is not allowed in the Church of Scotland;" and lifting his hat, he made a low bow, and passed on.

Scottish congregations, in some parts of the country, contain an element in their composition quite unknown in English churches. In pastoral parts of the country, it was an established practice for each shepherd to bring his faithful *collie* dog—at least it was so some years ago. In a district of Sutherland, where the population is very scanty, the congregations are made up one-half of dogs, each human member having his canine companion. These dogs sit out the Gaelic services and sermon with commendable patience, till towards the end of the last psalm, when there is a universal stretching and yawning, and are all prepared to scamper out, barking in a most excited manner whenever the blessing is commenced. The congregation of one of these churches determined that the service should close in a more decorous manner, and steps were taken to attain this object. Accordingly, when a stranger clergyman was officiating, he found the people all sitting when he was about to pronounce the blessing. He hesitated, and paused, expecting them to rise, till an old shepherd, looking up to the pulpit, said, "Say awa', sir, we're a' sittin' to cheat the dowgs."

I remember in the parish church of Fettercairn, though it must be sixty years ago, a custom—still lingering, I believe, in some parts of the country—of the precentor reading each single line before it was sung by the congregation. This practice gave rise to a somewhat unlucky introduction of a line from the first psalm. In most churches in Scotland the communion-tables are placed in the centre of the church. After sermon and prayer, the seats round these tables are occupied by the communicants while a psalm is being sung. One communion Sabbath, the precentor observed the noble family of Eglantine approaching the tables, and likely to be kept out by those pressing in before them. Being very zealous for their accommodation, he called out to an individual whom he considered to be the principal obstacle in clearing the passage, "Come back, Jock, and let in the noble family of Eglantine;" and then turning to his psalm-book, took up his duty, and went on to read the line, "Nor stand in sinners' way."

There must have been some curious specimens of Scottish humour brought out at the examinations or catechisings by ministers of the flock before the administrations of the communion. Thus, with reference to human nature before the fall, a man was asked, "What kind of man was Adam?" "Ou, just like ither fouk." The minister insisted on having a more special description of the first man, and pressed for more explanation. "Weel," said the catechumen, "he was just like Joe Simson the horse-couper." "How so?" asked the minister. "Weel, naebody got onything by him, and mony lost."

A lad had come for examination previous to his receiving his first communion. The pastor, knowing that his young friend was not very profound in his theology, and not wishing to discourage him, or keep him from the table unless compelled to do so, began by asking what he thought a safe question, and what would give him confidence. So he took the Old Testament, and asked him, in reference to the Mosaic law, how many commandments there were. After a little thought, he put his answer in the modest form of a supposition, and replied, cautiously, "Aiblins* a hunner." The clergyman was vexed, and told him such ignorance was intolerable, that he could not proceed in examination, and that the youth must wait and learn more; so he went away. On returning home he met a friend on his way to the manse, and on learning that he too was going to the minister for examination, shrewdly asked him, "Weel, what will ye say noo if the minister speers hoo mony commandments there are?" "Say! why, I shall say ten to be sure." To which the other rejoined, with great triumph, "Ten! Try ye him wi' ten! I tried him wi' a hunner, and he wasna satisfeed." A better example of an answer to catechetical examination was offered in the very conclusive reply made by an auld body to the minister who proposed the question of the shorter catechism, "What are the decrees of God?" Wisely he replied, "Deed, sir, he kens that best himsel'." Another answer from a little girl was shrewd and reflective. The question was, "Why did the Israelites make a golden calf?" "They hadna as muckle siller as wad mak a coo."

A kind correspondent has sent me, from personal knowledge, an admirable pendant to stories of Scottish child acuteness and shrewd observation. A young lady friend of his, resident in a part of Ayrshire rather remote from any very satisfactory administration of the gospel, is in the habit of collecting the children of the neighbourhood on Sundays at the "big house," for religious instruction. On one occasion, the class had repeated the paraphrase of the Lord's Prayer, which contains these lines—

> "Give us this day our daily bread,
> And raiment *fit* provide."

---

* Perhaps.

There being no question as to what "daily bread" was, the teacher proceeded to ask: "What do you understand by 'raiment fit,' or, as we might say, 'fit raiment?'" For a short time the class remained puzzled at the question; but at last one little girl sung out "stockings and shune." The child knew that "fit," was Scotch for feet, so her natural explanation of the phrase was equivalent to "feet raiment," or "stockings and shune," as she termed it.

On the point of changes in religious feelings there comes within the scope of these Reminiscences a character in Aberdeenshire, which has now gone out—I mean the popular and universally well-received Roman Catholic priest. Although we cannot say that Scotland is a more PROTESTANT nation than it was in past days, still religious differences, and strong prejudices, seem at the present time to draw a more decided line of separation between the priest and his Protestant countrymen. As examples of what is past, I would refer to the case of a genial and Romish bishop in Ross-shire. It is well known that private stills were prevalent in the Highlands fifty or sixty years ago, and no one thought there was any harm in them. This good bishop, whose name I forget, was (as I heard the late W. Mackenzie of Muirton assure a party at Dunrobin Castle) several years previously a famous hand at brewing a good glass of whisky, and that he distributed his mountain-dew with a liberal and impartial hand alike to Catholic and to Protestant friends. Of this class, I recollect certainly forty-five years ago, Priest Gordon, a genuine Aberdonian, and a man beloved by all, rich and poor. He was a sort of chaplain to Menzies of Pitfodels, and visited in all the country families round Aberdeen. I remember once his being at Banchory Lodge, and thus apologising to my aunt for going out of the room:—"I beg your pardon, Mrs. Forbes, for leaving you, but I maun just gae doun to the garden and say mi bit wordies"—these "bit wordies" being in fact the portion of the Breviary which he was bound to recite—so easily and pleasantly were those matters then referred to.

The following, however, is a still richer illustration, and I am assured it is genuine :—" Towards the end of the last century, a worthy Roman Catholic clergyman, well known as 'Priest Matheson,' and universally respected in the district, had charge of a mission in Aberdeenshire, and for a long time made his journeys on a piebald pony, the priest and his 'pyet shelty' sharing an affectionate recognition wherever they came. On one occasion, however, he made his appearance on a steed of a different description, and passing near a Seceding meeting-house, he forgathered with the minister, who, after the usual kindly greetings, missing the familiar pony said, 'Ou, Priest! fat's come o' the auld Pyet?' 'He's deid, minister.' 'Weel, he was an auld faithfu' servant, and ye wad nae doot gie him the offices o' the church?' 'Na, minister,' said his friend, not quite liking this allusion to his priestly offices, 'I didna dee that, for ye see he *turned Seceder afore he deed, an' I buried him like a beast.*' He then rode quietly away. This worthy man, however, could, when occasion required, rebuke with seriousness as well as point. Always a welcome guest at the houses of both clergy and gentry, he is said on one occasion to have met with a laird, whose hospitality he had thought it proper to decline, and on being asked the reason for the interruption of his visits, answered, 'Ye ken, an' I ken, but, laird, God kens!'"

One question connected with religious feeling, and the manifestation of religious feeling, has become a more settled point amongst us, since fifty years have expired. I mean the question of attendance by clergymen on theatrical representations. Dr. Carlyle had been prosecuted before the General Assembly in 1757 for being present at the performance of the tragedy of Douglas, written by his friend John Home. He was acquitted, however, and writes thus on the subject in his memoirs :—

" Although the clergy in Edinburgh and its neighbourhood had abstained from the theatre because it gave offence yet the more remote clergymen, when occasionally in town, had almost universally attended the playhouse. It is remarkable that in the year 1784, when the great actress Mrs. Siddons first appeared in Edinburgh, during the sitting of the General Assembly, that court was obliged to fix all its important business for the alternate days when she did not act, as all the younger members, clergy as well as laity, took their stations in the theatre on those days by three in the afternoon."

Drs. Robertson and Blair, although they cultivated the acquaintance of Mrs. Siddons in private, were amongst those clergymen, referred to by Dr. Carlyle, who abstained from attendance in the theatre ; but Dr. Carlyle states, that they regretted not taking the opportunity of witnessing a display of her talent, and of giving their sanction to the theatre as a place of recreation. Dr. Carlyle evidently considered it a narrow-minded intolerance and bigoted fanaticism, that clergymen should be excluded from that amusement. At a period far later than 1784, the same opinion prevailed in some quarters. I recollect when such indulgence on the part of clergymen was treated with much leniency, especially for Episcopalian clergy. I do not mean to say that there was anything like a general feeling in favour of clerical theatrical attendance ; but there can be no question of a feeling far less strict than what exists in our own time. As I have said, thirty-six years ago some clergymen went to the theatre ; and a few years before that, when my brothers and I were passing through Edinburgh, in going backwards and forward to school, at Durham, with our tutor, a licentiate of the Established Church of Scotland, and who afterwards attained considerable eminence in the Free Church, we certainly went with him to the theatre there, and at Durham very frequently I feel quite assured, however, that no clergyman could expect to retain the respect of his people or of the public, of whom it was known that he frequently or habitually attended theatrical representations. It is so understood. I had opportunities of conversing with the late Mr. Murray of the Theatre Royal, Edinburgh, and with Mr. Charles Kean on the subject. Both admitted the fact, and certainly if any men of the profession *could* have removed the feeling from the public mind, these were the men to have done it.

There is a phase of religious observances which has undergone a great change amongst us within fifty years—I mean the services and circumstances connected with the administration of the Holy Communion. When these occurred in a parish they were called "occasions," and the great interest excited by these sacramental solemnities may be gathered from "Peter's Letters," "The Annals of the Parish," and Burns' poem. Such ceremonials are now conducted, I believe, just as the ordinary church services. Some years back they were considered a sort of preaching-matches. Ministers vied with each other in order to bear away the bell in popularity, and hearers embraced the opportunity in exhibiting to one another their powers of criticism on what they heard and saw. In the parish of Urr, Dumfriesshire, on one sacramental occasion, some of the assistants invited were eminent ministers in Edinburgh; Dr. Scot, of St. Michael's, Dumfries, was the only local one who was asked, and he was, in his own sphere, very popular as a preacher. A brother clergyman, complimenting him upon the honour of being so invited, the old bald-headed divine modestly replied, "Gude bless you, man, what can I do? They are a' han' wailed* this time; I need never show face among them." "Ye're quite mista'en," was the soothing encouragement; "tak' your *Resurrection* (a well-known service used for such occasions by him), an I'll lay my lug ye'll beat every clute o' them." The Doctor did as suggested, and exerted himself to the utmost, and it appears he did not exert himself in vain. A batch

* Carefully selected.

of old women, on their way home after the conclusion of the services, were overheard discussing the merits of the several preachers who had that day addressed them from the tent. "Leeze me abune them a'," said one of the company, who had waxed warm in the discussion, "for yon auld clear-headed (bald) man, that said, 'Raphael sings an' Gabriel strikes his goolden harp, an' a' the angels clap their wings wi' joy.' O but it was gran', it just put me in min' o' our geese at Dunjarg when they turn their nebs to the south an' clap their wings when they see the rain's comin' after lang drooth."

There is a subject closely allied with the religious feelings of a people, and that is the subject of their *superstitions.* To enter upon that question, in a general view, especially in reference to the Highlands, would not be consistent with our present purpose, but I am induced to mention the existence of a singular superstition regarding swine which existed some years ago among the lower orders of the east coast of Fife. I can observe, in my own experience, a great change to have taken place amongst Scotch people generally on this subject. The old aversion to the "unclean animal" still lingers in the Highlands, but seems in the Lowland districts to have yielded to a sense of its thrift and usefulness.* The account given by my correspondent of the Fife swinophobia is as follows :—

Among the many superstitious notions and customs prevalent among the lower orders of the fishing towns on the east coast of Fife, till very recently, that class entertained a great horror of swine, and even at the very mention of the word. If that animal crossed their path when about to set out on a sea voyage, they considered it so unlucky an omen that they would not venture off. A clergyman of one of these fishing villages having mentioned

---

* I recollect an old Scottish gentleman, who shared this horror, asking very gravely, "Were not swine forbidden under the law, and cursed under the gospel?"

this superstition to a clerical friend, and finding that he was rather incredulous on the subject, in order to convince him told him he would allow him an opportunity of testing the truth of it by allowing him to preach for him the following day. It was arranged that his friend was to read the chapter relating to the herd of swine into which the evil spirits were cast. Accordingly, when the first verse was read in which the unclean beast was mentioned, a slight commotion was observable among the audience, each one of them putting his or her hand on any near piece of iron—a nail on the seat or bookboard, or to the nails on their shoes. At the repetition of the word again and again, more commotion was visible, and the words "cauld airn" (cold iron) the antidote to this baneful spell, were heard issuing from various corners of the church. And finally, on his coming over the hated word again, when the whole herd ran violently down the bank into the sea, the alarmed parishioners, irritated beyond bounds, rose and all left the church in bodies.

It is some time now, however, since the Highlanders have begun to appreciate the thrift and comfort of swine-keeping and swine-killing. A Scottish minister had been persuaded by the laird to keep a pig, and the gudewife had been duly instructed in the mysteries of black puddings, pork chops, and pig's head ; "Oh !" said the minister, "nae doubt there's a hantle o' miscellawneous eating aboot a pig."

Amongst a people so deeply impressed with the great truths of religion, and so earnest in their religious profession, any persons whose principles were known to be of an *infidel* character would naturally be looked on with abhorrence and suspicion. There is a story traditionary in Edinburgh regarding David Hume, which illustrates this feeling in a very amusing manner, and which, I have heard it said, Hume himself often narrated. The philosopher had fallen from the path into the swamp at the back of the Castle, the existence of which I recollect hearing of from old persons forty years ago. He fairly stuck fast, and called to a woman who was passing, and begged her assistance. She passed on apparently without attending to the request; at his earnest entreaty, however, she came where he was, and asked him, "Are na ye Hume the Atheist?" "Well, weel, no matter," said Hume; "Christian charity commands you to do good to every one." "Christian charity here, or Christian charity there," replied the woman, "I'll do naething for you till ye turn a Christian yoursell' —ye maun repeat the Lord's Prayer and the Creed, or faith I'll let ye grafel * there as I fand ye." The sceptic, really afraid for his life, rehearsed the required formulas.

Notwithstanding the high character borne for so many years by our countrymen as a people, and as specially attentive to all religious observances, still there can be no doubt that there has sprung up amongst the inhabitants of our crowded cities, wynds, and closes, a class of persons quite unknown in the old Scottish times. It is a great difficulty to get them to attend divine worship at all, and their circumstances combine to break off all associations with public services. Their going to church becomes a matter of persuasion and of missionary labour.

A lady, who is most active in visiting the houses of these outcasts from the means of grace, gives me an amusing instance of self-complacency arising from performance of the duty. She was visiting in the West Port, not far from the church established by my illustrious friend the late Dr. Chalmers. Having asked a poor woman if she ever attended there for divine service—"Ou ay," she replied; "there's a man ca'd Chalmers preaches there, and I whiles gang in and hear him, just to encourage him, puir body!"

From the religious opinions of a people, the transition is natural to their political partialities. One great political change has passed over Scotland, which none now living can hardly be said to have actually *witnessed;*

* Lie in a grovelling attitude. See Jamieson.

but they remember those who were contemporaries of the anxious scenes of '45, and many of us have known determined and thorough Jacobites. The poetry of that political period still remains, but we hear only as pleasant songs those words and melodies which stirred the hearts and excited the deep enthusiasm of a past generation. Jacobite anecdotes also are fading from our knowledge. To many young persons they are unknown. Of these stories illustrative of Jacobite feelings and enthusiasm, many are of a character not fit for me to record. The good old ladies who were violent partisans of the Stuarts had little hesitation in referring without reserve to the future and eternal destiny of William of Orange. One anecdote which I had from a near relative of the family may be adduced in illustration of the powerful hold which the cause had upon the views and consciences of Jacobites.

A former Mr. Stirling of Keir had favoured the Stuart cause, and had in fact attended a muster of forces at the Brig of Turk previous to the '15. This symptom of a rising against the Government occasioned some uneasiness, and the authorities were very active in their endeavours to discover who were the leaders of the movement. Keir was suspected. The miller of Keir was brought forward as a witness, and swore positively that the laird was *not* present. Now, as it was well known that he was there, and that the miller knew it, a neighbour asked him privately, when he came out of the witness-box, how he could on oath assert such a falsehood. The miller replied, quite undaunted, and with a feeling of confidence in the righteousness of his cause approaching the sublime—"I would rather trust my soul in God's mercy than trust Keir's head into their hands."

A correspondent has sent me an account of a curious ebullition of Jacobite feeling and enthusiasm, now I suppose quite extinct. My correspondent received it himself from Alexander, fourth Duke of Gordon, and he had entered it in a common-place book when he heard it, in 1826.

"David Tulloch, tenant in Drumbenan, under the second and third Dukes of Gordon, had been "*out*" in the '45—or the *fufteen, or both*—and was a great favourite of his respective landlords. One day David having attended the young Lady Susan Gordon (afterwards Duchess of Manchester) to the "Chapel" at Huntly, David, perceiving that her ladyship had neither hassock nor carpet to protect her garments from the earthen floor, respectfully spread his plaid for the young lady to kneel upon, and the service proceeded; but when the prayer for the King and Royal Family was commenced, David, *sans cerêmonie,* drew, or rather "twitched," the plaid from under the knees of the astonished young lady, exclaiming *not* sotto voce, "The deil a ane shall pray for *them* on *my* plaid!"

I have a still more pungent demonstration against praying for the king, which a friend in Aberdeen assures me he received from the son of the gentleman who *heard* the protest. In the Episcopal Chapel in Aberdeen, of which Primus *John* Skinner was incumbent, they commenced praying in the service for George III. immediately on the death of Prince Charles Edward. On the first Sunday of the prayer being used, this gentleman's father, walking home with a friend whom he knew to be an old and determined Jacobite, said to him, "What do you think of that, Mr. ——?" The reply was, "Indeed, the less we say about that prayer the better." But he was pushed for "further answer as to his own views and his own ideas on the matter," so he came out with the declaration, "Weel, then, I say this—they may pray the kenees* aff their breeks afore I join in that prayer."

The following is a characteristic Jacobite story. It must have happened shortly after 1745, when all manner of devices were fallen upon to display Jacobitism, without committing the safety of the Jacobite, such as having white knots on gowns; drinking, "The king, ye ken wha I mean;'

* So pronounced in Aberdeen.

uttering the toast "the king" with much apparent loyalty, and passing the glass on the one side of the water-jug from them, indicating the esoteric meaning of majesty *beyond* the sea,—etc. etc.; and various toasts, which were most important matters in those times, and were often given as tests of loyalty, or the reverse, according to the company in which they were given. Miss Carnegy of Craigo, well known and still remembered amongst the old Montrose ladies as an uncompromising Jacobite, had been vowing that she would drink King James and his son in a company of staunch Brunswickers, and being strongly dissuaded from any such foolish and dangerous attempt by some of her friends present, she answered them with a text of Scripture, "The tongue no man can tame—James *Third* and *Aucht*," and drank off her glass !*

---

* Implying that there was a James Third of England, Eighth of Scotland.

CHAPTER THE THIRD.

ON OLD SCOTTISH CONVIVIALITY.

The next change in manners which has been effected in the memory of many now living, regards the habits of conviviality, or, to speak more plainly, regards the banishment of *drunkenness* from polite society. It is indeed a most important and blessed change. But it is a change the full extent of which many persons now alive can hardly estimate. Indeed it is scarcely possible to realise the scenes which took place seventy or eighty years back, or even less. In many houses, when a party dined, the ladies going away was the signal for the commencement of a system of compulsory conviviality. No one was allowed to shirk—no daylight—no heeltaps—was the wretched jargon in which were expressed the propriety and the duty of seeing that the glass, when filled, must be emptied and drained. We have heard of glasses having the bottoms knocked off, so that no shuffling tricks might be played with them, and that they could only be put down—empty.

One cannot help looking back with amazement at the infatuation which could for a moment tolerate such a sore evil. To a man of sober inclinations, it must have been an intolerable nuisance to join a dinner party at many houses, where he knew he should have to witness the most disgusting excesses in others, and to fight hard to preserve himself from a compliance with the example of those around him.

The scenes of excess which occurred in the houses

where deep drinking was practised must have been most revolting to sober persons who were unaccustomed to such conviviality; as in the case of a drinking Angus laird, entertaining as his guest a London merchant of formal manners and temperate habits. The poor man was driven from the table when the drinking set in hard, and stole away to take refuge in his bedroom. The company, however, were determined not to let the worthy citizen off so easily, but proceeded in a body, with the laird at their head, and invaded his privacy by exhibiting bottles and glasses at his bed-side. Losing all patience, the wretched victim gasped out his indignation—"Sir, your hospitality borders upon brutality." It must have had a fatal influence also on may persons to whom drinking was most injurious, and who were yet not strong-minded enough to resist the temptations to excess. Poor James Boswell, who certainly required no *extraordinary* urging to take a glass too much, is found in his letters which have recently come to light, laying the blame of his excesses to "falling into a habit which still prevails in Scotland;" and then he remarks, with censorious emphasis, on the "drunken manners of his countrymen." This was about 1770.

A friend of mine, however, lately departed—Mr. Boswell of Balmuto—showed more spirit than the Londoner, when he found himself in a similar situation. Challenged by the host to drink, urged and almost forced to swallow a quantity of wine against his own inclination, he proposed a counter-challenge in the way of eating, and made the following ludicrous and original proposal to the company, that two or three legs of mutton should be prepared, and he would then contest the point of who could devour most meat; and certainly it seems as reasonable to compel people to *eat*, as to compel them to drink, beyond the natural cravings of nature.

The situation of ladies, too, must frequently have been very disagreeable—when, for instance, gentlemen came up stairs in a condition most unfit for female society. Indeed they were often compelled to fly from scenes which were most unfitting for them to witness. They were expected to get out of the way at the proper time, or when a hint was given them to do so. At Glasgow sixty years ago, when the time had come for the *bowl* to be introduced, some jovial and thirsty member of the company proposed as a toast, "The trade of Glasgow and *the outward bound!*" the hint was taken, and silks and satins moved off to the drawing-room.

In my part of the country the traditionary stories of drinking prowess are quite marvellous. On Deeside there flourished a certain Saunders Paul (whom I remember an old man), an innkeeper at Banchory. He was said to have drank whisky, glass for glass, to the claret of Mr. Maule and the Laird of Skene for a whole evening; and in those days there was a traditional story of his despatching, at one sitting, in company with a character celebrated for conviviality—one of the men employed to float rafts of timber down the Dee—three dozen of porter. Of this Mr. Paul it was recorded, that on being asked if he considered porter as a wholesome beverage, he replied, "Oh yes, if you don't take above a dozen." Saunders Paul was, as I have said, the innkeeper at Banchory; his friend and *porter* companion was drowned in the Dee, and when told that the body had been found down the stream below Crathes, he coolly remarked, "I am surprised at that, for I never kenn'd him pass the inn before without comin' in for a glass."

Some relatives of mine travelling in the Highlands were amused by observing in a small road-side public-house a party drinking, whose apparatus for conviviality called forth the dry quaint humour which is so thoroughly Scottish. Three drovers had met together and were celebrating their meeting by a liberal consumption of whisky; the inn could only furnish one glass without a bottom, and this the party passed on from one to another. A queer-looking pawky chield, whenever the glass came to his turn, remarked most gravely, "I think we wadna be the waur o' some water," taking care, however, never to add any of the simple element, but quietly drank off his glass.

There was a sort of infatuation in the supposed dignity and manliness attached to powers of deep potation, and the fatal effects of drinking were spoken of in a manner both reckless and unfeeling. Thus, I have been assured that a well-known old laird of the old school expressed himself with great indignation at the charge brought against hard drinking that it had actually *killed* people. "Na, na, I never knew onybody killed wi' drinking, but I hae kend some that deed in the training." A positive *éclat* was attached to the accomplished and well-trained consumer of claret or of whisky toddy, which gave an importance and even merit to the practice of drinking, and which had a most injurious effect. I am afraid some of the Pleydells of the old school would have looked with the most ineffable contempt on the degeneracy of the present generation in this respect, and that the temperance movement would be little short of insanity in their eyes; and this leads me to a remark.—In considering this portion of our subject, we should bear in mind a distinction. The change we now speak of involves more than a mere change of a custom or practice in social life. It is a change in men's sentiments and feelings on a certain great question of morals. Except we enter into this distinction we cannot appreciate the extent of the change which has really taken place in regard to intemperate habits.

I have an anecdote from a descendant of Principal Robertson, of an address made to him, which showed the real importance attached to all that concerned the system of drinking in his time. The Principal had been invited to spend some days in a country-house, and the minister of the parish (a jovial character) had been asked to meet him. Before dinner he went up to Dr. Robertson and addressed him confidentially, "Doctor, I understand ye are a brother of my gude freend Peter Robertson of Edinburgh, therefore I'll gie you a piece of advice,—Bend* weel to the Madeira at dinner, for here ye'll get little o't after." I have known persons who held that a man who could not drink must have a degree of feebleness and imbecility of character. But as this is an important point, I will adduce the higher authority of Lord Cockburn, and quote from him two examples, very different certainly in their nature, but both bearing upon the question. I refer to what he says of Lord Hermand—"With Hermand drinking was a virtue; he had a sincere respect for drinking, indeed a high moral approbation, and a serious compassion for the poor wretches who *could* not indulge in it, and with due contempt of those who could but did not;" and, secondly, I refer to Lord Cockburn's pages for an anecdote which illustrates the perverted feeling I refer to, now happily no longer existing. It relates the opinion expressed by an old drunken writer of Selkirk (whose name is not mentioned) regarding his anticipation of professional success for Mr. Cranstoun, afterwards Lord Corehouse. Sir Walter Scott, William Erskine, and Cranstoun, had dined with this Selkirk writer, and Scott—of hardy, strong, and healthy frame—had matched the writer himself in the matter of whisky punch. Poor Cranstoun, of refined and delicate mental and bodily temperament, was a bad hand at such work, and was soon off the field. On the party breaking up, the Selkirk writer expressed his admiration of Scott, assuring him that *he* would rise high in the profession, and adding: "I'll tell ye what, Maister Walter, that lad Cranstoun may get to the tap o' the bar, if he can; but tak my word for't, it's no be by drinking."

There was a sort of dogged tone of apology for excess in drinking, which marked the hold which the practice had gained on ordinary minds. Of this we have a remarkable example in the unwilling testimony of a witness who was examined as to the fact of drunkenness

* Old Scotch for drink hard.

being charged against a minister. The person examined was beadle or one of the church-officials. He was asked, "Did you ever see the minister the worse of drink?" "I canna say I've seen him the waur o' drink, but nae doubt I've seen him the *better* o't," was the evasive answer. The question, however, was pushed further; and when he was urged to say if this state of being "the better for drink" ever extended to a condition of absolute helpless intoxication, the reply was: "Indeed afore that cam' I was blind fou mysel', and I could see naething."

A legal friend has told me of a celebrated circuit where Lord Hermand was judge, and Clephane depute-advocate. The party got drunk at Ayr, and so continued (although quite able for their work) till the business was concluded at Jedburgh. Some years after my informant heard that this circuit had, at Jedburgh, acquired the permanent name of the "*daft* circuit."

Lord Cockburn was fond of describing a circuit scene at Stirling, in his early days at the bar, under the presidency of his friend and connection Lord Hermand. After the circuit dinner, and when drinking had gone on for some time, young Cockburn observed places becoming vacant in the social circle, but no one going out at the door. He found that the individuals had dropped down under the table. He took the hint, and by this ruse retired from the scene. He lay quiet till the beams of the morning sun penetrated the apartment. The judge and some of his staunch friends coolly walked up stairs, washed their hands and faces, came down to breakfast, and went into court quite fresh and fit for work.

The feeling of importance frequently attached to powers of drinking was formally attested by a well-known western baronet of convivial habits and convivial memory. He was desirous of bearing testimony to the probity, honour, and other high moral qualities of a friend whom he wished to commend. Having fully stated these claims to consideration and respect, he deemed it proper to notice also his *convivial* attainments; he added accordingly, with cautious approval on so important a point—"And he is a fair drinker." *

The following anecdote is an amusing example of Scottish servant humour and acuteness in measuring the extent of consumption by a convivial party in Forfarshire. The party had met at a farmer's house not far from Arbroath, to celebrate the reconciliation of two neighbouring farmers who had long been at enmity. The host was pressing and hospitable; the party sat late, and consumed a vast amount of whisky toddy. The wife was penurious, and grudged the outlay. When at last, at a morning hour, the party dispersed, the lady, who had not slept in her anxiety, looked over the stairs and eagerly asked the servant girl, "How many bottles of whisky have they used, Betty?" The lass, who had not to pay for the whisky, but had been obliged to go to the well to fetch the water for the toddy, coolly answered, "I dinna ken, mem, but they've drucken sax gang o' watter."

We cannot imagine a better illustration of the general habits that prevailed in Scottish society in regard to drinking about the time we speak of than one which occurs in the recently-published "Memoirs of a Banking House," that of the late Sir William Forbes, Bart. of Pitsligo. The book comprises much that is interesting to the family, and to Scotchmen. It contains a pregnant hint as to the manners of polite society and business habits in those days. Of John Coutts, one of four brothers connected with the house, Sir William records how he was "more correct in

---

* A friend learned in Scottish history suggests an ingenious remark, that this might mean more than a mere *full drinker*. To drink "fair," used to imply that the person drank in the same proportion as the company; to drink more would be unmannerly; to drink less might imply some unfair motive. Either interpretation shows the importance attached to drinking and all that concerned it.

his conduct than the others ; so much so, that Sir William *never but once* saw him in the counting-house disguised with liquor, and incapable of transacting business."

In the Highlands this sort of feeling extended to an almost incredible extent, even so much as to obscure the moral and religious sentiments. Of this a striking proof was afforded in a circumstance which took place in my own church soon after I came into it. One of our Gaelic clergy had so far forgotten himself as to appear in the church somewhat the worse of liquor. This having happened so often as to come to the ears of the bishop, he suspended him from the performance of divine service. Against this decision the people were a little disposed to rebel, because, according to their Highland notions, "a gentleman was no the waur for being able to tak a gude glass o' whisky." These were the notions of a people in whose eyes the power of swallowing whisky conferred distinction, and with whom inability to take the fitting quantity was a mark of a mean and futile character. Sad to tell, the funeral rites of Highland chieftains were not supposed to have been duly celebrated except there was an immoderate and often fatal consumption of whisky. It has been related that at the last funeral in the Highlands, conducted according to the traditions of the olden times, several of the guests fell victims to the usage, and actually died of the excesses.

This phase of old and happily almost obsolete Scottish intemperance at funeral solemnities must have been peculiarly revolting. Instances of this horrid practice being carried to a great extent are traditionary in every part of the country. I am assured of the truth of the following anecdote by a son of the gentleman who acted as chief mourner on the occasion :—About seventy years ago, an old maiden lady died in Strathspey. Just previous to her death, she sent for her grand-nephew, and said to him, "Willy, I'm deein', and as ye'll hae the charge o' a' I have, mind now that as much whisky is to be used at my funeral as there was at my baptism." Willy neglected to ask the old lady what the quantity of whisky used at the baptism was, but when the day of the funeral arrived, believed her orders would be best fulfilled by allowing each guest to drink as much as he pleased. The churchyard where the body was to be deposited was about ten miles distant from where the death occurred. It was a short day in November, and when the funeral party came to the churchyard, the shades of night had considerably closed in. The grave-digger, whose patience had been exhausted in waiting, was not in the least willing to accept of Captain G——'s (the chief mourner) apology for delay. After looking about him he put the anxious question, "But, Captain, whaur's Miss Ketty?" The reply was, "In her coffin, to be sure, and get it into the earth as fast as you can." There, however, was no coffin; the procession had sojourned at a country inn by the way—had rested the body on a dyke—started without it—and had to postpone the interment until next day. My correspondent very justly adds the remark, "What would be thought of indulgence in drinking habits now that could lead to such a result?"

Many scenes of a similar incongruous character are still traditionally connected with such occasions. Within the last thirty years, a laird of Dundonald, a small estate in Ross-shire, died at Inverness. There was open house for some days, and great eating and drinking. Here the corpse commenced its progress towards its appointed home on the coast, and people followed in multitudes to give it a partial convoy, all of whom had to be entertained. It took altogether a fortnight to bury poor Dundonald, and great expense must have been incurred. This, however, is looked back to at Inverness as the last of the real grand old Highland funerals. Such notions of what is due to the memory of the departed have now become unusual if not obsolete. I myself witnessed the first decided change in this matter. I officiated at the funeral of the late Duke of Sutherland. The procession was a mile long. Refreshments were provided for 7000 persons: beef, bread, and beer ; but not one glass of whisky was allowed on the property that day !

It may, perhaps, be said that the change we speak of is not peculiar to Scotland ; that in England the same change has been apparent; and that drunkenness has passed away in the higher circles, as a matter of course, as refinement and taste made an advancement in society. This is true. But there were some features of the question which were peculiar to Scotland, and which at one time rendered it less probable that intemperance would give way in the north. It seemed in some quarters to have taken deeper root amongst us. The system of pressing, or of *compelling*, guests to drink seemed more inveterate. Nothing can more powerfully illustrate the deep-rooted character of intemperate habits in families than an anecdote which was related to me, as coming from the late Mr. Mackenzie, author of the "Man of Feeling." He had been involved in a regular drinking party. He was keeping as free from the usual excesses as he was able, and as he marked companions around him falling victims to the power of drink, he himself dropped off under the table among the slain, as a measure of precaution, and lying there, his attention was called to a small pair of hands working at his throat ; on asking what it was, a voice replied, " Sir, I 'm the lad that 's to lowse the neckcloths." Here, then, was a family, where, on drinking occasions, it was the appointed duty of one of the household to attend, and, when the guests were becoming helpless, to untie their cravats in fear of apoplexy or suffocation. We ought certainly to be grateful for the change which has taken place from such a system ; for this change has made a great revolution in Scottish social life. The charm and the romance long attached in the minds of some of our countrymen to the whole system and concerns of hard drinking was indeed most lamentable and absurd. At tavern suppers, where, nine times out of ten, it was the express *object* of those who went to get drunk, such stuff as "regal purple stream," "rosy wine," "quaffing the gob let," "bright sparkling nectar," "chasing the rosy hours," and so on, tended to keep up the delusion, and make it a monstrous fine thing for men to sit up drinking half the night, to have frightful headachs all next day, to make maudlin idiots of themselves as they were going home, and to become brutes amongst their family when they arrived. And here I may introduce the mention of a practice connected with the convivial habits of which we have been speaking, but which has for some time passed away, at least from private tables—I mean the absurd system of calling for toasts and sentiments each time the glasses were filled. During dinner not a drop could be touched, except in conjunction with others, and with each drinking to the health of each. But toasts came *after* dinner. I can just remember the practice in partial operation; and my astonishment as a mere boy, when accidentally dining at table and hearing my mother called upon to "give the company a gentleman," is one of my earliest reminiscences. Lord Cockburn must have remembered them well, and I will quote his most amusing account of the effects:—"After dinner, and before the ladies retired, there generally began what was called '*Rounds*' of toasts, when each gentleman named an absent lady, and each lady an absent gentleman, separately; or one person was required to give an absent lady, and another person was required to match a gentleman with that lady, and the persons named were toasted, generally, with allusions and jokes about the fitness of the union. And worst of all, there were 'Sentiments.' These were short epigrammatic sentences expressive of moral feelings and virtues, and were thought refined and elegant productions. A faint conception of their nauseousness may be formed from the following examples, every one of which I have heard given a thousand times, and which indeed I only recollect from their being favourites. The glasses being filled, a person was asked for his or for her sentiment, when this, or something similar, was committed, 'May the pleasures of the evening bear the reflections of the morning;' or, 'may the friends of our youth be the companions of our old age;' or, 'delicate pleasures to susceptible minds;' 'may the honest heart never feel distress;' 'may the hand of charity wipe the tear from the eye of sorrow.' The conceited, the ready, or the reckless, hackneyed in the art, had a knack of making new sentiments applicable to the passing incidents with great ease. But it was a dreadful oppression on the timid or the awkward. They used to shudder, ladies particularly; for nobody was spared when their turn in the *round* approached. Many a struggle and blush did it cost; but this seemed only to excite the tyranny of the masters of the craft; and compliance could never be avoided, except by more torture than yielding. . . . It is difficult for those who have been under a more natural system to comprehend how a sensible man, a respectable matron, a worthy old maid, and especially a girl, could be expected to go into company easily, on such conditions."*

This accompaniment of domestic drinking, I mean of accompanying each glass by a toast or sentiment—the practice of which is now confined to public entertainments—was then invariable in private parties, and was supposed to enliven and promote the good fellowship of the social circle. Thus Ferguson, in one of his poems, in describing a dinner, says—

> "The grace is said; it's nae ower lang,
> The claret reams in bells.
> Quo' Deacon, 'Let the toast round gang;
> Come, here's our noble sels
> Weel met the day.'"

There was a great variety of these toasts, some of them exclusively Scottish. A correspondent has favoured me with a few reminiscences of such incentives to inebriety.

* Lord Cockburn's Memorials of his Time, p. 37, *et seq.*

The ordinary form of drinking a health was in the address, "Here's t'eye."

Then such as the following were named by successive members of the company at the call of the host :—

The land o' cakes (*Scotland*).
Mair freens and less need o' them.
Thumping luck and fat weans.
When we're gaun up the hill o' fortune may we ne'er meet a frien' coming doun.
May ne'er waur be amang us.
May the hinges o' friendship never rust, or the wings o' luve lose a feather.
Here's to them that lo'es us, or lenns us a lift.
Here's health to the sick, stilts to the lame ; claise to the back, and brose to the wame.
Here's health, wealth, wit, and meal.
The deil rock them in a creel that does na' wish us a' weel.
Horny hands and weather-beaten haffets (*cheeks*).
The rending o' rocks and the pu'in' doun o' auld houses.

The above two belong to the mason craft ; the first implies a wish for plenty of work, and health to do it ; the second, to erect new buildings and clear away old ones.

May the winds o' adversity ne'er blaw open our door.
*May poortith ne'er throw us in the dirt, or gowd into the high saddle.**
May the mouse ne'er leave our meal-pock wi' the tear in its e'e.
Blythe may we a' be.
Ill may we never see.
Breeks and brochan (*brose*).
May we ne'er want a freend or a drappie to gie him.

---

* May we never be cast down by adversity, or unduly elevated by prosperity.

Gude een to you a', an' tak your nappy.
*A willy-waught's a gude night cappy.**
May we a' be canty an' cosy.
An' ilk hae a wife in his bosy.
A cosy but, and a canty ben,
To couthie † women and trusty men.
The ingle neuk wi' routh ‡ o' bannocks and bairns.
Here's to him wha winna beguile ye.
Mair sense and mair siller.
Horn, corn, wool, an' yarn.§

The system of giving toasts was so regularly established, that collections of them were published to add brilliancy to the festive board. By the kindness of the librarian, I have seen a little volume which is in the Writers' Library of Edinburgh. It is entitled, "The Gentleman's New Bottle Companion," Edinburgh, printed in the year MDCCLXXVII. It contains various toasts and sentiments which the writer considered to be suitable to such occasions. Of the taste and decency of the companies where some of them could be made use of, the less is said the better.

I have heard also of large traditionary collections of toasts and sentiments, belonging to old clubs and societies, extending back above a century, but I have not seen any of them, and I believe my readers will think they have had quite enough.

The favourable reaction which has taken place in regard to the whole system of intemperance may very fairly, in the first place, be referred to an improved *moral* feeling. But other causes have also assisted; and it is curious to observe how the different changes in the modes of society bear upon one another. The alteration in the convivial habits which we are noticing in our own country may be partly due to alteration of hours. The old plan

* A toast at parting or breaking up of the party.

† Loving. ‡ Plenty. § Toast for agricultural dinners.

of early dining favoured a system of suppers, and after supper was a great time for convivial songs and sentiments. This of course induced drinking to a late hour. Most drinking songs imply the night as the season of conviviality —thus in a popular madrigal :—

"By the gaily circling glass,
We can tell how minutes pass ;
By the hollow cask we're told,
How the waning *night* grows old."

And Burns thus marks the time :—

"It is the moon, I ken her horn,
That's blinkin' in the lift sae hie ;
She shines sae bright, to wyle us hame,
But by my sooth she'll wait a wee."

The young people of the present day have no idea of the state of matters in regard to the supper system when it was the normal condition of society. The late dining hours may make the social circle more formal, but they have been far less favourable to drinking propensities. After such dinners as ours are now, suppers are clearly out of the question. One is astonished to look back and recal the scenes to which were attached associations of hilarity, conviviality, and enjoyment. Drinking parties were protracted beyond the whole Sunday, having begun by a dinner on Saturday ; imbecility and prostrate helplessness were a common result of these bright and jovial scenes ; and by what perversion of language, or by what obliquity of sentiment, the notions of pleasure could be attached to scenes of such excess—to the nausea, the disgust of sated appetite, and the racking headache—it is not easy to explain. There were men of heads so hard, and of stomachs so insensible, that, like my friend Saunders Paul, they could stand anything in the way of drink. But to men in general, and to the more delicate constitutions, such a life must have been a cause of great misery. To a certain extent, and up to a certain point, wine may be a refreshment and a wholesome stimulant; nay it is a medicine, and a valuable one, and as such, comes recommended on fitting occasions by the physician. *Beyond* this point, as sanctioned and approved by nature, the use of wine is only degradation. Well did the sacred writer call wine, when thus taken in excess, "a mocker." It makes all men equal, because it makes them all idiotic. It allures them into a vicious indulgence, and then mocks their folly, by depriving them of any sense they may ever have possessed.

Reference has already been made to Lord Hermand's opinion of drinking, and to the high estimation in which he held a staunch drinker, according to the testimony of Lord Cockburn. There is a remarkable corroboration of this opinion in a current anecdote which is traditionary regarding the same learned judge. A case of some great offence was tried before him, and the counsel pleaded extenuation for his client in that he was *drunk* when he committed the offence. "Drunk!" exclaimed Lord Hermand, in great indignation; "if he could do such a thing when he was drunk, what might he not have done when he was *sober!*" evidently implying that the normal condition of human nature, and its most hopeful one, was a condition of intoxication.

Of the prevalence of hard drinking in certain houses as a system, a remarkable proof is given at page 55. The following anecdote still further illustrates the subject, and corresponds exactly with the story of the "loosing the cravats," which was performed for guests in a state of helpless inebriety by one of the household. There had been a carousing party at Castle Grant, many years ago, and as the evening advanced towards morning, two Highlanders were in attendance to carry the guests up stairs, it being understood that none could by any other means arrive at their sleeping apartments. One or two of the guests, however, whether from their abstinence or their superior strength of head, were walking up stairs, and declined the proffered assistance. The attendants were quite astonished, and indignantly exclaimed, "Agh, it's sare cheenged times at Castle Grant, when gentlemens can gang to bed on their ain feet."

There was a practice in many Scottish houses which favoured most injuriously the national tendency to spirit-drinking, and that was a foolish and inconsiderate custom of offering a glass on all occasions as a mark of kindness or hospitality. I mention the custom only for the purpose of offering a remonstrance. It should never be done. Even now, I am assured, small jobs (carpenter's or black-smith's, or such like) are constantly remunerated in the West Highlands of Scotland—and doubtless in many other parts of the country—not by a pecuniary payment, but by a *dram ;* if the said dram be taken from a *speerit*-decanter out of the family press or cupboard, the compliment is esteemed the greater, and the offering doubly valued.

A very amusing dialogue between a landlord and his tenant on this question of the dram has been sent to me. John Colquhoun, an aged Dumbartonshire tenant, is asked by the Laird of C. on Loch Lomond side, his landlord, to stay a minute till he *tastes.* "Now, John," says the laird. "Only half a glass, Camstraddale," meekly pleads John. "Which half?" rejoins the laird, "the upper or the lower?" John grins, and turns off *both—the upper and lower* too.

The upper and lower portions of the glass furnish another drinking anecdote. A very greedy old lady employed another John Colquhoun to cut the grass upon the lawn, and enjoined him to cut it very close, adding, as a reason for the injunction, that one inch at the bottom was worth two at the top. Having finished his work much to her satisfaction, the old lady got out the whisky bottle and a tapering wine glass, which she filled about half full ; John suggested that it would be better to fill it up, slily adding, "Fill it up, mem, for it's no like the gress ; an inch at the tap's worth twa at the bottom."

But the most whimsical anecdote connected with the subject of drink, is one traditionary in the south of Scotland, regarding an old Gallowegian lady disclaiming more drink, under the following circumstances:—The old generation of Galloway lairds were a primitive and hospitable race, but their conviviality sometimes led to awkward occurrences. In former days, when roads were bad, and wheeled vehicles almost unknown, an old laird was returning from a supper party, with his lady mounted behind him on horseback. On crossing the river Urr, at a ford at a point where it joins the sea, the old lady dropped off, but was not missed till her husband reached his door, when, of course, there was an immediate search made. The party who were despatched in quest of her arrived just in time to find her remonstrating with the advancing tide, which trickled into her mouth, in these words, "No anither drap ; neither het nor cauld."

I would now introduce, as a perfect illustration of this portion of our subject, two descriptions of clergymen, well-known men in their day, which are taken from Dr. Carlyle's work, already referred to. Of Dr. Alexander Webster, a clergyman, and one of his contemporaries, he writes thus—"Webster, leader of the high-flying party, had justly obtained much respect amongst the clergy, and all ranks indeed, for having established the Widows' Fund. . . . His appearance of great strictness in religion, to which he was bred under his father, who was a very popular minister of the Tolbooth Church, not acting in restraint of his convivial humour, he was held to be excellent company even by those of dissolute manners ; while, being a five-bottle man, he could lay them all under the table. This had brought on him the nickname of Dr. Bonum Magnum in the time of faction. But never being indecently the worse of liquor, and a love of claret, to any degree, not being reckoned in those days a sin in Scotland, all his excesses were pardoned."

Dr. Patrick Cumming, also a clergyman and a contemporary, he describes in the following terms :—" Dr. Patrick Cumming was, at this time (1751), at the head of the moderate interest, and had his temper been equal to his talents, might have kept it long, for he had both learning and sagacity, and very agreeable conversation, *with a constitution able to bear the conviviality of the times.*"

Now, of all the anecdotes and facts which I have collected, or of all which I have ever heard to illustrate the state of Scottish society in the past times, as regards its habits of intemperance, this assuredly surpasses them all.— Of two well-known, distinguished, and leading clergymen in the middle of the eighteenth century, one who had "obtained much respect," and "had the appearance of great strictness in religion," is described as an enormous drinker of claret ; the other, an able leader of a powerful section in the church, is described as *owing* his influence to his power of meeting the conviviality of the times. Suppose for a moment a future biographer should write in this strain of eminent divines, and should apply to distinguished members of the Scottish Church in 1863 such description as the following :—" Dr. —— was a man who took a leading part in all church affairs at this time, and was much looked up to by the evangelical section of the General Assembly ; he could always carry off without difficulty his five bottles of claret. Dr. —— had great influence in society, and led the opposite party in the General Assembly, as he could take his place in all companies, and drink on fair terms at the most convivial tables ! !" Why, this seems to us so monstrous, that we can scarcely believe Dr. Carlyle's account of matters in his day to be possible.

There is a story which illustrates, with terrible force, the power which drinking had obtained in Scottish social life. I have been deterred from bringing it forward, as too shocking for production. But as the story is pretty well known, and its truth vouched for on high authority, I venture to give it, as affording a proof that, in those days, no consideration, not even the most awful that affects human nature, could be made to outweigh the claims of a determined conviviality. It may, I think, be mentioned also, in the way of warning men generally against the hardening and demoralizing effects of habitual drunkenness. The story is this :—At a prolonged drinking bout, one of the party remarked, "What gars the laird of Garskadden luk sae gash ?"* "Ou," says his neighbour, the laird of Kilmardinny, "Garskadden's been wi' his Maker these twa hours ; I saw him step awa, but I didna like to disturb gude company !"†

Before closing this subject of excess in *drinking*, I may refer to another indulgence in which our countrymen are generally supposed to partake more largely than their neighbours :—I mean snuff-taking. The popular southern ideas of a Scotchman and his snuff-box are inseparable. Smoking does not appear to have been practised more in Scotland than in England, and if Scotchmen are sometimes intemperate in the use of snuff, it is certainly a more innocent excess than intemperance in whisky. I recollect, amongst the common people in the north, a mode of taking snuff which showed a determination to make the *most* of it, and which indicated somewhat of intemperance in the enjoyment ; this was to receive it, not through a pinch between the fingers, but through a quill or little bone laddle, which forced it up the nose. But besides smoking and snuffing, I have a reminiscence of a *third* use to tobacco, which I apprehend is now quite obsolete. Some of my readers will be surprised when I name this forgotten luxury. It was called *plugging*, and consisted (*horresco referens*) in poking a piece of pig-tail tobacco right into the nostril. I remember this distinctly, and now, at a distance of more than sixty years, I recal my utter astonishment as a boy, at seeing my grand-uncle, with whom I lived

---

* Ghastly.

† The scene is described and place mentioned in Dr. Strang's account of Glasgow Clubs, p. 104, 2d edit.

in early days, put a thin piece of tobacco fairly up his nose. I suppose the plug acted as a continued stimulant on the olfactory nerve, and was, in short, like taking a perpetual pinch of snuff.

The inveterate snuff-taker, like the dram-drinker, felt severely the being deprived of his accustomed stimulant, as in the following instance:—A severe snow-storm in the Highlands, which lasted for several weeks, having stopped all communication betwixt neighbouring hamlets, the snuff-boxes were soon reduced to their last pinch. Borrowing and begging from all the neighbours within reach were first resorted to, but when these failed, all were alike reduced to the longing which unwillingly-abstinent snuff-takers alone know. The minister of the parish was amongst the unhappy number; the craving was so intense, that study was out of the question, and he became quite restless. As a last resort, the beadle was despatched, through the snow, to a neighbouring glen, in the hope of getting a supply; but he came back as unsuccessful as he went. "What's to be dune, John?" was the minister's pathetic inquiry. John shook his head, as much as to say that he could not tell; but immediately thereafter started up, as if a new idea had occurred to him. He came back in a few minutes, crying, "Hae!" The minister, too eager to be scrutinizing, took a long, deep pinch, and then said, "Whaur did you get it?" "I soupit* the poupit," was John's expressive reply. The minister's accumulated superfluous Sabbath snuff now came into good use.

It does not appear that at this time a similar excess in *eating* accompanied this prevalent tendency to excess in drinking. Scottish tables were at that period plain and abundant, but epicurism or gluttony do not seem to have been handmaids to drunkenness. A humorous anecdote, however, of a full-eating laird, may well accompany those which appertain to the *drinking* lairds.—A lady in the

---

* Swept.

north having watched the proceedings of a guest, who ate long and largely, she ordered the servant to take away, as he had at last laid down his knife and fork. To her surprise, however, he resumed his work, and she apologised to him, saying, "I thought, Mr. ——, you had done." "Oh, so I had, mem; but I just fan' a doo in the *redd* o' my plate." He had discovered a pigeon lurking amongst the bones and refuse of his plate, and could not resist finishing it.

CHAPTER THE FOURTH.

ON THE OLD SCOTTISH DOMESTIC SERVANT.

We come now to a subject on which a great change has taken place in this country during my own experience. I allude to the third division which we proposed of these desultory remarks—viz., those peculiarities of intercourse which some years back marked the connection between masters and servants. In many Scottish houses a great familiarity prevailed between members of the family and the domestics. For this many reasons might have been assigned. Indeed, when we consider the simple modes of life which discarded the ideas of ceremony or etiquette; the retired and uniform style of living which afforded few opportunities for any change in the domestic arrangements; and when we add to these a free, unrestrained, unformal, and natural style of intercommunion, which seems rather a national characteristic, we need not be surprised to find in quiet Scottish families a sort of intercourse with old domestics which can hardly be looked for at a time when habits are so changed, and where much of the quiet eccentricity belonging to us as a national characteristic is almost necessarily softened down or driven out. Many circumstances conspired to promote familiarity with old domestics which are now entirely changed. We take the case of a domestic coming early into service and passing year after year in the same family. The servant grows up into old age and confirmed habits when the laird is becoming a man, a husband, father of a family. The domestic cannot forget the days when his master was a child, riding on his back, applying to him for help in difficulties about his fishing, his rabbits, his pony, his going to school. All the family know how attached he is; nobody likes to speak harshly to him. He is a privileged man. The faithful old servant of thirty, forty, or fifty years, if with a tendency to be jealous, cross, and interfering, becomes a great trouble. Still the relative position was the result of good feelings. If the familiarity sometimes became a nuisance, it was a wholesome nuisance, and relic of a simpler time gone by. But the case of the old servant, whether agreeable or troublesome, was often so fixed and established in the households of past days, that there was scarce a possibility of getting away from it. The well-known story of the answer of one of these domestic tyrants to the irritated master, who was making an effort to free himself from the thraldom, shows the idea entertained, by *one* of the parties at least, of the permanency of the tenure. I am assured by a friend that the true edition of the story was this:—An old Mr. Erskine of Dun had one of these old retainers, under whose language and unreasonable assumption he had long groaned. He had almost determined to bear it no longer, when, walking out with his man, on crossing a field, the master exclaimed, "There's a hare." Andrew looked at the place, and coolly replied, "What a big lee, it's a cauff." The master, quite angry now, plainly told the old domestic that they *must* part. But the tried servant of forty years, not dreaming of the possibility of *his* dismissal, innocently asked, "Ay, sir; whare ye gaun? I'm sure ye're aye best at hame;" supposing that, if there were to be any disruption, it must be the master who would change the place. An example of a similar fixedness of tenure in an old servant was afforded in an anecdote related of an old coachman long in the service of a noble lady, and who gave all the trouble and annoyance which he conceived were the privileges of his position in the family. At last the lady fairly gave him notice to quit, and told him he must go. The only satisfaction she got was the quiet answer, "Na, na, my lady; I druve ye to your marriage, and I shall stay to drive ye to your burial." Indeed, we have heard of a still stronger assertion of his official position by one who met an order to quit his master's service by the cool reply, "Na, na; I'm no gangin'. If ye dinna ken whan ye've a gude servant, I ken whan I've a gude place."

It is but fair, however, to give an anecdote in which the master and the servant's position was *reversed*, in regard to a wish for change:—An old servant of a relation of my own with an ungovernable temper, became at last so weary of his master's irascibility, that he declared he must leave, and gave as his reason the fits of anger which came on and produced such great annoyance that he could not stand it any longer. His master, unwilling to lose him, tried to coax him by reminding him that the anger was soon off. "Ay," replied the other very shrewdly, "but it's nae suner aff than it's on again." I remember well an old servant of the old school, who had been fifty years domesticated in a family. Indeed I well remember the celebration of the half-century service completed. There were rich scenes with Sandy and his mistress. Let me recal you both to memory. Let me think of you, the kind, generous, warm-hearted mistress; a gentlewoman by descent and by feeling; a true friend, a sincere Christian. And let me think, too, of you, Sandy, an honest, faithful, and attached member of the family. For you were in that house rather as an humble friend than a servant. But out of this fifty years of attached service there sprang a sort of domestic relation and freedom of intercourse which would surprise people in these days. And yet Sandy knew his place. Like Corporal Trim, who, although so familiar and admitted to so much familiarity with my Uncle Toby, never failed in the respectful address—never forgot to say "your honour." At a dinner-party Sandy was very active about changing his mistress's plate, and whipped it off when he saw that she had got a piece of rich pattee upon it. His mistress not liking such rapid movements, and at the same time knowing that remonstrance was in vain, exclaimed, "Hout, Sandy, I'm no dune," and dabbed her fork into the pattee as it disappeared, to rescue a morsel. I remember her praise of English mutton was a great annoyance to the Scottish prejudices of Sandy. One day she was telling me of a triumph Sandy had upon that subject. The smell of the joint roasting had become very offensive through the house. The lady called out to Sandy to have the doors closed, and adding, "That must be some horrid Scotch mutton you have got." To Sandy's delight, this was a leg of *English* mutton his mistress had expressly chosen, and, as she significantly told me, "Sandy never let that down upon me."

On Deeside there existed, in my recollection, besides the Saunders Paul I have alluded to, a number of extraordinary acute and humorous Scottish characters amongst the lower classes. The native gentry enjoyed their humour, and hence arose a familiarity of intercourse which called forth many amusing scenes and quaint rejoinders. A celebrated character of this description bore the soubriquet of "Boaty." He had acted as Charon of the Dee at Banchory, and passed the boat over the river before there was a bridge. Boaty had many curious sayings recorded of him. When speaking of the gentry around, he characterized them according to their occupations and activity of habits—thus: "As to Mr. Russell of Blackha', he just works himsell like a paid labourer; Mr. Duncan's a' the day fish, fish; but Sir Robert's a perfect gentleman—he does naething, naething." Boaty was a first-rate salmon-fisher himself, and was much sought after by amateurs who came to Banchory for the sake of the sport afforded by the beautiful Dee. He was, perhaps, a little spoiled, and presumed upon the indulgence and familiarity shown to him in the way of his craft—as, for example, he was in attendance with his boat on a sportsman who was both skilful and successful, for he caught salmon after salmon. Between each fish catching he solaced himself with a good pull from a flask, which he returned to his pocket, however, without offering to let Boaty have any participation in the refreshment. Boaty, partly a little professionally jealous, perhaps, at the success, and partly indignant at receiving less than his usual attention on such occasions, and seeing no prospect of amendment, deliberately pulled the boat to shore, shouldered the oars, rods, landing-nets, and all the fishing apparatus which he had provided, and set off homewards. His companion, far from considering his day's work to be over, and keen for more sport, was amazed, and peremptorily ordered him to come back. But all the answer made by the offended Boaty was, "Na, na; them 'at drink by themsells may just fish by themsells."

The charge these old domestics used to take of the interests of the family, and the cool way in which they took upon them to protect those interests, sometimes led to very provoking, and sometimes to very ludicrous exhibitions of importance. A friend told me of a dinner scene illustrative of this sort of interference which had happened at Airth in the last generation. Mrs. Murray of Abercairney had been amongst the guests, and at dinner one of the family noticed that she was looking for the proper spoon to help herself with salt. The old servant Thomas was appealed to, that the want might be supplied. He did not notice the appeal. It was repeated in a more peremptory manner, "Thomas, Mrs. Murray has not a salt-spoon;" to which he replied most emphatically, "Last time Mrs. Murray dined here we *lost* a salt-spoon." An old servant who took a similar charge of everything that went on in the family, having observed that his master thought that he had drunk wine with every lady at table, but had overlooked one, jogged his memory with the question, "What ails ye at her wi' the green gown?"

In my own family I know a case of a very long service, and where, no doubt, there was much interest and attachment; but it was a case where the temper had not softened under the influence of years, but had rather assumed that form of disposition which we denominate *crusty*. My grand-uncle, Sir A. Ramsay, died in 1806, and left a domestic who had been in his service since he was ten years of age; and being at the time of his master's death past fifty or well on to sixty, he must have been more than forty years a servant in the family. From the retired life my grand-uncle had been leading, Jamie Layal had much of his own way, and, like many a domestic so situated, he did not like to be contradicted, and, in fact, could not bear to be found fault with. My uncle, who had succeeded to a part of my grand-uncle's property, succeeded also to Jamie Layal, and from respect to his late master's memory and Jamie's own services, he took him into his house, intending him to act as house servant. However, this did not answer, and he was soon kept on, more with the form than the reality of any active duty, and took any light work that was going on about the house. In this capacity it was his daily task to feed a flock of turkeys which were growing up to maturity. On one occasion, my aunt having followed him in his work, and having observed such a waste of food, that the ground was actually covered with grain which they could not eat, and which would soon be destroyed and lost, naturally remonstrated, and suggested a more reasonable and provident supply. But all the answer she got from the offended Jamie was a bitter rejoinder, "Weel, then, neist time they sall get *nane ava!*" On another occasion a family from a distance had called whilst my uncle and aunt were out of the house. Jamie came into the parlour to deliver the cards, or to announce that they had called. My aunt, somewhat vexed at not having been in the way, inquired what message Mr. and Mrs. Innes had left, as she had expected one "No; no message." She returned to the charge, and asked again if they had not told him *anything* he was to repeat. Still, "No; no message." "But did they say nothing? Are you sure they said nothing?" Jamie, sadly put out and offended at being thus interrogated, at last burst forth, "They neither said ba nor bum," and indignantly left the room, banging the door after him. A characteristic anecdote of one of these old domestics I have from a friend who was acquainted with the parties concerned. The old man was standing at the sideboard and attending to the demands of a pretty large dinner party: the calls made for various wants from the company became so numerous and frequent that the attendant got quite bewildered, and lost his patience and temper; at length he gave vent to his indignation in a remonstrance addressed to the whole company, "Cry a' thegither, that's the way to be served."

I have two characteristic and dry Scottish answers, traditional in the Lothian family, supplied to me by the present excellent and highly-gifted young Marquis. A Marquis of Lothian of a former generation observed in his walk two workmen very busy with a ladder to reach a bell, on which they next kept up a furious ringing. He asked what was the object of making such a din; to which the answer was, "Oh, juist, my lord, to ca' the workmen together." "Why, how many are there?" asked his lordship. "Ou, juist Sandy and me," was the quiet rejoinder. The same Lord Lothian, looking about the garden, directed his gardener's attention to a particular plum-tree, charging him to be careful of the produce of that tree, and send the *whole* of it in marked, as it was of a very particular kind. "Ou," said the gardener, "I'll do that, my lord; there's juist twa o' them."

These dry answers of Newbattle servants remind us of a similar state of communication in a Yester domestic. Lord Tweeddale was very fond of dogs, and on leaving Yester for London he instructed his head keeper, a quaint bodie, to give him a periodical report of the kennel, and particulars of his favourite dogs. Among the latter was an *especial* one, of the true Skye breed, called "Pickle," from which sobriquet we may form a tolerable estimate of his qualities.

It happened one day, in or about the year 1827, that poor Pickle during the absence of his master was taken unwell; and the watchful guardian immediately warned the marquis of the sad fact, and of the progress of the disease, which lasted three days—for which he sent the three following laconic despatches:—

Yester, *May* 1*st*, 18—.

MY LORD,

Pickle's no weel

Your Lordship's humble servant, etc.

Yester, 2*d May* 18—.

MY LORD,

Pickle will no do!

I am your Lordship's, etc.

Yester, 3*d May* 18—.

MY LORD,

Pickle's dead!

I am your Lordship's, etc.

I have heard of an old Forfarshire lady who, knowing the habits of her old and spoilt servant, when she wished a note to be taken without loss of time, held it open and read it over to him, saying, "There, noo, Andrew, ye ken a' that's in't; noo dinna stop to open it, but just send it aff." Of another servant, when sorely tried by an unaccustomed bustle and hurry, a very amusing anecdote has been recorded. His mistress, a woman of high rank, who had been living in much quiet and retirement for some time, was called upon to entertain a large party at dinner. She consulted with Nichol, her faithful servant, and all the arrangements were made for the great event. As the company were arriving, the lady saw Nichol running about in great agitation, and in his shirt sleeves. She remonstrated, and said that as the guests were coming in he must put on his coat. "Indeed, my lady," was his excited reply, "indeed, there's sae muckle rinnin' here and rinnin' there, that I'm just distrackit. I hae cuist'n my coat and waistcoat, and faith I dinna ken how lang I can thole* my breeks." There is often a ready wit in this class of character, marked by their replies. I have the following communicated from an ear-witness: "Weel, Péggy," said a man to an old family servant, "I wonder ye're aye single yet!" "Me marry," said she indignantly; "I wadna gie my single life for a' the double anes I ever saw."

An old woman was exhorting a servant once about her ways. "You serve the deevil," said she. "Me!" said the girl; "Na, na, I dinna serve the deevil; I serve ae single lady."

A baby was out with the nurse, who walked it up and down the garden. "Is't a laddie or a lassie?" said the gardener. "A laddie," said the maid. "Weel," says he, "I'm glad o' that, for there's ower money women in the world." "Hech, man," said Jess, "div ye no ken there's aye maist sawn o' the best crap?"

The answers of servants used curiously to illustrate habits and manners of the time,—as the economical modes of her mistress' life were well touched by the lass who thus described her ways and domestic habits with her household: "She's vicious upo' the wark; but eh, she's vary mysterious o' the victualling."

A country habit of making the gathering of the congregation in the churchyard previous to and after divine service an occasion for gossip and business, which I remember well, is thoroughly described in the following:— A lady, on hiring a servant-girl in the country, told her, as a great indulgence, that she should have the liberty of attending the church every Sunday, but that she would be expected to return home always immediately on the conclusion of service. The lady, however, rather unex-

---

* Bear.

pectedly found a positive objection raised against this apparently reasonable arrangement. "Then I canna engadge wi' ye, mem ; for 'deed I wadna gie the crack i' the kirkyard for a' the sermon."

There is another story which shows that a greater importance might be attached to the crack i' the kirkyard than was done even by the servant lass mentioned above. A rather rough subject, residing in Galloway, used to attend church regularly, as it appeared, for the *sake* of the crack. For on being taken to task for his absenting himself he remarked, "There's nae need to gang to the kirk noo, for everybody gets a newspaper."

The changes that many of us have lived to witness in this kind of intercourse between families and old servants is a part of a still greater change—the change in that modification of the feudal system, the attachment of clans. This, also, from transfers of property and extinction of old families in the Highlands, as well as from more general causes, is passing away ; and it includes also changes in the intercourse between landed proprietors and cottagers, and abolition of harvest-homes, and such meetings. People are now more independent of each other, and service has become a pecuniary and not a sentimental question. The extreme contrast of that old-fashioned Scottish intercourse of families with their servants and dependants, of which I have given some amusing examples, is found in the modern manufactory system. There the service is a mere question of personal interest. One of our first practical engineers, and one of the first engine-makers in England, stated that he employed and paid handsomely on an average 1200 workmen ; but that they held so little feeling for him as their master, that not above half a dozen of the number would notice him when passing him, either in the works or out of work hours. Contrast this advanced state of dependants' indifference with the familiarity of domestic intercourse we have been describing !

It has been suggested by my esteemed friend, Dr. W

Lindsay Alexander, that Scottish anecdotes deal too exclusively with the shrewd, quaint, and pawky *humour* of our countrymen, and have not sufficiently illustrated the deep pathos and strong loving-kindness of the "kindly Scot,"—qualities which, however little appreciated across the Border, abound in Scottish poetry and Scottish life. For example, to take the case before us of these old retainers, although snappy and disagreeable to the last degree in their replies, and often most provoking in their ways, they were yet deeply and sincerely attached to the family where they had so long been domesticated; and the servant who would reply to her mistress' order to mend the fire by the short answer "The fire's weel eneuch," would at the same time evince much interest in all that might assist her in sustaining the credit of her domestic economy; as, for example, whispering in her ear at dinner, "Press the jeelies; they winna keep;" and had the hour of real trial and of difficulty come to the family, would have gone to the death for them, and shared their greatest privations. Dr. Alexander gives a very interesting example of kindness and affectionate attachment in an old Scottish domestic of his own family, whose quaint and odd familiarity was charming. I give it in his own words:—"When I was a child, there was an old servant at Pinkieburn, where my early days were spent, who had been all her life, I may say, in the house—for she came to it a child, and lived, without ever leaving it, till she died in it, seventy-five years of age. Her feeling to her old master, who was just two years younger than herself, was a curious compound of the deference of a servant and the familiarity and affection of a sister. She had known him as a boy, lad, man, and old man, and she seemed to have a sort of notion, that without her he must be a very helpless being indeed. 'I aye keepit the house for him, whether he was hame or awa', was a frequent utterance of hers; and she never seemed to think the intrusion even of his own nieces, who latterly lived with him, at all legitimate. When on her deathbed, he hobbled to her room with difficulty, having just got over a severe attack of gout, to bid her farewell. I chanced to be present, but was too young to remember what passed, except one thing, which probably was rather recalled to me afterwards than properly recollected by me. It was her last request. 'Laird,' said she (for so she always called him, though his lairdship was of the smallest), 'will ye tell them to bury me whaur I'll lie across at your feet.' I have always thought this characteristic of the old Scotch servant, and as such I send it to you."

And here I would introduce another story which struck me very forcibly as illustrating the union of the qualities referred to by Dr. Alexander. In the following narrative, how deep and tender a feeling is expressed in a brief dry sentence! I give Mr. Scott's language :*—"My brother and I were, during our High School vacation, some forty years ago, very much indebted to the kindness of a clever young carpenter employed in the machinery workshop of New Lanark Mills, near to which we were residing during our six weeks' holidays. It was he—Samuel Shaw, our dear companion—who first taught us to saw, and to plane, and to turn too ; and who made us the bows and arrows in which we so much delighted. The vacation over, and our hearts very sore, but bound to Samuel Shaw for ever, our mother sought to place some pecuniary recompense in his hand at parting, for all the great kindness he had shown her boys. Samuel looked in her face, and gently moving her hand aside, with an affectionate look cast upon us, who were by, exclaimed, in a tone which had sorrow in it, "Noo, Mrs. Scott, *ye ha'e spoilt a'*." After such an appeal, it may be supposed no recompense, in silver or in gold, remained with Samuel Shaw.

On the subject of the old Scottish domestic, I have to acknowledge a kind communication from Lord Kinloch,

* Rev. R. Scott of Cranwell.

which I give in his Lordship's words :—" My father had been in the counting-house of the well-known David Dale, the founder of the Lanark Mills, and eminent for his benevolence. Mr. Dale, who it would appear was a short stout man, had a person in his employment named Matthew, who was permitted that familiarity with his master which was so characteristic of the former generation. One winter day Mr. Dale came into the counting-house, and complained that he had fallen on the ice. Matthew, who saw that his master was not much hurt, grinned a sarcastic smile. 'I fell all my length,' said Mr. Dale. 'Nae great length, sir,' said Matthew. 'Indeed, Matthew, ye need not laugh,' said Mr. Dale ; 'I have hurt the sma' of my back.' 'I wunner whaur *that* is,' said Matthew." Indeed, specimens like Matthew of serving-men of the former time have latterly been fast going out, but I remember one or two specimens. A lady of my acquaintance had one named John in her house at Portobello. I remember how my modern ideas were offended by John's familiarity when waiting at table. " Some more wine, John," said his mistress. " There 's some i' the bottle, mem," said John. A little after, " Mend the fire, John." " The fire's weel aneuch, mem," replied the impracticable John. Another " John" of my acquaintance was in the family of Mrs. Campbell of Ardnave, mother of the Princess Polignac and the Honourable Mrs. Archibald Macdonald. A young lady visiting in the family asked John at dinner for a potato. John made no response. The request was repeated ; when John, putting his mouth to her ear, said, very audibly " There 's jist twa in the dish, and they maun be keepit for the strangers."

The following was sent me by a kind correspondent—a learned Professor in India—as a sample of *squabbling* between Scottish servants. A mistress observing something peculiar in her maid's manner, addressed her, " Dear me, Tibbie, what are you so snappish about, that you go knocking the things as you dust them ?" " Ou, mem, it's

Jock." "Well, what has Jock been doing?" "Ou (with an indescribable, but easily imaginable toss of the head), he was angry at me, an' misca'd me, an' I said I was juist as the Lord had made me, an' ——." "Well, Tibbie?" "An' he said the Lord could hae had little to do whan he made me." The idea of Tibbie being the work of an idle moment was one, the deliciousness of which was not likely to be relished by Tibbie.

The following characteristic anecdote of a Highland servant I have received from the same correspondent. An English gentleman, travelling in the Highlands, was rather late of coming down to dinner. Donald was sent up stairs to intimate that all was ready. He speedily returned, nodding significantly, as much as to say that it was all right. "But, Donald," said the master, after some further trial of a hungry man's patience, "are ye sure ye made the gentleman understand?" "*Understand?*" retorted Donald (who had peeped into the room and found the guest engaged at his toilet), "I'se warrant ye he understands; he's *sharping* his teeth,"—not supposing the tooth-brush could be for any other use.

There have been some very amusing instances given of the matter-of-fact obedience paid to orders by Highland retainers when made to perform the ordinary duties of domestic servants; as when Mr. Campbell, a Highland gentleman, visiting in a country house, and telling Donald to bring everything out of the bedroom, found all its movable articles—fender, fire-irons, etc.—piled up in the lobby; so literal was the poor man's sense of obedience to orders! And of this he gave a still more extraordinary proof during his sojourn in Edinburgh, by a very ludicrous exploit. When the family moved into a house there, Mrs. Campbell gave him very particular instructions regarding visitors, explaining that they were to be shown into the drawing-room, and no doubt used the Scotticism, "*Carry* any ladies that call up stairs." On the arrival of the first visitors, Donald was eager to show his strict attention to the mistress' orders. Two ladies came together, and Donald, seizing one in his arms, said to the other, "Bide ye there till I come for ye," and, in spite of her struggles and remonstrances, ushered the terrified visitor into Mrs. Campbell's presence in this unwonted fashion.

Another case of *literal* obedience to orders produced a somewhat startling form of message. A servant of an old maiden lady, a patient of Dr. Poole, formerly of Edinburgh, was under orders to go to the doctor every morning to report the state of her health, how she had slept, etc., with strict injunctions *always* to add, "with her compliments." At length, one morning the girl brought this extraordinary message :—"Miss S——'s compliments, and she de'ed last night at aicht o'clock !"

I recollect, in Montrose (that fruitful field for old Scottish stories !), a most naïve reply from an honest lass, servant to old Mrs. *Captain* Fullerton. A party of gentlemen had dined with Mrs. Fullerton, and they had a turkey for dinner. Mrs. F. proposed that one of the legs should be *deviled*, and the gentlemen have it served up as a relish for their wine. Accordingly one of the company skilled in the mystery prepared it with pepper, cayenne, mustard, ketchup, etc. He gave it to Lizzy, and told her to take it down to the kitchen, supposing, as a matter of course, she would know that it was to be broiled, and brought back in due time. But in a little while, when it was rung for, Lizzy very innocently replied that she had ate it up. As it was sent back to the kitchen, her only idea was that it must be for herself. But on surprise being expressed that she had eaten what was so highly peppered and seasoned, she very quaintly answered, "Ou, I liket it a the better."

A well-known servant of the old school was John, the servant of Pitfour, Mr. Ferguson, M.P., himself a most eccentric character, long father of the House of Commons, and a great friend of Pitt. John used to entertain the tenants on Pitfour's brief visits to his estate with numerous anecdotes of his master and Mr. Pitt; but he always prefaced them with something in the style of Cardinal Wolsey's *Ego et rex meus*, with "Me, and Pitt, and Pitfour," went somewhere, or performed some exploit. The famous Duchess of Gordon once wrote a note to John (the name of this eccentric valet), and said, "John, put Pitfour into the carriage on Tuesday, and bring him up to Gordon Castle to dinner." After sufficiently scratching his head, and considering what he should do, he showed the letter to Pitfour, who smiled, and said dryly, "Well, John, I suppose we must go."

An old domestic of this class gave a capital reason to his *young* master for his being allowed to do as he liked:—"Ye needna find faut wi' me, Maister Jeems, *I hae been langer about the place than yersel'.*"

CHAPTER THE FIFTH.

ON HUMOUR PROCEEDING FROM SCOTTISH LANGUAGE, INCLUDING SCOTTISH PROVERBS.

WE come next to reminiscences chiefly connected with peculiarities which turned upon our Scottish LANGUAGE, whether contained in words or in expressions. I am quite aware that the difference between the anecdotes belonging to this division and to the division termed "Wit and Humour" is very indistinct, and must, in fact, in many cases, be quite arbitrary. Much of what we enjoy most in Scottish stories is not on account of wit or humour, properly so called, in the speaker, but, I should say rather from the odd and unexpected view which is taken of some matter, or from the quaint and original turn of the expression made use of, or from the simple and matter-of-fact reference made to circumstances which are unusual. I shall not, therefore, be careful to preserve any strict line of separation between this division and the next. Each is conversant with what is amusing and with what is Scotch. What we have now chiefly to illustrate by suitable anecdotes is peculiarities of Scottish language—its various humorous turns and odd expressions.

We have now to consider stories where words and expressions which are peculiarly Scotch impart the humour and the point. Sometimes they are altogether untranslatable into another language. As for example, a parishioner in an Ayrshire village, meeting his pastor, who had just returned after a considerable absence on account of ill health, congratulated him on his convalescence, and added anticipatory of the pleasure he would have in hearing him again, "I'm unco yuckie to hear a blaud o' your gab." This is an untranslatable form of saying how glad he should be to hear his minister's voice again speaking to him the words of salvation and of peace from the pulpit.

The two following are good examples of that Scottish style of expression which has its own character. They are kindly sent by Sir Archibald Dunbar. The first illustrates Scottish acute discernment. A certain titled lady well known around her country town for her long-continued and extensive charities, which are not withheld from those who least deserve them, had a few years since, by the unexpected death of her brother and of his only son, become possessor of a fine estate. The news soon spread in the neighbourhood, and a group of old women were overheard in the street of Elgin discussing the fact. One of them said, "Ay, she may prosper, for she has baith the prayers of the good and of the bad."

The second anecdote is a delightful illustration of Mrs. Hamilton's "Cottagers of Glenburnie," and of the old-fashioned Scottish pride in the *midden.* About twenty years ago, under the apprehension of cholera, committees of the most influential inhabitants of the county of Moray were formed to enforce a more complete cleansing of its towns and villages, and to induce the cottagers to remove their dunghills or dung-pits from too close a proximity to their doors or windows. One determined woman, on the outskirts of the town of Forres, no doubt with her future potato crop in view, met the M.P., who headed one of these committees, thus, "Noo, Major, you may tak our lives, but ye'll no tak our middens."

The change of language which has taken place in Scotland during the last seventy years has been a very important change, and must affect in a greater degree than many persons would imagine, the turn of thought and general modes and aspects of society. In losing the old racy Scottish tongue no doubt much originality of *character* was lost. I suppose at one time the two countries of England and Scotland were considered as almost speaking different languages, and I suppose also, that from the period of the union of the crowns the language has been assimilating. We see the process of assimilation going on, and ere long amongst persons of education and birth very little difference will be perceptible. With regard to that class a great change has taken place in my time. I recollect old Scottish ladies and gentlemen who really *spoke Scotch.* It was not, mark me, speaking English with an accent. No; it was downright Scotch. Every tone and every syllable was Scotch. For example, I recollect old Miss Erskine of Dun, a fine specimen of a real lady, and daughter of an ancient Scottish house, so speaking. Many people now would not understand her. She was always *the lady*, notwithstanding her dialect, and to none could the epithet vulgar be less appropriately applied. I speak of nearly forty years ago, and yet I recollect her accost to me as well as if it were yesterday: "I didna ken ye were i' the toun." Taking words and accents together, an address how totally unlike what we now meet with in society. Some of the old Scottish words which we can remember are delicious; but how strange they would sound to the ears of the present generation! Fancy that in walking from church, and discussing the sermon, a lady of rank should now express her opinion of it by the description of its being, "but a hummelcorn discourse." Many living persons can remember Angus old ladies who would say to their nieces and daughters, "Whatna hummeldoddie o' a mutch hae ye gotten?" meaning a flat and low-crowned cap. In speaking of the dryness of the soil on a road in Lanarkshire, a farmer said, "It stoors* in an oor."† How would this be as tersely translated into English? The late Duchess of Gordon sat at dinner next an English

---

* Stoor is, Scotticé, *dust in motion*, and there is really no synonym for it in English.

† Hour.

gentleman who was carving, and who made it a boast that he was thoroughly master of the Scottish language. Her Grace turned to him and said, "Rax me a spaul o' that bubbly jock."* The unfortunate man was completely *nonplussed.* A Scottish gentleman was entertaining at his house an English cousin who professed himself as rather knowing in the language of the north side of the Tweed. He asked him what he supposed to be the meaning of the expression, "ripin' the ribs."† To which he readily answered, "Oh, it describes a very fat man." I profess myself an out and out Scotchman. I have strong national partialities—call them if you will national prejudices. I cherish a great love of old Scottish language. Some of our pure Scottish ballad poetry is unsurpassed in any language for grace and pathos. How expressive, how beautiful are its phrases! You can't translate them. Take an example of power in a Scottish expression, to describe with tenderness and feeling what is in human life. Take one of our most familiar phrases; as thus,—We meet an old friend, we talk over bygone days, and remember many who were dear to us both, once bright and young and gay, of whom some remain, honoured, prosperous, and happy—of whom some are under a cloud of misfortune or disgrace—some are broken in health and spirits—some sunk into the grave; we recal old familiar places—old companions, pleasures, and pursuits; as Scotchmen our hearts are touched with these remembrances of

AULD LANG SYNE.

Match me the phrase in English. You can't translate it. The fitness and the beauty lie in the felicity of the language. Like many happy expressions, it is not transferable into another tongue, just like the "simplex munditiis" of Horace, which describes the natural grace of female elegance, or the ἀνηρίθμον γέλασμα of Æschylus,

* Reach me a leg of that turkey.

† Clearing ashes out of the bars of the grate.

which describes the bright sparkling of the ocean in the sun.

I think the power of Scottish dialect was happily exemplified by the late Dr. Adam, rector of the High School of Edinburgh, in his translation of the Horatian expression, "desipere in loco," which he turned by the Scotch phrase "Weel-timed daffin';" a translation, however, which no one but a Scotchman could appreciate. The following humorous Scottish translation of an old Latin aphorism has been assigned to the late Dr. Hill of St. Andrews:—"*Qui bene cepit dimidium facti fecit*," the witty Principal expressed in Scotch, "Weel saipet (well soaped) is half shaven."

What mere *English* word could have expressed a distinction so well in such a case as the following? I heard once a lady in Edinburgh objecting to a preacher that she did not understand him. Another lady, his great admirer, insinuated that probably he was too "deep" for her to follow. But her ready answer was, "Na, na, he's no just deep, but he's *drumly*."*

We have just received a testimony to the value of our Scottish language from the illustrious Chancellor of the University of Edinburgh, the force and authority of which no one will be disposed to question. Lord Brougham, in speaking of improvements upon the English language, makes these striking remarks:—

"The pure and classical language of Scotland must on no account be regarded as a provincial dialect, any more than French was so regarded in the reign of Henry V., or Italian in that of the first Napoleon, or Greek under the Roman Empire. Nor is it to be in any manner of way considered as a corruption of the Saxon; on the contrary, it contains much of the old and genuine Saxon, with an intermixture from the Northern nations, as Danes and Norse, and some, though a small portion, from the Celtic.

* Mentally confused. Muddy when applied to water.

But in whatever way composed, or from whatever sources arising, it is a national language, used by the whole people in their early years, by many learned and gifted persons throughout life, and in which are written the laws of the Scotch, their judicial proceedings, their ancient history; above all, their poetry.

"There can be no doubt that the English language would greatly gain by being enriched with a number both of words and of phrases, or turns of expression, now peculiar to the Scotch. It was by such a process that the Greek became the first of tongues, as well written as spoken. . . .

"Would it not afford means of enriching and improving the English language, if full and accurate glossaries of improved Scotch words and phrases—those successfully used by the best writers, both in prose and verse—were given, with distinct explanation and reference to authorities? This has been done in France and other countries, where some dictionaries accompany the English, in some cases with Scotch synonyms, in others with varieties of expression."—*Installation Address*, p. 63.

The Scotch as a people, from their more guarded and composed method of speaking, are not so liable to fall into that figure of speech for which our Irish neighbours are celebrated—usually called the Bull; some specimens, however, of that confusion of thought, very like a bull, have been recorded of Scottish interlocutors.

Of this the two following examples have been sent to me by a kind friend.

It is related of a Scottish judge (who has supplied several anecdotes of Scottish stories), that on going to consult a dentist, who, as is usual, placed him in the professional chair, and told his lordship that he must let him put his fingers into his mouth, he exclaimed, "Na! na! ye'll aiblins *bite me*."

A Scottish laird, singularly enough the grandson of the learned judge mentioned above, when going his round to canvass for the county, at the time when the electors were chiefly confined to resident proprietors, was asked at one house where he called if he would not take some refreshment, hesitated, and said, "I doubt it's treating, and may be ca'd *bribery*."

But a still more amusing specimen of this figure of speech was supplied by an honest Highlander, in the days of sedan chairs. For the benefit of my young readers I may describe the sedan chair as a comfortable little carriage fixed to two poles, and carried by two men, one behind and one before. A dowager lady of quality had gone out to dinner in one of these "leathern conveniences," and whilst she herself enjoyed the hospitality of the mansion upstairs, her bearers were profusely entertained downstairs, and partook of the abundant refreshment offered to them. When my lady was to return, and had taken her place in the sedan, her bearers raised the chair, but she found no progress was made—she felt herself sway first to one side, then to the other, and soon came bump upon the ground, when Donald behind was heard shouting to Donald before (for the bearers of sedans were always Highlanders), "Let her down, Donald man, *for she's drunk*."

I cannot help thinking that a change of national language involves to some extent change of national character. Numerous examples of great power in Scottish phraseology, to express the picturesque, the feeling, the wise, and the humorous, might be taken from the works of Robert Burns, Ferguson, or Allan Ramsay, and which lose their charm altogether when *unscottified*. The speaker certainly seems to take a strength and character from his words. We must now look for specimens of this racy and expressive tongue in the more retired parts of the country. It is no longer to be found in high places. It has disappeared from the social circles of our cities. In my early days the intercourse with the peasantry of Forfarshire, Kincardineshire, and especially Deeside, was most amusing—not that the things said were so much out of the common, as that the language in which they were conveyed was picturesque, and odd, and taking. And certainly it does appear to me that as the language grows more uniform and conventional, less marked and peculiar in its dialect and expressions, so does the character of those who speak it become so. I have a rich sample of Mid-Lothian Scotch from a young friend in the country, who describes the conversation of an old woman on the property as amusing her by such specimens of genuine Scottish raciness and humour. On one occasion, for instance, the young lady had told her humble friend that she was going to Ireland, and would have to undergo a sea voyage. "Weel, noo, ye dinna mean that! Ance I thocht to gang across to tither side o' the Queensferry wi' some ither folks to a fair, ye ken; but juist when e'er I pat my fit in the boat, the boat gie wallop, and my heart gie a loup, and I thocht I'd gang oot o' my judgment athegither, so says I, Na, na, ye gang awa by yoursells to tither side, and I'll bide here till sic times as ye come awa back." When we hear our Scottish language at home, and spoken by our own countrymen, we are not so much struck with any remarkable effects; but it takes a far more impressive character when heard amongst those who speak a different tongue, and when encountered in other lands. I recollect the late Sir Robert Liston expressing this feeling in his own case. When our ambassador at Constantinople, some Scotchmen had been recommended to him for some purpose of private or of government business; and Sir Robert was always ready to do a kind thing for a countryman. He found them out in a barber's shop waiting for being shaved in turn. One came in rather late, and seeing he had scarcely room at the end of the seat, addressed his countryman, "Neebour, wad ye sit a bit *wast*?" What strong associations must have been called up, by hearing in a distant land such an expression in Scottish tones.

We may observe here, that marking the course any

person is to take, or the direction in which any object is to be met with, by the points of the compass, was a prevailing practice amongst the older Scottish race. There could hardly be a more ludicrous application of the test, than was furnished by an honest Highlander in describing the direction which his medicine would *not* take. Jean Cumming, of Altyre, who, in common with her three sisters, was a true sœur de charité, was one day taking her rounds as usual, visiting the poor sick, among whom there was a certain Donald MacQueen, who had been some time confined to his bed. Miss Cumming, after asking him how he felt, and finding that he was "no better," of course inquired if he had taken the medicine which she had sent him; "Troth no, me lady," he replied. "But why not, Donald?" she answered, "it was *very wrong;* how can you expect to get better if you do not help yourself with the remedies which Heaven provides for you?" "*V*right or *V*rang," said Donald, "it wadna gang *wast* in spite o' me." In all the north country, it is always said, "I'm ganging east or west," etc., and it happened that Donald on his sick bed was lying east and west, his feet pointing to the latter direction, hence his reply to indicate that he could not swallow the medicine!

We may fancy the amusement of the officers of a regiment in the West Indies at the innocent remark of a young lad who had just joined from Scotland. On meeting at dinner, his salutation to his Colonel was, "Anither het day, Cornal," as if "het days" were in Barbadoes few and far between, as they were in his dear old stormy cloudy Scotland. Or take the case of a Scottish saying, which indicated at once the dialect and the economical habits of a hardy and struggling race. A young Scotchman, who had been some time in London, met his friend recently come up from the north to pursue his fortune in the great metropolis. On discussing matters connected with their new life in London, the more experienced visitor remarked upon the greater *expenses* there than in the retired

Scottish town which they had left. "Ay," said the other, sighing over the reflection, "when ye get cheenge for a saxpence here, it's soon slippit awa'." I recollect a story of my father's which illustrates the force of dialect, although confined to the inflections of a single monosyllable. On riding home one evening, he passed a cottage or small farm-house, where there was a considerable assemblage of people, and an evident incipient merry-making for some festive occasion. On asking one of the lasses standing about what it was, she answered, "Ou, it's just a wedding o' Jock Thamson and Janet Frazer." To the question, "Is the bride rich?" there was a plain quiet "Na." Is she young?" a more emphatic and decided "Naa!" but to the query, "Is she bonny?" a most elaborate and prolonged shout of "Naaa!"

It has been said that the Scottish dialect is peculiarly powerful in its use of *vowels*, and the following dialogue between a shopman and a customer has been given as a specimen. The conversation relates to a plaid hanging at the shop door—

Cus. (inquiring the material), Oo? (wool?)
Shop. Ay, oo (yes, of wool).
Cus. A' oo? (all wool?)
Shop. Ay, a' oo (yes, all wool).
Cus. A' ae oo? (all same wool?)
Shop. Ay, a' *ae* oo (yes, all same wool).

An amusing anecdote of a pithy and jocular reply, comprised in one syllable, is recorded of an eccentric legal Scottish functionary of the last century. An advocate, of whose professional qualifications he had formed rather a low estimate, was complaining to him of being passed over in a recent appointment to the bench, and expressed his sense of the injustice with which he had been treated. He was very indignant at his claims and merit being overlooked in their not choosing him for the new judge, adding with much acrimony. "And I can tell you they might have got a 'waur.'"* To which, as if merely coming over the complainant's language again, the answer was a grave "Whaur?"† The merit of the impertinence was, that it sounded as if it were merely a repetition of his friend's last words, waur and whaur. It was as if "*echo* answered whaur?" As I have said, the oddity and acuteness of the speaker arose from the manner of expression, not from the thing said. In fact, the same thing said in plain English would be mere commonplace. I recollect being much amused with a dialogue between my brother and his man, the chief manager of a farm which he had just taken, and, I suspect, in a good measure, manager of the *farmer* as well. At any rate he committed to this acute overseer all the practical details; and on the present occasion had sent him to market to dispose of a cow and a pony, a simple enough transaction, and with a simple enough result. The cow was brought back, the pony was sold. But the man's description of it forms the point. "Well, John, have you sold the cow?" "Na, but I *grippit* a chiel for the powny!" "*Grippit*" was here most expressive! Indeed, this word has a significance hardly expressed by any English one, and used to be very prevalent to indicate keen and forcible tenacity of possession; thus a character noted for avarice or sharp looking to self-interest was termed "grippy." In mechanical contrivances, anything taking a close adherence was called having a gude *grip*. I recollect in boyish days when on Deeside taking wasp-nests, an old man looking on was sharply stung by one, and his description was, "Ane o' them's grippit me fine." The following had an indescribable piquancy, which arose from the *Scotticism* of the terms and the manners. Many years ago, when accompanying a shooting party on the Grampians, not with a gun like the rest, but with a botanical box for collecting specimens of mountain plants, the party had got very hot, and very tired, and very cross

---

* Worse † Where.

On the way home, whilst sitting down to rest, a gamekeeper sort of attendant, and a character in his way, said, "I wish I was in the dining-room of Fasque." An old laird very testily replied, "Ye'd soon be kickit out o' that;" to which the other replied, not at all daunted, "Weel, weel, then I wadna be far frae the kitchen." A quaint and characteristic reply, I recollect from another farm-servant. My eldest brother had just been constructing a piece of machinery, which was driven by a stream of water running through the home farm-yard. There was a thrashing machine, a winnowing machine, and circular saw for splitting trees into paling, and other contrivances of a like kind. Observing an old man, who had long been about the place, looking very attentively at all that was going on, he said, "Wonderful things people can do now, Robby?" "Ay," said Robby; "indeed, Sir Alexander, I'm thinking if Solomon was alive noo he'd be thocht naething o'!"

The two following derive their force entirely from the Scottish turn of the expressions. Translated into English, they would lose all point—at least, much of the point which they now have:—

At the sale of an antiquarian gentleman's effects in Roxburghshire, which Sir Walter Scott happened to attend, there was one little article, a Roman *patina*, which occasioned a good deal of competition, and was eventually knocked down to the distinguished baronet at a high price.

Sir Walter was excessively amused during the time of bidding, to observe how much it excited the astonishment of an old woman, who had evidently come there to buy culinary utensils on a more economical principle. "If the parritch-pan," she at last burst out—"If the parritch-pan gans at that, what will the kail-pat gang for?"

An ancestor of Sir Walter Scott joined the Pretender, and, with his brother, was engaged in that unfortunate adventure which ended in a skirmish and captivity at Preston, 1715. It was the fashion of those times for all persons of the rank of gentlemen to wear scarlet waistcoats. A ball had struck one of the brothers, and carried part of this dress into his body, and in this condition he was taken prisoner with a number of his companions, and stript, as was too often the practice in those remorseless wars. Thus wounded, and nearly naked, having only a shirt on, and an old sack about them, the ancestor of the great poet was sitting, along with his brother and a hundred and fifty unfortunate gentlemen, in a granary at Preston. The wounded man fell sick, as the story goes, and vomited the scarlet cloth which the ball had passed into the wound. "O man, Wattie," cried his brother, "if you have a wardrobe in your wame, I wish you would vomit me a pair o' breeks." But, after all, it was amongst the old ladies that the great abundance of choice pungent Scottish expressions, such as you certainly do not meet with in these days, was to be sought. In their position of society, education either in England, or education conducted by English teachers, has so spread in Scottish families, and intercourse with the south has been so increased, that all these colloquial peculiarities are fast disappearing. Some of the ladies of this older school felt some indignation at the change which they lived to see was fast going on. One of them being asked if an individual whom she had lately seen was "Scotch," answered with some bitterness, "I canna say; ye a' speak sae *genteel* now that I dinna ken wha's Scotch." It was not uncommon to find, in young persons, examples, some years ago, of an attachment to the Scottish dialect, like that of the old lady. In the life of P. Tytler, lately published, there is an account of his first return to Scotland from a school in England. His family were delighted with his appearance, manners, and general improvement; but a sister did not share this pleasure unmixed, for being found in tears, and the remark being made, "Is he not charming?" her reply was, in great distress, "Oh yes, but he speaks English!"

The class of old Scottish ladies marked by so many

peculiarities generally lived in provincial towns, and never dreamt of going from home. Many had never been in London, or had even crossed the Tweed. But as Lord Cockburn's experience goes back further than mine, and as he had special opportunities of being acquainted with their characteristic peculiarities, I will quote his animated description at page 57 of his Memorials. "There was a singular race of old Scotch ladies. They were a delightful set—strong-headed, warm-hearted, and high-spirited—merry even in solitude; very resolute; indifferent about the modes and habits of the modern world, and adhering to their own ways, so as to stand out like primitive rocks above ordinary society. Their prominent qualities of sense, humour, affection, and spirit, were embodied in curious outsides, for they all dressed, and spoke, and did exactly as they chose. Their language, like their habits, entirely Scotch, but without any other vulgarity than what perfect naturalness is sometimes mistaken for."*

This is a masterly description of a race now all but passed away. I have known several of them in my early days; and amongst them we must look for the racy Scottish peculiarities of diction and of expression which, with them, are also nearly gone. Lord Cockburn has given some illustrations of these peculiarities; and I have heard others, especially connected with Jacobite partialities, of which I say nothing, as they are in fact rather *strong* for such an occasion as the present. One, however, I heard lately as coming from a Forfarshire old lady of this class, which bears upon the point of "resolute" determination referred to in Lord Cockburn's description. She had been very positive in the disclaiming of some assertion which had been attributed to her, and on being asked if she had not written it, or something very like it, she replied, "Na, na; I never *write* onything of consequence—I may deny what I say, but I canna deny what I write."

* Lord Cockburn's Memorials, p. 58.

Mrs. Baird of Newbyth, the mother of our distinguished countryman the late General Sir David Baird, was always spoken of as a grand specimen of the class. When the news arrived from India of the gallant but unfortunate action of '84 against Hyder Ali, in which her son, then Captain Baird, was engaged, it was stated that he and other officers had been taken prisoners and chained together two and two. The friends were careful in breaking such sad intelligence to the mother of Captain Baird. When, however, she was made fully to understand the position of her son and his gallant companions, disdaining all weak and useless expressions of her own grief, and knowing well the restless and athletic habits of her son, all she said was, "Lord pity the chiel that's chained to our Davy."*

The ladies of this class had certainly no affectation in speaking of those who came under their displeasure, even when life and death were concerned. I had an anecdote illustrative of this characteristic, in a well-known old lady of the last century, Miss Johnstone of Westerhall. She had been extremely indignant that, on the death of her brother, his widow had proposed to sell off the old furniture of Westerhall. She was attached to it from old associations, and considered the parting with it little short of sacrilege. The event was, however, arrested by death, or, as she describes the result, "The furniture was a' to be roupit, and we couldna persuade her. But before the sale cam' on, in God's gude providence, she just clinkit aff hersell." Of this same Miss Johnstone, another characteristic anecdote has been preserved in the family. She came into possession of Hawkhill, near Edinburgh, and died there. When dying, a tremendous storm of rain and thunder came on, so as to shake the house. In her own quaint eccentric

---

* It is but due to the memory of "our Davie" to state that "the chiel" to whom he was chained, in writing home to his friends, bore high testimony to the kindness and consideration with which he was treated by Captain Baird.

spirit, and with no thought of profane or light allusions, she looked up, and, listening to the storm, quietly remarked, in reference to her departure, "Ech, sirs! what a night for me to be fleeing through the air!" Of fine acute sarcasm I recollect hearing an expression from a *modern* sample of the class, a charming character, but only to a certain degree answering to the description of the *older* generation. Conversation turning, and with just indignation, on the infidel remarks which had been heard from a certain individual, and on his irreverent treatment of Holy Scripture, all that this lady condescended to say of him was, "Gey impudent of him, I think."

A recorded reply of old Lady Perth to a French gentleman is quaint and characteristic. They had been discussing the respective merits of the cookery of each country. The Frenchman offended the old Scottish peeress by some disparaging remarks on Scottish dishes, and by highly preferring those of France. All she would answer was, "Weel, weel, some fowk like parritch, and some like paddocks."*

Of this older race—the ladies who were aged fifty years ago—the description is given by Lord Cockburn in strong and bold outline. I would pretend to nothing more than giving a few illustrative details from my own experience, which may assist the description by adding some practical realities to the picture. Several of them whom I knew in my early days certainly answered to many of those descriptions of Lord Cockburn. Their language and expressions had a zest and peculiarity which is gone, and which would not, I fear, do for modern life and times.

I have spoken of Miss Erskine of Dun, which is near Montrose. She, however, resided in Edinburgh. But those I knew best had lived many years in the then retired society of a country town. Some were my own relations; and in boyish days (for they had not generally much patience with boys) were looked up to with considerable

* Frogs.

awe as very formidable personages. Their characters and modes of expression in many respects remarkably corresponded with Lord Cockburn's description. There was a dry Scottish humour which we fear their successors do not inherit. One of these Montrose ladies had many anecdotes told of her quaint ways and sayings. Walking in the street one day, slippery from frost, she fairly fell down. A young officer with much politeness came forward and picked her up, earnestly asking her at the same time, "I hope, ma'am, you are no worse?" to which she replied, looking at him very steadily, "Indeed, sir, I'm just as little the better." A few days after, she met her military supporter in a shop. He was a fine tall youth, upwards of six feet high, and by way of making some grateful recognition for his late polite attention, she eyed him from head to foot; and as she was of the opinion of the old Scotch lady, who declared she "aye liked bonny fowk," she viewed her young friend with much satisfaction, but which she only evinced by the dry remark, "Od, ye're a lang lad; God gie ye grace."

I had from a relative or intimate friend of two sisters of this school, well known about Glasgow, an odd account of what it seems from their own statement had passed between them at a country house, where they had attended a sale by auction. As the business of the day went on, a dozen of silver spoons had to be disposed of; and before they were put up for competition, they were, according to the usual custom, handed round for inspection to the company. When returned into the hands of the auctioneer, he found only eleven. In great wrath, he ordered the door to be shut, that no one might escape, and insisted on every one present being searched, to discover the delinquent. One of the sisters, in consternation, whispered to the other, "Esther, ye hae nae gotten the spune?" to which she replied, "Na; but I hae gotten Mrs. Siddons in my pocket." She had been struck by a minature of the great actress, and had quietly pocketed it. The cautious reply of the sister was, "Then just drop her, Esther." One of the sisterhood, a connection of my own, had much of this dry Scottish humour. She had a lodging in the house of a respectable grocer; and on her niece most innocently asking her, "if she was not very fond of her landlord," in reference to the excellence of her apartments and the attention he paid to her comfort, she demurred to the question on the score of its propriety, by replying, "Fond of my landlord! that would be an *unaccountable* fondness."

An amusing account was given of an interview and conversation between this lady and the provost of Montrose. She had demurred at paying some municipal tax with which she had been charged, and the provost was anxious to prevent her getting into difficulty on the subject, and kindly called to convince her of the fairness of the claim, and the necessity of paying it. In his explanation he referred back to his own bachelor days when a similar payment had been required from him. "I assure you, ma'am," he said, "when I was in your situation I was called upon in a similar way for this tax;" to which she replied, in quiet scorn, "In my situation! an' whan were ye in my situation—an auld maid leevin' in a flat wi' an ae lass?" But the complaints of such imposts were urged in a very humorous manner by another Montrose old lady, Miss Helen Carnegy of Craigo; she hated paying taxes, and always pretended to misunderstand their nature. One day, receiving a notice of such payment signed by the provost (Thom), she broke out: "I dinna understand thae taxes; but I just think that when Mrs. Thom wants a new gown, the provost sends me a tax paper!" The good lady's naïve rejection of the idea that she could be in any sense "fond of her landlord," already referred to, was somewhat in unison with a similar feeling recorded to have been expressed by the late Mr. Wilson, the celebrated Scottish vocalist. He was taking lessons from the late Mr. Finlay Dun, one of the most accomplished musicians of the day. Mr. Dun had just returned from Italy, and, impressed with admiration of the deep pathos, sentiment, and passion of the Italian school of music, he regretted to find in his pupil so lovely a voice and so much talent losing much of its effect for want of feeling. Anxious, therefore, to throw into his friend's performance something of the Italian expression, he proposed to bring it out by this suggestion : "Now, Mr. Wilson, just suppose that I am your lady love, and sing to me as you could imagine yourself doing were you desirous of impressing her with your earnestness and affection." Poor Mr. Wilson hesitated, blushed, and under doubt how far such a personification even in his case was allowable, at last remonstrated, "Aye, Mr. Dun, ye forget I'm a married man !"

A case has been reported of a country girl, however, who thought it possible there might be an excess in such scrupulous regard to appearances. On her marriage-day, the youth to whom she was about to be united said to her in a triumphant tone, "Weel, Jenny, haven't I been unco ceevil," alluding to the fact that during their whole courtship he had never even given her a kiss. Her quiet reply was, "Ou, ay, man ; senselessly ceevil."

One of these Montrose ladies and a sister lived together ; and in a very quiet way they were in the habit of giving little dinner-parties, to which occasionally they invited their gentlemen friends. However, gentlemen were not always to be had ; and on one occasion, when such a difficulty had occurred, they were talking over the matter with a friend. The one lady seemed to consider such an acquisition almost essential to the having a dinner at all. The other, who did not see the same necessity, quietly adding, "But, indeed, oor Jean thinks a man perfect salvation."

Very much of the same class of remarks was the following sly remark of one of the sisterhood. At a well-known tea-table in a country town in Forfarshire, the events of the day, grave and gay, had been fully discussed by the assembled sisterhood. The occasion was improved by an elderly spinster, as follows:—"Weel, weel, sirs, these are solemn events—death and marriage—but ye ken they're what we must all come till." "Eh, Miss Jeany! ye have been lang spared," was the arch reply of a younger member.

There was occasionally a pawky semi-sarcastic humour in the replies of some of the ladies we speak of that was quite irresistible, of which I have from a friend a good illustration in an anecdote well known at the time. A late well-known member of the Scottish bar, when a youth, was somewhat of a dandy, and, I suppose, somewhat short and sharp in his temper. He was going to pay a visit in the country, and was making a great fuss about his preparing and putting up his habiliments. His old aunt was much annoyed at all this bustle, and stopped him by the somewhat contemptuous question, "Whar's this you're gaun, Robby, that ye mak sic a grand wark about yer claes?" The young man lost temper, and pettishly replied, "I'm going to the devil." "'Deed, Robby, then," was the quiet answer, "ye needna be sae nice, he'll juist tak' ye as ye are."

Ladies of this class had a quiet mode of expressing themselves on very serious subjects, which indicated their quaint power of description, rather than their want of feeling. Thus, of two sisters, when one had died, it was supposed that she had injured herself by an imprudent indulgence in strawberries and cream, of which she had partaken in the country. A friend was condoling with the surviving sister, and, expressing her sorrow, had added, "I had hoped your sister was to live many years." To which her relative replied—"Leeve! hoo could she leeve! she juist felled* hersell at Craigo wi' strawberries and cream!" However, she spoke with the same degree of coolness of her own decease. For when her friend was comforting her in illness, by the hopes that she would, after winter, enjoy again some of their country spring butter, she exclaimed, without the slightest idea of being

* Killed.

guilty of any irreverence, "Spring butter! by that time I shall be buttering in heaven." When really dying, and when friends were round her bed, she overheard one of them saying to another, "Her face has lost its colour; it grows like a sheet of paper." The quaint spirit even then broke out in the remark, "Then I'm sure it maun be *broon* paper." A very strong-minded lady of the class, and, in Lord Cockburn's language, "indifferent about modes and habits," had been asking from a lady the character of a cook she was about to hire. The lady naturally entered a little upon her moral qualifications, and described her as a very decent woman; the response which was, "Oh, d—n her decency; can she make good collops?"—an answer which would somewhat surprise a lady of Moray Place now, if engaged in a similar discussion of a servant's merits.

The Rev. Dr. Cook of Haddington supplies an excellent anecdote, of which the point is in the dry Scottish answer: An old lady of the Doctor's acquaintance, about seventy, sent for her medical attendant to consult him about a sore throat, which had troubled her for some days. Her medical man was ushered into her room, decked out with the now-prevailing fashion, a mustache and flowing beard. The old lady, after exchanging the usual civilities, described her complaint to the worthy son of Æsculapius. "Well," says he, "do you know, Mrs. Macfarlane, I used to be much troubled with the very same kind of sore throat, but ever since I allowed my mustache and beard to grow, I have never been troubled with it." "Aweel, aweel," said the old lady drily, "that may be the case, but ye maun prescribe some other method for me to get quit o' the sair throat; for ye ken, doctor, I canna adopt *that* cure."

But how exquisite the answer of old Mrs. Robison, widow of the eminent professor of natural philosophy, and who had a morbid dislike to everything which she thought savoured of *cant*. She had invited a gentleman to dinner on a particular day, and he had accepted, with the reservation, "If I am spared"—"Weel, weel," said Mrs Robison, "if ye're dead, I'll no expect ye."

I had two grand-aunts living at Montrose at that time—two Miss Ramsays of Balmain. They were somewhat of the severe class—Nelly especially, who was an object rather of awe than of affection. She certainly had a very awful appearance to young apprehensions, from the strangeness of her head gear. Ladies of this class Lord Cockburn has spoken of as "having their peculiarities embodied in curious outsides, as they dressed, spoke, and did exactly as they chose." As a sample of such curious outside and dress, my good aunt used to go about the house with an immense pillow strapped over her head—warm but formidable. These two maiden grand-aunts had invited their niece to pay them a visit—an aunt of mine, who had made what they considered a very imprudent marriage, and where considerable poverty was likely to accompany the step she had taken. The poor niece had to bear many a slap directed to her improvident union, as for example : One day she had asked for a piece of tape for some work she had in hand as a young wife expecting to become a mother. Miss Nelly said, with much point, "Ay, Kitty, ye shall get a bit knittin' (*i.e.*, a bit of tape). We hae a'thing ; we're no married." It was this lady who, by an inadvertent use of a term, showed what was passing in her mind in a way which must have been quite transparent to the bystanders. At a supper which she was giving, she was evidently much annoyed at the reckless and clumsy manner in which a gentleman was operating upon a ham which was at table, cutting out great lumps, and distributing them to the company. The lady said in a very querulous tone, "Oh, Mr. *Divet*, will you help Mrs. So and So ?"—divet being a provincial term for a turf or sod cut out of the green, and the resemblance of it to the pieces carved out by the gentleman evidently having taken possession of her imagination. Mrs. Helen Carnegy of

Craigo was a thorough specimen of this class of old Scottish ladies. She lived in Montrose, and died in 1818, at the advanced age of 91. She was a Jacobite, and very aristocratic in her feelings, but on social terms with many burghers of Montrose, or Munross, as it was called. She preserved a very nice distinction of addresses, suited to different individuals in the town, according as she placed them in the scale of her consideration. She liked a party at quadrille, and sent out her servant every morning to invite the ladies required to make up the game, and her directions were graduated thus—"Nelly, ye'll ging to Lady Carnegy's, and mak my compliments, and ask the *honour* of her ladyship's company, and that of the Miss Carnegies, to tea this evening; and if they canna come, ging to the Miss Mudies, and ask the *pleasure* of their company; and if they canna come, ye may ging to Miss Hunter and ask the *favour* of her company; and if she canna come, ging to Lucky Spark and *bid her come*."

A great confusion existed in the minds of some of those old-fashioned ladies on the subject of modern inventions and usages. A Montrose old lady protested against the use of steam-vessels, as counteracting the decrees of Providence in going against wind and tide, vehemently asserting, "I would *hae* naething to say to thae impious vessels." Another lady was equally discomposed by the introduction of gas, asking with much earnestness, "What's to become o' the puir whales?" deeming their interests materially affected by this superseding of their oil. A lady of this class, who had long lived in country retirement, coming up to Edinburgh, was, after an absence of many years, going along Princes Street about the time when the water-carts were introduced for preventing the dust, and seeing one of them passing, rushed from off the pavement to the driver, saying, "Man, ye're *skailin'* a' the water." Such being her ignorance of modern improvements.

There is a point and originality in the expressions on common matters of the old Scottish ladies, unlike what one finds now ; for example : A country minister had been invited, with his wife, to dine and spend the night at the house of one of his lairds. Their host was very proud of one of the very large beds which had just come into fashion, and in the morning asked the lady how she had slept in it. "O vary well, sir ; but, indeed, I thought I'd lost the minister athegither."

Nothing, however, in my opinion comes up to the originality and point of the Montrose old maiden lady's most "exquisite reason" for not subscribing to the proposed fund for organizing a volunteer corps in that town. It was at the time of expected invasion at the beginning of the century, and some of the town magistrates called upon her and solicited her subscription to raise men for the service of the king—"Indeed," she answered right sturdily, "I'll dae nae sic thing ; I ne'er could raise a man *for mysell*, and I'm no gaen to raise men for King George."

Some curious stories are told of ladies of this class, as connected with the novelties and excitement of railway travelling. Missing their luggage, or finding that something has gone wrong about it, often causes very terrible distress, and might be amusing, were it not to the sufferer so severe a calamity. I was much entertained with the earnestness of this feeling, and the expression of it from an old Scotch lady, whose box was not forthcoming at the station where she was to stop. When urged to be patient, her indignant exclamation was—"I can bear ony pairtings that may be ca'ed for in God's providence ; but I canna stan' pairtin' frae ma claes."

The following anecdote from the west exhibits a curious confusion of ideas arising from the old-fashioned prejudice against Frenchmen and their language, which existed in the last generation. During the long French war, two old ladies in Stranraer were going to the kirk ; the one said to the other, "Was it no a wonderfu' thing that the Breetish were aye victorious ower the French in battle." "Not a bit," said the other old lady, "dinna ye ken the Breetish aye say their prayers before ga'in into battle." The other replied, "But canna the French say their prayers as weel." The reply was most characteristic, "Hoot! jabbering bodies, wha could *understan'* them."

Some of these ladies, as belonging to the old county families, had very high notions of their own importance, and a great idea of their difference from the burgher families of the town. I am assured of the truth of the following naïve specimen of such family pride:—One of the olden maiden ladies of Montrose called one day on some ladies of one of the families in the neighbourhood, and on being questioned as to the news of the town, said, "News! oh, Baillie ——'s eldest son is to be married." "And pray," was the reply, "and pray, Miss ——, an' fa' ever heard o' a merchant i' the toon o' Montrose *ha'in'* an *eldest son?*" The good lady thought that any privilege of primogeniture belonged only to the family of *laird.*

It is a dangerous experiment to try passing off ungrounded claims upon characters of this description. Many a clever sarcastic reply is on record from Scottish ladies, directed against those who wished to impose upon them some false sentiment. I often think of the remark of the outspoken ancient lady, who, when told by her pastor, of whose disinterestedness in his charge she was not quite sure, that he "had a call from his Lord and Master to go," replied—"Deed, sir, the Lord micht hae ca'ed and ca'ed to ye lang eneuch, and ye'd ne'er hae lippened* till him an the steepen' hadnae been better."

At the beginning of this century, when the fear of invasion was rife, it was proposed to mount a small battery at the water-mouth by subscription, and Miss Carnegy was waited on by a deputation from the town-council. One of them having addressed her on the subject, she heard him with some impatience, and when he had finished, she said, "Are ye ane o' the toon council?" He replied, "I have

* Trusted.

that honour, ma'am." To which she rejoined, "Ye may hae that *profit*, but honour ye hae nane;" and then to the point, she added, "But I've been tell't that ae day's wark o' twa or three men wad mount the cannon, and that it may be a' dune for twenty shillings; now there's twa punds to ye." The councillor pocketed the money and withdrew. On one occasion, as she sat in an easy chair, having assumed the habits and privileges of age, Mr. Mollison, the minister of the Established Kirk, called on her to solicit for some charity. She did not like being asked for money, and, from her Jacobite principles, she certainly did not respect the Presbyterian Kirk. When he came in she made an inclination of the head, and he said, "Don't get up, madam." She replied, "Get up! I wadna rise out of my chair for King George himself, let abee a Whig minister."

This was plain speaking enough, but there is something quite inimitable in the matter-of-factness of the following story of an advertisement, which may tend to illustrate the Antiquary's remark to Mrs. Macleuchar, anent the starting of the coach or fly to Queensferry. A carrier, who plied his trade between Aberdeen and a village considerably to the north of it, was asked by one of the villagers, "Fan are ye gaun to the town" (Aberdeen)? To which he replied, "I'll be in on Monanday, God willin' and weather permittin', an' on Tiseday, *fither or no*."

It is a curious subject the various shades of Scottish dialect and Scottish expressions, commonly called Scotticisms. We mark in the course of fifty years how some disappear altogether; others become more and more rare, and of all of them we may say, I think, that the specimens of them are to be looked for every year more in the descending classes of society. What was common amongst peers, judges, lairds, advocates, and people of family and education, is now found in humbler ranks of life. There are few persons perhaps who have been born in Scotland, and who have lived long in Scotland, whom a nice southern ear might not detect as from the north. But far beyond such nicer shades of distinction, there are strong and characteristic marks of a Caledonian origin with which some of us have had practical acquaintance. I possess two curious, and now, I believe, rather scarce, publications on the prevalent Scotticisms of our speaking and writing. One is entitled "Scotticisms designed to Correct Improprieties of Speech and Writing," by Dr. Beattie of Aberdeen. The other is to the same purpose, and is entitled, "Observations on the Scottish Dialect," by the late Right Honourable Sir John Sinclair. Expressions which were common in their days, and used by persons of all ranks, are not known by the rising generation. Many amusing equivoques used to be current, arising from Scotch people in England applying terms and expressions in a manner rather surprising to Southern ears. Thus, the story was told of a public character dear to the memory of Scotland, Henry Dundas (Viscount Melville), applying to Mr. Pitt for the loan of a horse "*the length* of Highgate;" a very common expression in Scotland, at that time, to signify the distance to which the ride was to extend. Mr. Pitt good humouredly wrote back to say that he was afraid he had not a horse in his possession quite so long as Mr. Dundas had mentioned, but he had sent the longest he had. There is a well-known case of mystification, caused to English ears by the use of Scottish terms, which took place in the House of Peers during the examination of the Magistrates of Edinburgh touching the particulars of the Porteous Mob in 1736. The Duke of Newcastle having asked the Provost with what kind of shot the town-guard, commanded by Porteous, had loaded their muskets, received the unexpected reply, "Ou, juist sic as ane shutes dukes and sic like fules wi'." The answer was considered as a contempt of the House of Lords, and the poor Provost would have suffered from misconception of his patois, had not the Duke of Argyle (who must have been exceedingly amused) explained that the worthy magistrate's expression when rendered into English meant to describe the shot used for *ducks and water-fowl*. The circumstance is referred to by Sir W. Scott in the notes to the Heart of Mid-Lothian. A similar equivoque upon the double meaning of "Deuk" in Scottish language supplied material for a poor woman's honest compliment to a benevolent Scottish nobleman. John Duke of Roxburghe was one day out riding, and at the gate of Floors he was accosted by an importunate old beggar woman. He gave her half-a-crown, which pleased her so much that she exclaimed, "Weel's me on your *guse* face, for Deuk's our little to ca' ye."

A very curious list may be made of words used in Scotland in a sense which would be quite unintelligible to southerns. Such applications are going out, but I remember them well amongst the old-fashioned people of Angus and the Mearns quite common in conversation. I subjoin some specimens :—

Bestial signifies amongst Scottish agriculturists cattle generally, the whole aggregate number of beasts on the farm. Again, a Scottish farmer when he speaks of his "hogs," or of buying "hogs," has no reference to swine, but means young sheep, *i.e.*. sheep before they have lost their first fleece.

Discreet does not bear the meaning of prudent or cautious, but of civil, kind, attentive. Such application of the word is said to have been made by Dr. Chalmers to the Bishop of Exeter. These two eminent individuals had met for the first time at the hospitable house of the late Mr. Murray the publisher. On the introduction taking place, the bishop expressed himself so warmly as to the pleasure it gave him to meet so distinguished and excellent a man as Dr. Chalmers, that the Doctor was quite overcome, and in a deprecating tone, said, "Oh, I am sure your lordship is very 'discreet.'"

Enterteening has in olden Scottish usage the sense not of amusing, but interesting. I remember an honest Dandie Dinmont on a visit to Bath. A lady, who had taken a kind charge of him, accompanied him to the theatre, and in the most thrilling scene of Kemble's acting, what is usually termed the dagger scene in Macbeth, she turned to the farmer with a whisper, "Is not that fine?" to which the confidential reply was, "Oh, mem, it's verra *enterteening!*" Enterteening expressing his idea of the *interesting!*

Pig, in old-fashioned Scotch, was always used for a coarse earthenware jar or vessel. In the life of the late Patrick Tytler, the amiable and gifted historian of Scotland, there occurs an amusing exemplification of the utter confusion of ideas caused by the use of Scottish phraseology. The family, when they went to London, had taken with them an old Scottish servant who had no notion of any terms beside her own. She came in one day greatly disturbed at the extremely backward state of knowledge of domestic affairs amongst the Londoners. She had been to so many shops and could not get "a great broon pig* to haud the butter in."

From a relative of the family I have received an account of a still worse confusion of ideas caused by the inquiry of a Mrs. Chisholm of Chisholm, who died in London in 1825, at an advanced age. She had come from the country to be with her daughter, and was a genuine Scottish lady of the old school. She wished to purchase a table-cloth of a cheque pattern like the squares of a chess or draft-board. Now a draft-board used to be called (as I remember) by old Scotch people a "dam†-brod."‡ Accordingly, Mrs. Chisholm entered the shop of a linen-draper, and asked to be shown table-linen a *dam-brod pattern*. The shopman, although taken aback by a request, as he considered it, so strongly worded, by a respectable old lady, brought down what he assured her was the largest and widest made. No; that would not do. She repeated her wish for a dam-brod pattern, and left the shop surprised at

* Earthenware vessel.

† *Dam*, the game of drafts. ‡ *Brod*, the board.

the stupidity of the London shopman not having the pattern she asked for.

Silly has in genuine old Scottish use reference to weakness of body only, and not of mind. Before knowing the use of the word, I remember being much astonished at a farmer of the Mearns telling me of the strongest-minded man in the county that he was "growing uncommon silly," not insinuating any decline of mental vigour, but only meaning that his bodily strength was giving way.

Frail, in like manner, expresses infirmity of body, and implies no charge of any laxity in moral principle; yet I have seen English persons looking with considerable consternation when an old-fashioned Scottish lady, speaking of a young and graceful female, lamented her being so *frail.*

Fail is another instance of different use of words. In Scotland it used to be quite common to say of a person whose health and strength had declined, that he had *failed.* To say this of a person connected with mercantile business has a very serious effect upon Southern ears, as implying only bankruptcy and ruin. I recollect many years ago at Monmouth, a Scottish lady creating much consternation in the mind of the mayor, by saying of a worthy man, the principal banker in the town, whom they both concurred in praising, that she was "sorry to find he was *failing.*"

Honest has in Scotch a peculiar application, irrespective of any integrity of moral character. It is a kindly mode of referring to an individual, as we would say to a stranger, "Honest man, would you tell me the way to —— ?" or as Lord Hermand, when about to sentence a woman for stealing, began, remonstratively, "Honest woman, what garr'd ye steal your neighbour's tub?"

Superstitious: A correspondent informs me that in some parts of Mid-Lothian, the people constantly use the word "superstitious" for "bigoted;" thus, speaking of a very keen Free Church person, they will say, "he is awfu' supperstitious."

Kail in England simply expresses cabbage, but in Scotland represents the chief meal of the day. Hence the old-fashioned easy way of asking a friend to dinner was to ask him if he would take his kail with the family. In the same usage of the word, the Scottish proverb expresses distress and trouble in a person's affairs, by saying that "he has got his kail through the reek." In like manner haddock, in Kincardineshire and Aberdeenshire, used to express the same idea, as the expression is, "Will ye tak your haddock wi' us the day?" that fish being so plentiful and so excellent that it was a standing dish. There is this difference, however, in the local usage, that to say in Aberdeen, Will you take your haddock? implies an invitation to dinner; whilst in Montrose the same expression means an invitation to *supper*. Differences of pronunciation also caused great confusion and misunderstanding. Novels used to be pronounced *novels*; envy *envy*; a cloak was a clock, to the surprise of an English lady, to whom the maid said, on leaving the house, "Mem, winna ye tak the *clock* wi' ye?"

The names of children's diseases were a remarkable item in the catalogue of Scottish words:—Thus, in 1775, Mrs. Betty Muirheid kept a boarding-school for young ladies in the Trongate of Glasgow, near the Tron steeple. A girl on her arrival was asked whether she had had smallpox. "Yes, mem, I've had the sma'pox, the nirls,* the blabs,† the scaw,‡ the kinkhost § and the fever, the branks || and the worm."¶

There is indeed a case of Scottish pronunciation which adds to the force and copiousness of our language, by discriminating four words, which, according to English speaking, are undistinguishable in mere pronunciation. The words are—wright (a carpenter), to write (with a pen), right (the reverse of wrong), rite (a ceremony). The four are however distinguished in old-fashioned Scotch pronunciation thus—1, He's a wiricht; 2, to wireete; 3, richt; 4, rite;

* Measles. † Nettle-rash. ‡ The itch.
§ Whooping-cough. || Mumps. ¶ Toothache.

I can remember a peculiar Scottish phrase very commonly used, which now seems to have passed away. I mean the expression "to let on" indicating the notice or observation of some thing, or of some person.—For example, "I saw Mr. ——, at the meeting, but I never let on that I knew he was present." A form of expression which has been a great favourite in Scotland, in my recollection, has much gone out of practice—I mean the frequent use of diminutives, generally adopted either as terms of endearment or of contempt. Thus, it was very common to speak of a person whom you meant rather to undervalue, as a *mannie*, a *bodie*, a *bit bodie*, or a *wee bit mannie*. The bailie in Rob Roy, when he intended to represent his party as persons of no importance, used the expression, "We are bits o' Glasgow bodies." In a popular child's song, we have the endearing expression, "My wee bit laddie." We have known the series of diminutives, as applied to the canine race, very rich in diminution. There is—1. A dog; 2. A doggie; 3. A bit doggie; 4. A wee bit doggie; and even 5. A wee bit doggikie. A correspondent has supplied me with a diminutive, which is of a more extravagant degree of attenuation than any I ever met with. It is this—"A peerie wee bit o' a manikinie." We used to hear such expressions as these, which would not now be reckoned genteel: "Come in and get your bit dinner;" "I hope you are now settled in your ain bit housie." In the Caldwell papers (page 39) we have an interesting case of a diminutive happily applied. It is recorded in the family that Mrs. Mure, on receiving from David Hume, on his deathbed, the copy of his history which is still in the library of Caldwell, marked "From the Author," she thanked him very warmly, and added in her native dialect, which she and the historian spoke in great purity, "O David, that's a book ye may weel be proud o', but before ye dee ye should burn a' your wee bukies;" to which, raising himself, he replied with some vehemence, half offended half in joke—"What for should I burn a' my wee bukies?" He was too weak for discussion. He shook her hand and bade her farewell.

An admirable Scotch expression I recollect from one of the Montrose ladies before referred to. Her niece was asking a great many questions on some point concerning which her aunt had been giving her information, and coming over and over the ground, demanding an explanation how this had happened, and why something else was so and so. The old lady lost her patience, and at last burst forth: "I winna be *back-speired* noo, Pally Fullerton." Back-speired! how much more pithy and expressive than cross-examined! Another capital expression to mark that a person has stated a point rather under than over the truth, is "The less I lee," as in Guy Mannering, where the precentor exclaims to Mrs. MacCandlish, "Aweel, guidwife, then the less I lee." We have found it a very amusing task collecting together a number of these phrases, and forming them into a connected epistolary composition. We may imagine the sort of puzzle it would be to a young person of the present day—one of what we may call the new school. We will suppose an English young lady, or an English educated young lady, lately married, receiving such a letter as the following from the Scottish aunt of her husband. We may suppose it to be written by a very old lady, who, for the last fifty years, has not moved from home, and has changed nothing of her early days. I can safely affirm that every word of it I have either seen written in a letter, or have heard in ordinary conversation:—

"*Montrose.**

"MY DEAR NIECE—I am real glad to find my *nevy* has made so good a choice as to have secured you for his wife; and I am sure this step will add much to his comfort, and we *behove* to rejoice at it. He will now look forward to his evening at home, and you will be happy

---

* The Scotticisms are printed in italics.

when you find you never *want* him. It will be a great pleasure when you hear him in the *trance*, and wipe his feet upon the *bass*. But Willy is not strong, and you must look well after him. I hope you do not let him *snuff* so much as he did. He had a sister, poor thing, who died early. She was remarkably clever, and well read, and most intelligent, but was always uncommonly *silly*.* In the autumn of '40 she had a *sair host*, and was aye *speaking through a cold*, and at dinner never did more than to *sup a few family broth*. I am afraid she did not *change her feet* when she came in from the wet one evening. I never *let on* that I observed anything to be wrong ; but I remember asking her to come and *sit upon* the fire. But she went out and did not *take* the door with her. She lingered till next spring, when she had a great *income*,† and her parents were then too poor to take her south, and she died. I hope you will like the lassie Eppie we have sent you. She is a *discreet* girl, and comes of a decent family. She has a sister *married upon* a Seceding minister at Kirkcaldy. But I hear he expects to be *transported* soon. She was brought up in one of the *hospitals* here. Her father had been a *souter* and a *pawky chiel* enough, but was *doited* for many years, and her mother was *sair dottled*. We have been greatly interested in the hospital where Eppie was *educate*, and intended getting up a bazaar for it, and would have asked you to help us, as we were most anxious to raise some additional funds, when one of the Baillies died and left it *feuing-stances* to the amount of 5000 pounds, which was really a great *mortification*. I am not a good *hand of write*, and therefore shall stop. I am very tired, and have been *gantin'*‡ for this half hour, and even in correspondence gantin' may be *smittin'*.§ The *kitchen*‖ is just coming in, and I *feel a smell of tea*, so when I get my *four hours*, that

---

* Delicate in health. † Ailment.
‡ Yawning. § Catching. ‖ Tea-urn.

will refresh me and set me up again.—I am your affectionate aunt,

"ISABEL DINGWALL."

This letter, then, we suppose written by a very old Forfarshire lady to her niece in England, and perhaps the young lady who received it might answer it in a style as strange to her aunt as her aunt's is to her, especially if she belonged to that lively class of our young female friends who indulge a little in phraseology which they have imbibed from their brothers or male cousins, who have perhaps, for their amusement, encouraged them in its use. The answer, then, might be something like this; and without meaning to be severe or satirical upon our young lady friends, I may truly say that though I never heard from one young lady all these *fast terms*, I have heard the most of them separately from many :—

"MY DEAR AUNTY—Many thanks for your kind letter and its enclosure. From my not knowing Scotch, I am not quite up to the whole, and some of the expressions I don't twig at all. Willie is absent for a few days, but when he returns home he will explain it; he is quite awake on all such things. I am glad you are pleased that Willie and I are now spliced. I am well aware that you will hear me spoken of in some quarters as a fast young lady, but don't believe them. We get on famously at present. Willie comes home from the office every afternoon at five. We generally take a walk before dinner, and read and work if we don't go out; and I assure you we are very jolly. We don't know many people here yet. It is rather a swell neighbourhood; and if we can't get in with the nobs, depend upon it we will never take up with any society that is decidedly snobby. I daresay the girl you are sending will be very useful to us; our present one is an awful slow coach. But we hope some day to sport buttons. My father and mother paid us a visit last week.

The governor is well, and, notwithstanding years and infirmities, comes out quite a jolly old cove. He is, indeed, if you will pardon the partiality of a daughter, a regular brick. He says he will help us if we can't get on, and I make no doubt will in due time fork out the tin. I am busy working a cap for you, dear aunty ; it is from a pretty German pattern, and I think when finished will be quite a stunner. There is a shop in Regent Street where I hire patterns, and can get six of them for 5 bob. I then return them without buying them, which I think a capital dodge. I hope you will sport it for my sake at your first tea and turn out.

"I have nothing more to say particular, but am always "Your affectionate niece,

"ELIZA DINGWALL."

"*P.S.*—I am trying to break Willie off his horrid habit of taking snuff. I had rather see him take his cigar when we are walking. You will be told, I daresay, that I sometimes take a weed myself. It is not true, dear aunty."

Before leaving the question of change in Scottish expressions, it may be proper to add a few words on the subject of Scottish *dialects*—*i.e.*, on the differences which exist in different counties or localities in the Scottish tongue itself. These differences used to be as marked as different languages ; of course they still exist amongst the peasantry as before. The change consists in their gradual vanishing from the conversation of the educated and refined. The dialects with which I am most conversant are the two which present the greatest contrast, viz., the Angus and the Aberdeen, or the slow and broad Scotch—the quick and sharp Scotch. Whilst the one talks of "buuts and shoon," the other calls the same articles "beets and sheen." With the Aberdonian "what" is always "fat" or "fatten," "music" is "meesic," "brutes are breets ;" "What are ye duing ?" of Southern Scotch, in Aberdeen would be "Fat are ye deein' ?"* Thus, when a Southerner mentioned the death of a friend, a sharp lady of the granite city asked "Fat deed he o' ?" which being utterly incomprehensible to the person asked, another Aberdonian lady kindly ex-

* Fergusson, nearly a century ago, noted this peculiarity of dialect in his poem of The Leith Races :—

"The Buchan bodies through the beach,
Their bunch of Findrams cry ;
And skirl out bauld in Norland speech,
Gude speldans, *fa* will buy."

"Findon," or "Finnan haddies," are split, smoked, and partially dried haddocks. Fergusson, in using the word "*Findrams*," which is not found in our glossaries, has been thought to be in error, but his accuracy has been verified, singularly enough, within the last few days, by a worthy octogenarian Newhaven fisherman, bearing the characteristic name of Flucker, who remarked "that it was a word commonly used in his youth : and, above all," he added, "when Leith Races were held on the sands ye was like to be deeved wi' the lang-tongued hizzies skirling out, '*Aell a Findram Speldrains*,' and they jist ca'ed it that to get a better grip o't wi' their tongues."

In Galloway, in 1684, Symson, afterwards an ousted Episcopalian mininster (of Kirkinner), notes some peculiarities in the speech of the people in that district. "Some of the countrey people, especially those of the elder sort, do very often omit the letter 'h' after 't' as ting for thing ; tree for three ; tatch for thatch ; wit for with ; fait for faith ; mout for mouth, etc. ; and also, contrary to some north countrey people, they oftentimes pronounce 'w' for 'v,' as serwant for servant ; and so they call the months of February, March, and April, the *ware* quarter, from *ver*.* Hence their common proverb, speaking of the stormes in February, '*Winter never comes till ware comes.*'" These peculiarities of language have almost disappeared—the immense influx of Irish emigrants during late years having exercised a perceptible influence over the dialect of Wigtonshire.

* *Ver.* The spring months—*e. g.*,
"This was in *ver* quhen wynter tid."—*Barbour*

plained the question, and put it into language which she supposed *could* not be mistaken, as thus, "Fat did he dee o'?" If there was this difference between the Aberdeen and the Forfar dialect, how much greater must be that difference when contrasted with the *ore rotundo* language of an English southern dignitary. Such a one being present at a school examination in Aberdeen wished to put some questions on Scripture history himself, and asked an intelligent boy, "What was the ultimate fate of Pharaoh?" This the boy not understanding, the master put the same question Aberdonicé, "Jemmy, fat was the hinner end o' Pharaoh?" which called forth the ready reply, "He was drouned i' the Red Sea."

The power of Scottish phraseology, or rather of Scottish *language* could not be better displayed than in the follow- Aberdonian description of London theatricals:—Mr. Taylor, well known in London as having the management of the opera-house, had his father up from Aberdeen to visit him and see the wonders of the capital. When the old man returned home, his friends, anxious to know the impressions produced on his mind by scenes and characters so different from what he had been accustomed to at home, inquired what sort of business his son carried on? "Ou," said he (in reference to the operatic singers and the corps de ballet), "He just keeps a curn* o' quainies† and a wheen widdyfous,‡ and gars them fissle,§ and loup, and mak murgeons,|| to please the great fowk."

Another ludicrous interrogatory occurred regarding the death of a Mr. Thomas Thomson. It appeared there were two cousins of this name, both corpulent men. When it was announced that Mr. Thomas Thomson was dead, an Aberdeen friend of the family asked, "Fatten Thamas Thamson?" He was informed that it was a fat Thomas Thomson, upon which the Aberdeen query naturally arose,

---

* A number. † Young girls. ‡ Gallows birds.
§ Make whistling noises. || Distorted gestures.

"Aye, but fatten fat Thamas Thamson?" A young lady from Aberdeen had been on a visit to Montrose, and was disappointed at finding there a great lack of beaus, and balls, and concerts. This lack was not made up to her by the invitations which she had received to dinner parties. And she thus expressed her feelings on the subject in her native dialect, when asked how she liked Montrose, "Indeed there's neither men nor meesic, and fat care I for meat?" The dialect and the local feelings of Aberdeen were said to have produced some amusement in London, as displayed by the lady of the Provost of Aberdeen when accompanying her husband going up officially to the capital. Some persons to whom she had been introduced recommended her going to the opera as one of the sights worthy the attention of a stranger. The good lady, full of the greatness of her situation as wife of the provost, and knowing the sensation her appearance in public occasioned when in her own city, and supposing that a like excitement would accompany her with the London public, rather declined, under the modest plea, "Fat for should I gang to the opera, just to creat a confeesion?" An aunt of mine, who knew Aberdeen well, used to tell a traditionary story of two Aberdonian ladies who, by their insinuations against each other, finely illustrated the force of the dialect then in common use. They had both of them been very attentive to a sick lady in declining health, and on her death each had felt a distrust of the perfect disinterestedness of the other's attention. This created more than a coolness between them, and the bad feeling came out on their passing in the street. The one insinuated her suspicions of unfair dealing with the property of the deceased by ejaculating, as the other passed her, "Henny pig* and green tea," to which the other retorted, in the same spirit, "Silk coat and negligee!"† Aberdonian pronunciation produced on one occasion a curious equivoque between the minister

* Honey jar. † A female garment then in common use.

and a mother of a family with whom he was conversing in a pastoral way. The minister had said, "Weel, Margaret, I hope you're thoroughly ashamed of your *sins*." Now, in Aberdeenshire sons are pronounced sins; accordingly, to the minister's surprise, Margaret burst forth, "Ashamed o' ma sins! na, na, I'm proud o' ma sins. Indeed, gin it were na for thae cutties o' dauchters, I should be *ower* proud o' ma sins."

I have not had leisure to pursue, as I had intended, a further consideration of SCOTTISH DIALECT, and their differences from each other in the north, south, east, and west of Scotland. I merely remark now, that the dialect of one district is considered quite barbarous, and laughed at by the inhabitants of another district where a different form of language is adopted. I have spoken (p. 120) of the essential difference between Aberdeen and southern Scotch. An English gentleman had been visiting the Lord Provost of Edinburgh, and accompanied him to Aberdeen. His lordship of Edinburgh introduced his English friend to the Provost of Aberdeen, and they both attended a great dinner given by the latter. After grace had been said, the Provost kindly and hospitably addressed the company Aberdonicé—"Now, gentlemen, fah tee, fah tee." The Englishman whispered to his friend, and asked what was meant by "fah tee, fah tee;" to which his lordship replied—"Hout, he canna speak—he means fau too, fau too." Thus one Scotticism was held in terror by those who used a different Scotticism: as at Inverary, the wife of the chief writer of the place, seeking to secure her guest from the taint of inferior society, intimated to him, but somewhat confidentially, that Mrs. W. (the rival writer's wife) was quite a vulgar body, so much so as to ask any one leaving the room to "*snib* the door," instead of bidding them, as she triumphantly observed, "*sneck* the door."

Any of my readers not much conversant with Aberdeen dialect will find the following a good specimen:—A lady who resided in Aberdeen being on a visit to some friends in the country, joined an excursion on horseback. Not being much of an equestrian, she was mounted upon a Highland pony as being the *canniest baste.* He, however, had a trick of standing still in crossing a stream. A burn had to be crossed—the rest of the party passed on, while "Paddy" remained, pretending to drink. Miss More, in great desperation, called out to one of her friends—"Bell, 'oman, turn back an gie me your bit fuppie, for the breet's stannin' i' the peel wi' ma."

There is no class of men which stands out more prominent in the reminiscences of the last hundred years than that of our Scottish Judges. They form, in many instances, a type or representative of the leading *peculiarities* of Scottish life and manners. They are mixed up with all our affairs, social and political. There are to be found in the annals of the bench rich examples of pure Scottish humour, the strongest peculiarity of Scottish phraseology, acuteness of intellect, cutting wit, eccentricity of manners, and abundant powers of conviviality. Their successors no longer furnish the same anecdotes of oddity or of intemperance. The Courts of the Scottish Parliament House, without lacking the learning or the law of those who sat there sixty years ago, lack not the refinement and the dignity that have long distinguished the Courts of West minster Hall.

Stories still exist, traditionary in society, amongst its older members, regarding Lords Gardenstone, Monboddo, Hermand, Newton, Polkemmet, Braxfield, etc. But many younger persons do not know them. It may be interesting to some of my readers to devote a few pages to the subject, and to offer some judicial gleanings.*

* I have derived some information from a curious book, "Kay's Portraits," 2 vols. The work is scarcely known in England, and is becoming scarce in Scotland. "Nothing can be more valuable in the way of engraved portraits than these representations of the distinguished men who adorned Edinburgh in the latter part of the eighteenth century."—*Chambers.*

I have two anecdotes to show that, both in social and judicial life, a remarkable change must have taken place amongst the "fifteen." I am assured that the following scene took place at the *table* of Lord Polkemmet, at a dinner party in his house. When the covers were removed, the dinner was seen to consist of veal broth, a roast fillet of veal, veal cutlets, a florentine (an excellent old Scottish dish composed of veal), a calf's head, calf's foot jelly. The worthy judge could not help observing a surprise on the countenance of his guests, and perhaps a simper on some; so he broke out in explanation; "Ou ay, it's a cauf; when we kill a beast we just eat up ae side, and down the tither." The expressions he used to describe his own *judicial* preparations for the bench were very characteristic: "Ye see I first read a' the pleadings, and then, after letting them wamble in my wame wi' the toddy twa or three days, I gie my ain interlocutor." For a moment suppose such anecdotes to be told now of any of our high legal functionaries. Imagine the feelings of surprise that would be called forth were the present Justice-Clerk to adopt such imagery in describing the process of preparing *his* legal judgment on a difficult case in his court!

In regard to the wit of the Scottish *bar*.—It is a subject which I do not pretend to illustrate. It would require a volume for itself. One anecdote, however, I cannot resist, and I record it as forming a striking example of the class of Scottish humour which, with our dialect, has lost its distinctive characteristics. John Clerk (afterwards a judge by the title of Lord Eldin), was arguing a Scotch appeal case before the House of Lords. His client claimed the use of a mill-stream by a prescriptive right. Mr. Clerk spoke broad Scotch, and argued that "the *watter* had rin that way for forty years. Indeed naebody kenned how long, and why should his client now be deprived of the watter?" etc. The chancellor, much amused at the pronunciation of the Scottish advocate, in a rather bantering tone asked him, "Mr. Clerk, do you spell water in Scotland with two t's?" Clerk, a little nettled at this hit at his national tongue, answered "Na, my lord, we dinna spell watter (making the word as short as he could) wi' twa t's, but we spell mainners (making the word as long as he could) wi' twa n's."

John Clerk's vernacular version of the motto of the Celtic Club is highly characteristic of his humour and his prejudice. He had a strong dislike to the whole Highland race, and the motto assumed by the modern Celts, "Olim marte, nunc arte," Clerk translated "Formerly *rubbers*, now thieves." Very dry and pithy too was his legal *opinion* given to a claimant of the Annandale peerage, who, when pressing the employment of some obvious forgeries, was warned that if he persevered, nae doot he might be a peer, but it would be a peer o' anither *tree!*

The following account of his conducting a case is also highly characteristic. Two individuals, the one a mason, the other a carpenter, both residenters in West Portsburgh, formed a copartnery, and commenced building houses within the boundaries of the burgh corporation. One of the partners was a freeman, the other not. The corporation, considering its rights invaded by a non-freeman exercising privileges only accorded to one of their body, brought an action in the Court of Session against the interloper, and his partner as aiding and abetting. Mr. John Clerk, then an advocate, was engaged for the defendants. How the cause was decided matters little. What was really curious in the affair, was the naïvely droll manner in which the advocate for the defence opened his pleading before the Lord Ordinary. "My Lord," commenced John, in his purest Doric, at the same time pushing up his spectacles to his brow and hitching his gown over his shoulders, "I wad hae thocht naething o't (the action), had hooses been a new invention, and my clients been caught ouvertly impingin' on the patent richts o' the inventors!"

Of Lord Gardenstone (Francis Garden) I have many early *personal* reminiscences, as his property of Johnstone was in the Howe of the Mearns, not far from my early home. He was a man of energy, and promoted improvements in the county with skill and practical sagacity. His favourite scheme was to establish a flourishing town upon his property, and he spared no pains or expense in promoting the importance of his village of Laurencekirk. He built an excellent inn, to render it a stage for posting. He built and endowed an Episcopal chapel for the benefit of his English immigrants, in the vestry of which he placed a most respectable library; and he encouraged manufacturers of all kinds to settle in the place. Amongst others a *hatter* came to reconnoitre, and ascertain its capabilities for exercising his calling. But when, on going to public worship on Sunday after his arrival, he found only *three* hats in the kirk, viz., the minister's, Lord Gardenstone's, and his own—the rest of the congregation all wearing the old flat Lowland bonnet—he soon went off, convinced that Laurencekirk was no place for hatters to thrive in. He was much taken up with his hotel or inn, and for which he provided a large volume for receiving the written contributions of travellers who frequented it. It was the landlady's business to present this volume to the guests, and ask them to write in it, during the evenings, whatever occurred to their memory or their imagination. In the mornings it was a favourite amusement of Lord Gardenstone to look it over. I recollect Sir Walter Scott being much taken with this contrivance, and his asking me about it at Abbotsford. His son said to him, "You should establish such a book, sir, at Melrose;" upon which Sir W. replied, "No, Walter, I should just have to see a great deal of abuse of myself." On his son deprecating such a result, and on his observing my surprised look, he answered, "Well, well, I should have to read a great deal of foolish praise, which is much the same thing." An amusing account is given of the cause of Lord Gardenstone withdrawing this volume from the hotel, and of his determination to submit it no more to the tender mercies of the passing traveller. As Professor Stuart of Aberdeen was passing an evening at the inn, the volume was handed to him, and he wrote in it the following lines, in the style of the prophecies of Thomas the Rhymer :—

"Frae sma' beginnings Rome of auld
Became a great imperial city,
'T was peopled first, as we are tauld,
By bankrupts, vagabonds, banditti.
Quoth Thamas, Then the day may come,
When Laurencekirk shall equal Rome."

These lines so nettled Lord Gardenstone, that the volume disappeared, and was never seen afterwards in the inn of Laurencekirk. There is another lingering reminiscence which I retain connected with the inn at Laurencekirk. The landlord, Mr. Cream, was a man well known throughout all the county, and was distinguished, in his later years, as one of the few men who continued to wear a *pigtail.* On one occasion the late Lord Dunmore (grandfather or great-grandfather of the present peer), who also still wore his queue, halted for a night at Laurencekirk. On the host leaving the room, where he had come to take orders for supper, Lord Dunmore turned to his valet and said, "John-stone, do I look as like a fool in my pigtail as Billy Cream does?"—"Much about it, my lord," was the valet's imperturbable answer. "Then," said his lordship, "cut off mine to-morrow morning when I dress."

Lord Gardenstone seemed to have had two favourite tastes : he indulged in the love of pigs and the love of snuff. He took a young pig as a pet, and it became quite tame, and followed him about like a dog. At first the animal shared his bed, but when, growing up to advanced swinehood, it became unfit for such companionship, he had it to sleep in his room, in which he made a comfortable couch for it of his own clothes. His snuff he kept not in a box, but in a leathern waist-pocket made for the purpose. He took it in enormous quantities, and used to say that if he had a dozen noses he would feed them all. Lord Gardenstone died 1793.

Lord Monboddo (James Burnet, Esq. of Monboddo) is another of the well-known members of the Scottish Bench, who combined, with many eccentricities of opinion and habits, great learning and a most amiable disposition. From his paternal property being in the county of Kincardine, and Lord M. being a visitor at my father's house, and indeed a relation or clansman, I have many early reminiscences of stories which I have heard of the learned judge. His speculations regarding the origin of the human race have, in times past, excited much interest and amusement. His theory was that man emerged from a wild and savage condition, much resembling that of apes; that man had then a tail like other animals, but which, by progressive civilization and the constant habit of *sitting*, had become obsolete. This theory produced many a joke from facetious and superficial people, who had never read any of the arguments of an elaborate work, by which the ingenious and learned author maintained his theory.* Lord Kames, a brother judge, had his joke on it. On some occasion of their meeting, Lord Monboddo was for giving Lord Kames the precedency. Lord K. declined, and drew back, saying, "By no means, my lord; you must walk first, that I may *see your tail.*" I recollect Lord Monboddo's coming to dine at Fasque caused a great excitement of interest and curiosity. I was in the nursery, too young to take part in the investigations; but my elder brothers were on the alert to watch his arrival, and get a glimpse of his tail. Lord M. was really a learned man, read Greek and Latin authors—not as a mere exercise of classical scholarship—but because he identified himself with their philosophical opinions, and would have revived Greek customs and modes of life. He used to give suppers after the manner of the ancients, and used to astonish his guests by the ancient cookery of

* Origin and Progress of Language.

Spartan broth, and of *mulsum*. He was an enthusiastical Platonist. On a visit to Oxford, he was received with great respect by the scholars of the University, who were much interested in meeting with one who had studied Plato, as a pupil and follower. In accordance with the old custom at learned universities, Lord Monboddo was determined to address the Oxonians in Latin, which he spoke with much readiness. But they could not stand the numerous slips in prosody. Lord Monboddo shocked the ears of the men of Eton and of Winchester by dreadful false quantities—verse-making being, in Scotland, then quite neglected, and a matter little thought of by the learned judge.

Lord Monboddo was considered an able lawyer, and on many occasions exhibited a very clear and correct judicial discernment of intricate cases. It was one of his peculiarities that he never sat on the bench with his brother judges, but always at the clerk's table. Different reasons for this practice have been given, but the simple fact seems to have been, that he was deaf, and heard better at the lower seat. His mode of travelling was on horseback. He scorned carriages, on the ground of its being unmanly to "sit in a box drawn by brutes." When he went to London he rode the whole way. At the same period, Mr. Barclay of Ury (father of the well-known Captain Barclay), when he represented Kincardineshire in Parliament, always *walked* to London. He was a very powerful man, and could walk fifty miles a day, his usual refreshment on the road being a bottle of port wine, poured into a bowl, and drunk off at a draught. I have heard that George III. was much interested at these performances, and said, "I ought to be proud of my Scottish subjects, when my judges *ride*, and my members of Parliament *walk* to the metropolis."

On one occasion of his being in London, Lord Monboddo attended a trial in the Court of King's Bench. A cry was heard that the roof of the court-room was giving way, upon which judges, lawyers, and people made a rush to get to the door. Lord Monboddo viewed the scene from his corner with much composure. Being deaf and short-sighted, he knew nothing of the cause of the tumult. The alarm proved a false one; and on being asked why he had not bestirred himself to escape like the rest, he coolly answered that he supposed it was an *annual ceremony* with which, as an alien to the English laws, he had no concern, but which he considered it interesting to witness as a remnant of antiquity! Lord Monboddo died 1799.

Lord Rockville (the Hon. Alexander Gordon, third son of the Earl of Aberdeen) was a judge distinguished in his day by his ability and decorum. "He adorned the bench by the dignified manliness of his appearance, and polished urbanity of his manners." * Like most lawyers of his time, he took his glass freely, and a whimsical account which he gave, before he was advanced to the bench, of his having fallen upon his face, after making too free with the bottle, was commonly current at the time. Upon his appearing late at a convivial club with a most rueful expression of countenance, and on being asked what was the matter, he exclaimed with great solemnity, "Gentlemen, I have just met with the most extraordinary adventure that ever occurred to a human being. As I was walking along the Grassmarket, all of a sudden *the street rose up and struck me on the face.*" He had, however, a more serious *encounter* with the street after he was a judge. In 1792, his foot slipped as he was going to the Parliament House; he broke his leg, was taken home, fevered, and died.

Lord Braxfield (Robert M'Queen of Braxfield) was one of the judges of the old school, well known in his day, and might be said to possess all the qualities united, by which the class were remarkable. He spoke the broadest Scotch. He was a sound and laborious lawyer. He was fond of a glass of good claret, and had a great fund of good Scotch humour. He rose to the dignity of Justice-Clerk, and, in consequence, presided at many important political criminal

---

* Douglas' Peerage, vol. i., p. 22.

trials about the year 1793-4, such as those of Muir, Palmer, Skirving, Margarot, Gerrold, etc. He conducted these trials with much ability and great firmness, occasionally, no doubt, with more appearance of severity and personal prejudice than is usual with the judges who in later times are called on to preside on similar occasions. The disturbed temper of the times and the daring spirit of the political offenders seemed, he thought, to call for a bold and fearless front on the part of the judge, and Braxfield was the man to show it, both on the bench and in common life. He met, however, sometimes with a spirit as bold as his own from the prisoners before him. When Skirving was on trial for sedition he thought Braxfield was threatening him, and by gesture endeavouring to intimidate him; accordingly, he boldly addressed the bench :—" It is altogether unavailing for your Lordship to menace me, for I have long learnt not to fear the face of man." I have observed that he adhered to the *broadest* Scottish dialect. "Hae ye ony coonsel, man ?" he said to Maurice Margarot (who, I believe, was an Englishman). "No," was the reply. "Div ye want to hae ony appinted ?" "No," replied Margarot; "I only want an *interpreter* to make me understand what your Lordship says." Braxfield had much humour, and enjoyed wit in others. He was immensely delighted at a reply by Dr. M'Cubbin, the minister of Bothwell. Braxfield, when Justice-Clerk, was dining at Lord Douglas', and observed there was only port upon the table. In his usual off-hand brusque manner, he demanded of the noble host if "there was nae claret i' the castle." "Yes," said Lord Douglas; "but my butler tells me it is not good." "Let's pree't," said Braxfield in his favourite dialect. A bottle was produced, and declared by all present to be quite excellent. "Noo, minister," said the old judge, addressing Dr. M'Cubbin, who was celebrated as a wit in his day, "as a *fama clamosa* has gone forth against this wine, I propose that you *absolve* it,"—playing upon the terms made use of in the Scottish Church Courts. "Ay, my Lord," said the minister, "you are first-rate authority for a case of civil or criminal law but you do not quite understand our Church Court practice. We never absolve *till after three several appearances.*" The wit and the condition of absolution were alike relished by the judge. Lord Braxfield closed a long and useful life in 1799.

Of Lord Hermand we have spoken on several occasions, and his name has become in some manner identified with that conviviality which marked almost as a characteristic the Scottish bench of his time. He gained, however, great distinction as a judge, and was a capital lawyer. When at the bar, Lords Newton and Hermand were great friends, and many were the convivial meetings they enjoyed together. But Lord Hermand outlived all his old last-century contemporaries, and formed with Lord Balgray what we may consider the connecting links between the past and the present race of Scottish lawyers.

We could scarcely perhaps offer a more marked difference between habits *once* tolerated on the bench and those which now distinguish the august seat of senators of justice than by quoting, from Kay's Portraits, vol. ii., p. 278, a sally of a Lord of Session of those days, which he played off, when sitting as judge, upon a young friend whom he was determined to frighten. "On one occasion, a young counsel was addressing him on some not very important point that had arisen in the division of a common (or commonty, according to law phraseology), when having made some bold averment, the judge exclaimed, 'That's a lee, Jemmie.' 'My lord!' ejaculated the amazed barrister. 'Ay, ay, Jemmie; I see by your face ye're leein'.' 'Indeed, my lord, I am not.' 'Dinna tell me that; it's no in your memorial (brief)—awa wi' you;' and, overcome with astonishment and vexation, the discomfited barrister left the bar. The judge thereupon chuckled with infinite delight; and beckoning to the clerk who attended on the occasion, he said, 'Are ye no Rabbie H——'s man?' 'Yes, my lord.' 'Was na Jemmie —— leein'?' 'Oh no, my lord. 'Ye're quite sure?' 'Oh yes.' 'Then just write out what you want, and I'll sign it; my faith, but I made Jemmie stare.' So the decision was dictated by the clerk, and duly signed by the judge, who left the bench highly diverted with the fright he had given his young friend." Such scenes enacted in Court *now* would astonish the present generation, both of lawyers and of suitors.

Under this head of Scottish dialect, language, and phraseology, we naturally introduce some notice of that most interesting subject connected with our national literature which belongs to Scottish PROVERBIAL expressions. It is an old remark, that the characteristics of a people are always found in such sayings, and the expression of Bacon has been often quoted—"The genius, wit, and wisdom of a nation are discovered by their proverbs." Now, as there can be no doubt that there are proverbs exclusively Scottish, and that as in them we find also many traits of Scottish character, and many peculiar forms of Scottish thought and Scottish language, sayings of this kind, once so familiar, should have a place in our Scottish reminiscences. Indeed, proverbs are literally, in many instances, become *reminiscences.* They now seem to belong to that older generation whom we recollect, and who used them in conversation freely and constantly. To strengthen an argument or illustrate a remark by a proverb, was then a common practice in conversation. Their use, however, is now considered vulgar, and their formal application is almost prohibited by the rules of polite society. Lord Chesterfield denounced the practice of quoting proverbs as a palpable violation of all polite refinement in conversation. Notwithstanding all this, we acknowledge having much pleasure in recalling our national proverbial expressions. They are full of character, and we find amongst them important truths, expressed forcibly, wisely, and gracefully.

All nations have their proverbs, and a vast number of books have been written on the subject. We find, accordingly, that collections have been made of proverbs considered as belonging peculiarly to Scotland. The collections to which I have had access are the following :—

1. The fifth edition, by Balfour, of "Ray's Complete Collection of English Proverbs," in which is a separate collection of those which are considered Scottish Proverbs—1813. Ray professes to have taken these from Fergusson's work mentioned below.

2. A Complete Collection of Scottish Proverbs explained and made intelligible to the English reader, by James Kelly, M.A., published in London 1721.

3. Scottish Proverbs gathered together by David Fergusson, sometime minister at Dumfermline, and put *ordine alphabetico* when he departed this life anno 1598. Edinburgh, 1641.

4. A collection of Scots Proverbs, dedicated to the Tenantry of Scotland, by Allan Ramsay. This collection is found in the edition of his Poetical Works, 3 vols. post octavo, Edin. 1818, but is not in the handsome edition of 1800. London, 2 vols. 8vo.*

5. Scottish Proverbs, collected and arranged by Andrew Henderson. With an introductory Essay by W. Motherwell. Edin. 1832.

6. The Proverbial Philosophy of Scotland, an address to the School of Arts, by William Stirling of Keir, M.P. Stirling and Edin. 1855.

The collection of Ray, the great English naturalist, is well known. The two first editions, published at Cambridge in 1670 and 1678, were by the author; subsequent editions were by other editors.

The work by James Kelly professes to collect Scottish Proverbs only. It is a volume of nearly 400 pages, and contains a short explanation or commentary attached to

* This was pointed out to me by the late Sir John Melville, who kindly supplied me with the three volume edition.

each, and often parallel sayings from other languages.* Mr. Kelly bears ample testimony to the extraordinary free use made of proverbs in his time by his countrymen and by himself. He says that "there were current in society upwards of 3000 proverbs, exclusively Scottish." He adds, "the Scots are wonderfully given to this way of speaking, and as the consequence of that, abound with proverbs, many of which are very expressive, quick, and home to the purpose; and, indeed, this humour prevails universally over the whole nation, especially among the better sort of the commonalty, none of whom will discourse with you any considerable time, but he will affirm every assertion and observation with a Scottish proverb. To that nation I owe my birth and education; and to that manner of speaking I was used from my infancy, to such a degree that I became in some measure remarkable for it." This was written in 1721, and we may see from Mr. Kelly's account what a change has taken place in society as regards this mode of intercourse. Our author states that he has "omitted in his collection many popular proverbs which are very pat and expressive," and adds as his reason, that "since it does not become a man of manners to use them, it does not become a man of my age and profession to write them." What was Mr. Kelly's profession or what his age does not appear from any statements in this volume; but, judging by many proverbs which he has *retained,* those which consideration of years and of profession induced him to omit, must have been bad indeed, and unbecoming for *any* age or *any* profession.† The third collection by Mr. Fergusson is mentioned by Kelly as the only one which had been made

* Amongst many acts of kindness and essential assistance which I have received and am constantly receiving from my friend Mr. Hugh James Rollo, I owe my introduction to this interesting Scottish volume, now I believe rather scarce.

† Kelly's book is constantly quoted by Jamieson, and is, indeed, an excellent work for the study of good old Scotch.

before his time, and that he had not met with it till he had made considerable progress in his own collection. The book is now extremely rare, and fetches a high price. By the great kindness of the learned librarian, I have been permitted to see the copy belonging to the library of the Writers to the Signet. It is the first edition, and very rare. A quaint little thin volume, such as delight the eyes of true bibliomaniacs, unpaged, and published at Edinburgh, 1641—although on the title-page the proverbs are said to have been collected at Mr. Fergusson's death, 1598.* There is no preface or notice by the author, but an address from the printer, "to the merrie, judicious, and discreet reader."

The proverbs, amounting to 945, are given without any comment or explanation; many of them are of a very antique cast of language; indeed some would be to most persons quite unintelligible without a lexicon.

The printer, in his address, "to the merrie, judicious, and discreet reader," refers in the following quaint expressions to the author:—"Therefore manie in this realme that hath hard of David Fergusson, sometime minister at Dunfermline, and of his quick answers and speeches, both to great persons and others inferiours, and hath heard of his proverbs which hee gathered together in his time, and now we put downe according to the order of the alphabet; and manie of all ranks of persons, being verie desirous to have the said proverbs, I have thought good to put them to the presse for thy better satisfaction. . . . I know that there may be some that will say and marvell that a minister should have taken pains to gather such proverbs together; but they that knew his forme of powerfull preaching the word, and his ordinar talking, ever almost using proverbiall speeches, will not finde fault with this that hee hath done. And whereas there are some old Scottish

* This probably throws back the collection to about the middle of the century.

words not in use now, bear with that, because if ye alter those words, the proverb will have no grace ; and so, recommending these proverbs to thy good use, I bid thee farewell."

I now subjoin a few of Fergusson's Proverbs, verbatim, which are of a more obsolete character, and have appended explanations, of the correctness of which, however, I am not quite confident :—

A year a nurish,[1] *seven year a da.*[2] Refers, I presume, to fulfilling the maternal office

Anes payit never cravit. Debts once paid give no more trouble.

All wald[3] *have all, all wald forgie.*[4] Those who exact much should be ready to concede.

A gangang[5] *fit*[6] *is aye*[7] *gettin* (*gin*[8] *it were but a thorn*), or, as it sometimes runs, *gin it were but a broken tae, i.e.,* toe. A man of industry will certainly get a living ; though the proverb is often applied to those who went abroad and got a mischief when they might safely have stayed at home—(Kelly).

All crakes,[9] *all bears.*[10] Spoken against bullies who kept a great hectoring, and yet, when put to it, tamely pocket an affront—(Kelly).

Bourd[11] *not wi' bawtie*[12] (*lest he bite you*). Do not jest too familiarly with your superiors (Kelly), or with dangerous characters.

Bread's house skailed never.[13] While people have bread they need not give up housekeeping. Spoken when one has bread and wishes something better—(Kelly).

Crabbit[14] *was and cause had.* Spoken ironically of persons put out of temper without adequate cause.

Dame, deem[15] *warily ye* (*watna*[16] *wha wytes*[17] *yersell*).—

---

[1] Nurse. [2] Daw, a slut. [3] Would. [4] Forgive. [5] Going or moving. [6] Foot. [7] Always. [8] If. [9] Boasters. [10] Used as cowards (?) [11] Jest. [12] A dog's name. [13] To skail house, to disfurnish. [14] Being angry or cross. [15] Judge. [16] Know not. [17] Blames.

Spoken to remind those who pass harsh censures on others that they may themselves be censured.

Efter lang mint[1] *never dint.*[2] Spoken of long and painful labour producing little effect. Kelly's reading is "*Lang mint little dint.*" Spoken when men threaten much and dare not execute—(Kelly).

Fill fou[3] *and haud*[4] *fou maks a stark*[5] *man.* In Border language a *stark* man was one who takes and keeps boldly.

He that crabbs[6] *without cause should mease*[7] *without mends.*[8] Spoken to remind those who are angry without cause, that they should not be particular in requiring apologies from others.

He is worth na weill that may not bide na wae. He deserves not the sweet that will not taste the sour. He does not deserve prosperity who cannot meet adversity.

Kame[9] *sindle*[10] *kame sair.*[11] Applied to those who forbear for a while, but when once roused can act with severity.

Kamesters[12] *are aye creeshie.*[13] It is usual for men to look like their trade.

Let alane maks mony lurden.[14] Want of correction makes many a bad boy—(Kelly).

Mony tynes[15] *the half mark*[16] *whinger*[17] (*for the halfe pennie whang*). Another version of penny wise and pound foolish.

Na plie[19] *is best.*

---

[1] To aim at. [2] A stroke. [3] Full. [4] Hold. [5] Potent or strong. [6] Is angry. [7] Settle. [8] Amends. [9] Comb. [10] Seldom. [11] Painfully. [12] Wool combers. [13] Greasy. [14] Worthless fellow. [15] Loses. [16] Sixpenny.

[17] A sort of dagger or hanger which seems to have been used both at meals as a knife and in broils—

"And *whingers* now in friendship bare,
The social meal to part and share.
Had found a bloody sheath."—*Lay of the Last Minstrel.*

[18] Thong. [19] No lawsuit.

Reavers[1] *should not be rewers.*[2] Those who are so fond of a thing as to snap at it, should not repent when they have got it—(Kelly).

Sokand seill is best. The interpretation of this proverb is not obvious, and later writers do not appear to have adopted it from Fergusson. It is quite clear that Sok or Sock is the ploughshare. Seil is happiness, as in Kelly. "Seil comes not till sorrow be o'er;" and in Aberdeen they say, "Seil o' your face," to express a blessing. My reading is "the plough and happiness the best lot." The happiest life is the healthy country one. See Robert Burns' spirited song with the chorus—

"Up wi' my ploughman lad,
And hey my merry ploughman;
Of a' the trades that I do ken,
Commend me to the ploughman."

A somewhat different reading of this very obscure and now indeed obsolete proverb has been suggested by an esteemed and learned friend—"I should say rather it meant that the ploughshare, or country life, accompanied with good luck or fortune, was best; *i. e.*, that industry coupled with good fortune (good seasons and the like) was the combination that was most to be desired. *Sæl* in Anglo-Saxon as a noun means *opportunity*, and then good luck, happiness, etc.

There's mae[3] *madines*[4] *nor makines.*[5] Girls are more plentiful in the world than hares.

Ye bried[6] *of the gouk,*[7] *ye have not a rhyme*[8] *but ane.* Applied to persons who tire everybody by constantly harping on one subject.

The collection by Allan Ramsay is very good, and professes to correct the errors of former collectors. I have now before me the *first edition*, Edinburgh, 1737, with the

[1] Robbers. [2] Rue, to repent. [3] More. [4] Maidens. [5] Hares. [6] Take after. [7] Cuckoo. [8] Note.

appropriate motto on the title-page, "That maun be true that a' men say." This edition contains proverbs only, the number being 2464. Some proverbs in this collection I do not find in others, and one quality it possesses in a remarkable degree—it is very Scotch. The language of the proverbial wisdom has the true Scottish flavour; not only is this the case with the proverbs themselves, but the dedication to the tenantry of Scotland, prefixed to the collection, is written in pure Scottish dialect. From this dedication I make an extract, which falls in with our plan of recording Scotch reminiscences, as Allan Ramsay there states the great value set upon proverbs in his day, and the great importance which he attaches to them as teachers of moral wisdom, and as combining amusement with instruction. The prose of Allan Ramsay has, too, a spice of his poetry in its composition. His dedication is, To the tenantry of Scotland, farmers of the dales, and storemasters of the hills—

"Worthy friends—The following hoard of wise sayings and observations of our forefathers, which have been gathering through mony bygane ages, I have collected with great care, and restored to their proper sense. . . .

"As naething helps our happiness mair than to have the mind made up wi' right principles, I desire you, for the thriving and pleasure of you and yours, to use your een and lend your lugs to these guid *auld saws*, that shine wi' wail'd sense, and will as lang as the world wags. Gar your bairns get them by heart; let them have a place among your family-books, and may never a window-sole through the country be without them. On a spare hour, when the day is clear, behind a ruck, or on the green howm, draw the treasure frae your pouch, an' enjoy the pleasant companion. Ye happy herds, while your hirdsell are feeding on the flowery braes, you may eithly make yoursells master of the haleware. How usefou' will it prove to you (wha hae sae few opportunities of common clattering) when ye fergather wi' your friends at kirk or market, banquet or bridal! By your proficiency you'll be able, in the proverbial way, to keep up the saul of a conversation that is baith blyth an usefou'."

Mr. Henderson's work is a compilation from those already mentioned. It is very copious, and the introductory essay contains some excellent remarks upon the wisdom and wit of Scottish proverbial sayings.

Mr. Stirling's address, like everything he writes, indicates a minute and profound knowledge of his subject, and is full of picturesque and just views of human nature. He attaches much importance to the teaching conveyed in proverbial expressions, and recommends his readers even still to collect such proverbial expressions as may yet linger in conversation, because, as he observes, "If it is not yet registered, it is possible that it might have died with the tongue from which you took it, and so have been lost for ever." "I believe," he adds, "the number of good old saws still floating as waifs and strays on the tide of popular talk to be much greater than might at first appear."

One remark is applicable to all these collections, viz., that out of so large a number there are many of them on which we have little grounds for deciding that they are *exclusively* Scottish. In fact, some are mere translations of proverbs adopted by many nations; some of universal adoption. Thus we have—

A burnt bairn fire dreads.
Ae swallow makes nae simmer
Faint heart neer wan fair lady.
Ill weeds wax weel.
Mony smas mak a muckle.
O' twa ills chuse the least.
Set a knave to grip a knave.
Twa wits are better than ane.
There's nae fule to an auld fule.
Ye canna mak a silk purse o' a sow's lug.
Ae bird i' the hand is worth twa fleeing.
Mony cooks neer made gude kail.

Of numerous proverbs such as these, some may or may not be original in the Scottish. Mr. Stirling remarks, that many of the best and oldest proverbs may be common to all people—may have occurred to all. In our national collections, therefore, some of the proverbs recorded may be simply translations into Scotch of what have been long considered the property of other nations. Still, I hope, it is not a mere national partiality to say that many of the common proverbs *gain* much by such translation from other tongues. All that I would attempt now is, to select some of our more popular proverbial sayings, which many of us can remember as current amongst us, and were much used by the late generation in society, and to add a few from the collections I have named, which bear a very decided Scottish stamp either in turn of thought or in turn of language.

I remember being much struck the first time I heard the application of that pretty Scottish saying regarding a fair bride. I was walking in Montrose, a day or two before her marriage, with a young lady a connection of mine, who merited this description, when she was kindly accosted by an old friend, an honest fishwife of the town, "Weel, Miss Elizabeth, hae ye gotten a' yer claes ready?" to which the young lady modestly answered, "Oh, Janet, my claes are soon got ready;" and Janet replied, in the old Scottish proverb, "Ay, weel, *a bonny bride's sune buskit*."[1] In the old collection, an addition less sentimental is made to this proverb, *A short horse is sune wispit.*[2]

To encourage strenuous exertions to meet difficult circumstances, is well expressed by *Setting a stout heart to a stey brae.* This mode of expressing that the worth of a handsome woman outweighs even her beauty, has a very Scottish character—*She's better than she's bonny.* The opposite of this was expressed by a Highlander of his own

[1] Attired. [2] Curried.

wife, when he somewhat ungrammatically said of her, "*She's bonnier than she's better.*"

The frequent evil to harvest operations from autumnal rains and fogs in Scotland is well told in the saying, *A dry summer ne'er made a dear peck.*

There can be no question as to country in the following, which seems to express generally that persons may have the name and appearance of greatness without the reality—*A' Stuarts are na sib*[1] *to the king.*

There is an excellent Scottish version of the common proverb, "He that's born to be hanged will never be drowned."—*The water will never warr*[2] *the widdie, i.e.*, never cheat the gallows. This saying received a very naïve practical application during the anxiety and alarm of a storm. One of the passengers, a good simple-minded minister, was sharing the alarm that was felt round him, until spying one of his parishioners, of whose ignominious end he had long felt persuaded, exclaimed to himself, "Oh, we are all safe now," and accordingly accosted the poor man with strong assurances of the great pleasure he had in seeing him on board.

It's ill getting the breeks aff the Highlandman is a proverb that savours very strong of a Lowland Scotch origin. Having suffered loss at the hands of their neighbours from the hills, this was a mode of expressing the painful truth, that there was little hope of obtaining redress from those who had not the means of supplying it.

Proverbs connected with the bag-pipes I set down as legitimate Scotch, as thus, *Ye are as lang in tuning your pipes as anither wad play a spring.*[3] You are as long a setting about a thing as another would be in doing it.

There is a set of Scottish proverbs which we may group together as containing one quality in common, and that in reference to the Evil Spirit, and to his agency in the world. This is a reference often, I fear, too lightly

---

[1] Related. [2] Outrun. [3] Tune.

made; but I am not conscious of anything deliberately profane or irreverent in the following:—

The deil's nae sae ill as he's caaed. The most of people may be found to have some redeeming good point: applied in "Guy Mannering" by the Deacon to Gilbert Glossin, upon his intimating his intention to come to his shop soon for the purpose of laying in his winter stock of groceries.

To the same effect, *It's a sin to lee on the deil.* Even of the worst people, *truth* at least should be spoken.

He should hae a lang shafted spune that sups kail wi' the deil. He should be well guarded and well protected that has to do with cunning and unprincipled men.

Lang ere the deil dee by the dyke-side. Spoken when the improbable death of some powerful and ill-disposed person is talked of.

Let ae deil ding anither. Spoken when two bad persons are at variance over some evil work.

The deil's bairns hae deil's luck. Spoken enviously when ill people prosper.

The deil's a busy bishop in his ain diocie. Bad men are sure to be active in promoting their own bad ends. A quaint proverb of this class I have been told of as coming from the reminiscences of an old lady of quality, to recommend a courteous manner to every one: *It's aye gude to be ceevil, as the auld wife said when she beckit*[1] *to the deevil.*

Raise nae mair deils than ye are able to lay. Provoke no strifes which ye may be unable to appease.

The deil's aye gude to his ain. A malicious proverb, spoken as if those whom we disparage were deriving their success from bad causes.

Ye wad do little for God an the deevil was dead. A sarcastic mode of telling a person that fear, rather than love or principle, is the motive to his good conduct.

In the old collection already referred to is a proverb which I quote unwillingly, and yet which I do not like to

---

[1] Curtsied.

omit. It is doubtful against whom it took its origin, whether as a satire against the decanal order in general, or against some obnoxious dean in particular : *The Deil an the Dean begin wi' ae letter. When the Deil has the Dean the kirk will be the better.*

The deil's gane ower Jock Wabster, is a saying which I have been accustomed to in my part of the country from early years. It expresses generally misfortune or confusion, but I am not quite sure of the *exact* meaning, or who is represented by Jock Wabster. It was a great favourite with Sir Walter Scott, who quotes it twice in Rob Roy. Allan Ramsay introduces it in the Gentle Shepherd to express the misery of married life when the first dream of love has passed away :

" The 'Deil gaes ower Jock Wabster,' hame grows hell,
When Pate misca's ye waur than tongue can tell."

There are two very pithy Scottish proverbial expressions for describing the case of young women losing their chance of good marriages, by setting their aims too high. Thus an old lady, speaking of her granddaughter having made what she considered a poor match, described her as having "lookit at the moon, and lichtit[1] in the midden."

It is recorded again of a celebrated beauty, Becky Monteith, that being asked how she had not made a good marriage, having replied, "Ye see, I wadna hae the walkers, and the riders gaed by."

It's ill to wauken sleeping dogs. It is a bad policy to rouse dangerous and mischievous people, who are for the present quiet.

It is nae mair pity to see a woman greit than to see a goose go barefit. A harsh and ungallant reference to the facility with which the softer sex can avail themselves of tears to carry a point.

A Scots mist will weet an Englishman to the skin. A

---

[1] Fell.

proverb, evidently of Caledonian origin, arising from the frequent complaints made by English visitors of the heavy mists which hang about our hills, and which are found to annoy the southern traveller as it were downright rain.

Keep your ain fish guts to your ain sea maws. This was a favourite proverb with Sir Walter Scott when he meant to express the policy of first considering the interests that are nearest home. The saying savours of the fishing population of the east coast.

A Yule feast may be done at Pasch. Festivities although usually practised at Christmas, need not, on suitable occasions, be confined to any season.

It's better to sup wi' a cutty than want a spune. Cutty means anything short, stumpy, and not of full growth; frequently applied to a short-handled horn spoon. As Meg Merrilees says to the bewildered Dominie, "If ye dinna eat instantly, by the bread and salt, I'll put it down your throat wi' the *cutty spune.*"

"*Fules mak feasts and wise men eat 'em*, my Lord." This was said to a Scottish nobleman on his giving a great entertainment, and who readily answered, "Ay, and *Wise men make proverbs and fools repeat 'em.*"

A green Yule[1] *and a white Pays*[2] *mak a fat kirk-yard.* A very coarse proverb, but may express a general truth as regards the effects of season on the human frame. Another of a similar character is, *An air*[3] *winter maks a sair*[4] *winter.*

Wha will bell the cat? The proverb is used in reference to a proposal for accomplishing a difficult or dangerous task, and alludes to the fable of the poor mice proposing to put a bell about the cat's neck, that they might be apprised of his coming. The historical application is well known. When the nobles of Scotland proposed to go in a body to Stirling to take Cochrane, the favourite of James the Third, and hang him, the Lord Gray asked, "It is well said, but wha will bell the cat?" The Earl of Angus accepted the

---

[1] Christmas. [2] Pasch or easter. [3] Early. [4] Severe.

challenge, and effected the object. To his dying day he was called Archibald Bell-the-Cat.

Ye hae tint the tongue o' the trump. "Trump" is a Jew's harp. To lose the tongue of it is to lose what is essential to its sound.

Meat and mass hinders nae man. Needful food, and suitable religious exercises, should not be spared under greatest haste.

Ye fand it whar the highlandman fand the tangs (*i. e.*, at the fireside). A hit at our mountain neighbours, who occasionally took from the Lowlands—as having found—something that was never *lost.*

His head will ne'er fill his father's bonnet. A picturesque way of expressing that the son will never equal the influence and ability of his sire.

His bark is waur nor his bite. A good-natured apology for one who is good-hearted and rough in speech.

Do as the cow of Forfar did, tak a standing drink. This proverb relates to an occurrence which gave rise to a lawsuit and a whimsical legal decision. A woman in Forfar, who was brewing, set out her tub of beer to cool. A cow came by and drank it up. The owner of the cow was sued for compensation, but the bailies of Forfar, who tried the case, acquitted the owner of the cow, on the ground that the farewell drink, called in the Highlands the *dochan doris,** or stirrup cup, taken by the guest standing at the door, was never charged ; and as the cow had taken but a standing drink outside, it could not, according to the Scottish usage, be chargeable. Sir Walter Scott has humorously alluded to this circumstance in the notes to Waverley, but has not mentioned it as the subject of an old Scotch proverb.

Bannocks are better nor nae kind o' bread. Evidently

---

* The proper orthography of this expression is deoch-an-doruis (or dorais). *Deoch,* a drink ; *an,* of the ; *doruis* or *dorais,* possessive case of dorus or doras, a door.

Scottish. Better have oatmeal cakes to eat than be in want of wheaten loaves.

Folly is a bonny dog. Meaning, I suppose, that many are imposed upon by the false appearances and attractions of vicious pleasures.

The e'ening brings a' hame, is an interesting saying, meaning, that the evening of life, or the approach of death, softens many of our political and religious differences. I do not find this proverb in the older collections, but Mr. Stirling justly calls it "a beautiful proverb, which, lending itself to various uses, may be taken as an expression of faith in the gradual growth and spread of large-hearted Christian charity, the noblest result of our happy freedom of thought and discussion." The literal idea of the "e'ening bringing a' hame," has a high and illustrious antiquity, as in the fragment of Sappho, Ἑσπερε, παντα φέρεις—φέρεις ὄϊν (or οἶνον) φέρεις αἶγα, φέρεις ματέρι παῖδα—which is thus paraphrased by Lord Byron in Don Juan, iii. 107 :—

> "O Hesperus! thou bringest all good things—
> Home to the weary, to the hungry cheer;
> To the young bird the parent's brooding wings,
> The welcome stall to the o'erlaboured steer, etc.
> Thou bring'st the child, too, to the mother's breast."

A similar graceful and moral saying inculcates an acknowledgment of gratitude for the past favours which we have enjoyed when we come to the close of the day or the close of life—

Ruse the fair day at e'en.*

But a very learned and esteemed friend has suggested another reading of this proverb, in accordance with the celebrated saying of Solon (Arist. Eth. N. I. 10) : Κατὰ Σόλωνα χρεὼν τέλος ὁρᾶν—Do not praise the fairness of the day *till* evening ; do not call the life happy *till* you have seen the close ; or, in other matters, do not boast that

* Praise.

all is well till you have conducted your undertaking to a prosperous end.

Let him tak a spring on his ain fiddle. Spoken of a foolish and unreasonable person; as if to say, "We will for the present allow him to have his own way." Bailie Nicol Jarvie quotes the proverb with great bitterness, when he warns his opponent that *his* time for triumph will come ere long,—"Aweel, aweel, sir, you're welcome to a tune on your ain fiddle; but see if I dinna gar ye dance till't afore it's dune."

The kirk is meikle, but ye may say mass in ae end o't; or, as I have received it in another form, "If we canna preach in the kirk, we can sing mass in the quire." This intimates, where something is alleged to be too much, that you need take no more than what you have need for. I heard the proverb used in this sense by Sir Walter Scott at his own table. His son had complained of some quaighs which Sir Walter had produced for a dram after dinner, that they were too large. His answer was, "Well, Walter, as my good mother used to say, if the kirk is owre big, just sing mass in the quire." Here is another reference to kirk and quire—*He rives*[1] *the kirk to theik*[2] *the quire.* Spoken of unprofitable persons, who, in the English proverb, "rob Peter to pay Paul."

The king's errand may come the cadger's gate yet. A great man may need the service of a very mean one.

The maut is aboon the meal. His liquor has done more for him than his meat. The man is drunk.

Mak a kirk and a mill o't. Turn a thing to any purpose you like; or rather, spoken sarcastically, Take it, and make the best of it.

Like a sow playing on a trump. No image could be well more incongruous than a pig performing on a Jew's harp.

Mair by luck than gude guiding. His success is due

---

[1] Tears. [2] Thatch.

to his fortunate circumstances, rather than to his own discretion.

He's not a man to ride the water wi'. A common Scottish saying to express you cannot trust such an one in trying times. May have arisen from the districts where fords abounded, and the crossing them was dangerous.

He rides on the riggin o' the kirk. The rigging being the top of the roof, the proverb used to be applied to those who carried their zeal for church matters to the extreme point.

Leal heart never leed, well expresses that an honest loyal disposition will scorn, under all circumstances, to tell a falsehood.

A common Scottish proverb, *Let that flee stick to the wa',* has an obvious meaning,—"Say nothing more on that subject." But the derivation is not obvious.* In like manner, the meaning of *He that will to Cupar maun to Cupar,* is clearly that if a man is obstinate, and bent upon his own dangerous course, he must take it. But why Cupar? and whether is it the Cupar of Angus or the Cupar of Fife?

Kindness creeps where it canna gang, prettily expresses that where love can do little, it will do that little though it cannot do more.

In my part of the country a ridiculous addition used to be made to the common Scottish saying, *Mony a thing's made for the pennie,* i.e., Many contrivances are thought of to get money. The addition is, "As the old woman said when she saw a black man,"—taking it for granted that he was an ingenious and curious piece of mechanism made for profit.

---

* It has been suggested, and with much reason, that the reference is to a flee sticking on a wet or a newly painted wall; this is corroborated by the addition in Rob Roy, "When the dirt's dry, it will rub out," which seems to point out the meaning and derivation of the proverb.

Bluid is thicker than water, is a proverb which has a marked Scottish aspect, as meant to vindicate those family predilections to which, as a nation, we are supposed to be rather strongly inclined.

There's aye water where the stirkie drouns.* Where certain effects are produced, there must be some causes at work—a proverb used to show that a universal popular suspicion as to an obvious effect must be laid in truth.

Better a finger aff than aye waggin'. This proverb I remember as a great favourite with many Scotch people. Better experience the worst, than have an evil always pending.

Cadgers are aye cracking o' crook-saddles† has a very Scottish aspect, and signifies that professional men are very apt to talk too much of their profession.

As sure's deeth. A common Scottish proverbial expression to signify either the truth or certainty of a fact, or to pledge the speaker to a performance of his promise. In the latter sense an amusing illustration of faith in the superior obligation of this asseveration to any other, is recorded in the Eglinton Papers.‡ The Earl one day found a boy climbing up a tree, and called him to come down. The boy declined, because, he said, the Earl would thrash him. His Lordship pledged his honour that he would not do so. The boy replied, "I dinna ken onything about your honour, but if you say as sure's deeth, I'll come doun."

Proverbs are sometimes local in their application.

The men o' the Mearns manna do mair than they may. Even the men of Kincardineshire can only do their utmost—a proverb intended to be highly complimentary to the powers of the men of that county.

I'll mak Cathkin's covenant with you, Let abee for let abee. This is a local saying quoted often in Hamilton.

* A young bullock. † Saddle for supporting panniers.

‡ Vol. I., p. 134.

The laird of that property had—very unlike the excellent family who have now possessed it for more than a century—been addicted to intemperance. One of his neighbours, in order to frighten him on his way home from his evening potations, disguised himself, on a very dark night, and, personating the devil, claimed a title to carry him off as his rightful property. Contrary to all expectation, however, the laird showed fight, and was about to commence the onslaught, when a parley was proposed, and the issue was "Cathkin's covenant, Let abee for let abee."

When the castle of Stirling gets a hat, the carse of Corntown pays for that. This is a local proverbial saying; the meaning is, that when the clouds descend so low as to envelope Stirling Castle, a deluge of rain may be expected in the adjacent country.

I will conclude this notice of our proverbial reminiscences, by adding a cluster of Scottish proverbs, selected from an excellent article on the general subject in the "North British Review" of February 1858. The reviewer designates these as "broader in their mirth, and more caustic in their tone," than the moral proverbial expressions of the Spanish and Italian:—

A blate[1] cat maks a proud mouse.
Better a toom[2] house than an ill tenant.
Jouk[3] and let the jaw[4] gang by.
Mony ane speers the gate[5] he kens fu' weel.
The tod[6] ne'er sped better than when he gaed his ain errand.
A wilfu' man should be unco wise.
He that has a meikle nose thinks ilka ane speaks o't.
He that teaches himsel has a fule for his maister.
It's an ill cause that the lawyer thinks shame o'.
Lippen[7] to me, but look to yoursell.

---

[1] Shy. [2] Empty. [3] Stoop down
[4] Wave. [5] The way. [6] Fox. [7] Trust to.

Mair whistle than woo, as the souter said when shearing the soo.
Ye gae far about seeking the nearest.
Ye'll no sell your hen in a rainy day.
Ye'll mend when ye grow better.
*Ye'er nae chicken for a' your cheepin'.**

I have now adduced quite sufficient specimens to convince those who may not have given attention to the subject, how much of wisdom, knowledge of life, and good feeling are contained in these aphorisms which compose the mass of our Scottish proverbial sayings. No doubt, to many of my younger readers, proverbs are little known, and to all they are becoming more and more matters of reminiscence. I am quite convinced that much of the old quaint and characteristic Scottish talk which we are now endeavouring to recal, depended on a happy use of those abstracts of moral sentiment. And this feeling will be confirmed when we call to mind how often those of the old Scottish school of character, whose conversation we have ourselves admired, had most largely availed themselves of the use of its *proverbial* philosophy.

In connection with the division of our subject, the present seems to be a proper place for introducing the mention of a Scottish peculiarity—viz., that of naming individuals from lands which have been possessed long by the family, or frequently from the landed estates which they acquire. The use of this mode of discriminating individuals in the Highland districts is sufficiently obvious. Where the inhabitants of a whole country side are Campbells, or Frasers, or Gordons, nothing could be more convenient than addressing the individuals of each clan by the name of his estate. Indeed, some years ago, any other designation, as Mr. Campbell, Mr. Fraser, would have been resented as an indignity. Their consequence sprang from their posses-

* Chirping.

sion.* But all this is fast wearing away. The estates of old families have often changed hands, and Highlanders are most unwilling to give the names of old properties to new proprietors. The custom, however, lingers amongst us, in the northern districts especially. Farms also used to give their names to the tenants.† I can recal an amusing instance of this practice belonging to my early days. The oldest recollections I have are connected with the name, the figure, the sayings and doings, of the old cowherd at Fasque in my father's time; his name was Boggy, *i. e.*, his ordinary appellation; his true name was Sandy Anderson. But he was called Boggy from the circumstance of having once held a wretched farm on Deeside named Boggendreep. He had long left it, and been unfortunate in it, but the name never left him,—he was Boggy to his grave. The territorial appellation used to be reckoned complimentary, and more respectful than Mr. or any higher title to which the individual might be entitled. I recollect, in my brother's time, at Fasque, his showing off some of his home stock to Mr. Williamson, the Aberdeen butcher. They came to a fine stot, and Sir Alexander said, with some appearance of boast, "I was offered twenty guineas for that ox." "Indeed, Fasque," said Williamson, "ye should hae steekit your neive upo' that."

Sir Walter Scott had marked in his diary a territorial greeting of two proprietors which had amused him much. The laird of Kilspindie had met the laird of Tannachy-Tulloch, and the following compliments passed between them:—"Yer maist obedient hummil servant, Tannachy-Tulloch." To which the reply was, "Yer nain man, Kilspindie."

---

* Even in Forfarshire, where Carnegies abound, we had Craigo, Balnamoon, Pittarrow, etc.

† This custom is still in use in Galloway; and "Challoch," "Eschonchan," "Tonderghie," "Balsalloch," and "Drummorral," etc. etc., appear regularly at kirk and market.

In proportion as we advance towards the Highland districts this custom of distinguishing clans or races, and marking them out according to the district they occupied, became more apparent. There was the Glengarry country, the Fraser country, the Gordon country, etc. etc. These names carried also with them certain moral features as characteristic of each division. Hence the following anecdote :—The morning litany of an old laird of Cultoquhey, when he took his morning draught at the cauld well, was in these terms—"Frae the ire o' the Drummonds, the pride o' the Græmes, the greed o' the Campbells, and the wind o' the Murrays, guid Lord deliver us." On being reproved by the Duke of Athole for taking such liberties with noble names, his answer was—"There, my lord, there's the wind o' the Murrays!"

CHAPTER THE SIXTH.

ON SCOTTISH STORIES OF WIT AND HUMOUR.

The portion of our subject, which we proposed under the head of "Reminiscences of Scottish Stories of Wit or Humour," yet remains to be considered. This is closely connected with the question of Scottish dialect and expressions; indeed, on some points hardly separable, as the wit, to a great extent, proceeds from the quaint and picturesque modes of expressing it. But here we are met by a difficulty. On high authority it has been declared that no such thing as wit exists among us. What has no existence can have no change. We cannot be said to have lost a quality which we never possessed. Many of my readers are no doubt familiar with what Sydney Smith declared on this point, and certainly on the question of wit he must be considered an authority. He used to say (I am almost ashamed to repeat it), "It requires a surgical operation to get a joke well into a Scotch understanding. Their only idea of wit, which prevails occasionally in the north, and which, under the name of Wut, is so infinitely distressing to people of good taste, is laughing immoderately at stated intervals." Strange language to use of a country which has produced Smollett, Burns, Scott, Galt, and Wilson—all remarkable for the humour diffused through their writings. Indeed, we may fairly ask, have they equals in this respect amongst English writers? Charles Lamb had the same notion, or, I should rather say, the same prejudice, about Scottish people not being accessible to wit; and he tells a story of what happened to himself, in corroboration of the opinion. He had been asked to a party, and one object of the invitation had been to meet a son of Burns. When he arrived, Mr. Burns had not made his appearance, and in the course of conversation regarding the family of the poet, Lamb, in his lack-a-daisical kind of manner, said, "I wish it had been the father instead of the son;" upon which four Scotchmen present with one voice exclaimed, "That's impossible, for *he's dead*."* Now, there will be dull men and matter-of-fact men everywhere, who do not take a joke or enter into a jocular allusion; but surely, as a general remark, this is far from being a natural quality of our country. Sydney Smith and Charles Lamb say so. But at the risk of being considered presumptuous, I will say I think them entirely mistaken. I should say that there was, on the contrary, a strong *connection* between the Scottish temperament and, call it if you like, humour, if it is not wit. And what is the difference? My readers need not be afraid that they are to be led through a labyrinth of metaphysical distinctions between wit and humour. I have read Dr. Campbell's dissertation on the difference in his philosophy of rhetoric; I have read Sydney Smith's own two lectures; but I confess I am not much the wiser. Professors of rhetoric, no doubt, must have such discussions, but when you wish to be amused by the thing itself, it is somewhat disappointing to be presented with metaphysical analysis. It is like instituting an examination of the glass and cork of a champagne bottle, and a chemical testing of the wine. In the very process the volatile and sparkling draught which was to delight the palate, has become like ditch water, vapid and dead. What I mean is, that, call it wit or humour, or what you please,

* After all, the remark may not have been so absurd then as it appears now. Burns had not been long dead, nor was he then so noted a character as he is now. The Scotchmen might really have supposed a Southerner unacquainted with the *fact* of the poet's death.

there is a school of Scottish pleasantry, amusing and characteristic beyond all other. Don't think of *analysing* its nature, or the qualities of which it is composed; enjoy its quaint and amusing flow of oddity and fun; as we may, for instance, suppose it to have flowed on that eventful night so joyously described by Burns :—

> "The souter tauld his queerest stories,
> The landlord's laugh was ready chorus."

Or we may think of the delight it gave the good Mr. Balwhidder, when he tells, in his Annals of the Parish, of some such story, that it was a "jocosity that was just a kittle to hear." When I speak of changes in such Scottish humour which have taken place, I refer to a particular sort of humour, and I speak of the sort of feeling that belongs to Scottish pleasantry,—which is sly, and cheery, and pawky. It is, undoubtedly, a humour that depends a good deal upon the vehicle in which the story is conveyed. If, as we have said, our quaint dialect is passing away, and our national eccentric points of character, we must expect to find much of the peculiar humour allied with them to have passed away also. In other departments of wit and repartee, and acute hits at men and things, Scotchmen (whatever Sydney Smith may have said to the contrary) are equal to their neighbours, and, so far as I know, may have gained rather than lost. But this peculiar humour of which I now speak has not, in our day, the scope and development which were permitted to it by the former generation. Where the tendency exists, the exercise of it is kept down by the usages and feelings of society. For examples of it (in its full force at any rate), we must go back to a race who are departed. One remark, however, has occurred to me in regard to the specimens we have of this kind of humour—viz., that they do not always proceed from the wit or the cleverness of any of the individuals concerned in them. The amusement comes from the circumstances, from the concurrence or combination of the ideas, and in many cases from the mere expressions which describe the facts. The humour of the narrative is unquestionable, and yet no one has tried to be humorous. In short, it is the *Scottishness* that gives the zest. The same ideas differently expounded might have no point at all. There is, for example, something highly original in the notions of celestial mechanics entertained by an honest Scottish Fife lass regarding the theory of comets. Having occasion to go out after dark, and having observed the brilliant comet then visible (1858), she ran in with breathless haste to the house, calling on her fellow-servants to "Come oot and see a new star that hasna got its tail cuttit aff yet!" Exquisite astronomical speculation! Stars, like puppies, are born with tails, and in due time have them docked. Take an example of a story where there is no display of any one's wit or humour, and yet it is a good story, and one can't exactly say why:—An English traveller had gone on a fine Highland road so long, without having seen an indication of fellow-travellers, that he became astonished at the solitude of the country; and no doubt before the Highlands were so much frequented as they are in our time, the roads had a very striking aspect of solitariness. Our traveller at last coming up to an old man breaking stones, he asked him if there was any traffic on this road—was it at *all* frequented? "Ay," he said, "it's no ill at that; there was a cadger body yestreen, and there's yoursell the day." No English version of the story could have half such amusement, or have so quaint a character. An answer, even still more characteristic, is recorded to have been given by a countryman to a traveller. Being doubtful of his way, he inquired if he were on the right road to Dunkeld. With some of his national inquisitiveness about strangers, the countryman asked his inquirer where he came from. Offended at the liberty, as he considered it, he sharply reminded the man that where he came from was nothing to him; but all the answer he got, was the quiet rejoinder. "Indeed, it's just as little to me whar ye're gaen'." A friend has told me of an answer highly characteristic of this dry and unconcerned quality which he heard given to a fellow-traveller. A gentleman sitting opposite to him in the stage-coach at Berwick, complained bitterly that the cushion on which he sat was quite wet. On looking up to the roof he saw a hole through which the rain descended copiously, and at once accounted for the mischief. He called for the coachman, and in great wrath reproached him with the evil under which he suffered, and pointed to the hole which was the cause of it. All the satisfaction, however, that he got was the quiet unmoved reply, "Ay, mony a ane has complained o' *that* hole." Another anecdote I heard from a gentleman who vouched for the truth, which is just a case where the narrative has its humour, not from the wit which is displayed, but from that dry matter-of-fact view of things peculiar to some of our countrymen. The friend of my informant was walking in a street of Perth, when, to his horror, he saw a workman fall from a roof where he was mending slates, right upon the pavement. By extraordinary good fortune he was not killed, and, on the gentleman going up to his assistance, and exclaiming, with much excitement, "God bless me, are you much hurt?" all the answer he got was the cool rejoinder, "On the contrary, sir." A similar matter-of-fact answer was made by one of the old race of Montrose humorists. He was coming out of church, and, in the press of the kirk *skailing*, a young man thoughtlessly trod on the old gentleman's toe, which was tender with corns. He hastened to apologise, saying, "I am very sorry, sir; I beg your pardon." The only acknowledgment of which was the dry answer, "And ye've as muckle need, sir."

One of the best specimens of cool Scottish matter-of fact view of things has been supplied by a kind correspondent, who narrates it from his own personal recollection.

The back windows of the house where he was brought

up looked upon the Greyfriars' Church that was burnt down. On the Sunday morning in which that event took place, as they were all preparing to go to church, the flames began to burst forth; the young people screamed from the back part of the house, "A fire! a fire!" and all was in a state of confusion and alarm. The housemaid was not at home, it being her turn for the Sunday "out." Kitty, the cook, was taking her place, and performing her duties. The old woman was always very particular on the subject of her responsibility on such occasions, and came panting and hobbling up stairs from the lower regions, and exclaimed, "O what is't, what is't?" "Oh, Kitty, look here, the Greyfriars' Church is on fire!" "Is that a', Miss? What a fricht ye geed me! I thought ye said the parlour fire was out."

From a first-rate *Highland* authority I have been supplied with the following clever and crushing reply to what was intended as a sarcastic compliment and a smart saying:—

About the beginning of the present century, the then Campbell, of Combie, on Loch Awe side, in Argyleshire, was a man of extraordinary character, and of great physical strength, and such swiftness of foot that it is said he could "catch the best *tup* on the hill." He also looked upon himself as a "pretty man," though in this he was singular; also, it was more than whispered that the laird was not remarkable for his principles of honesty. There also lived in the same district a Miss MacNabb of Bar-a'-Chaistril, a lady who, before she had passed the zenith of life, had never been remarkable for her beauty—the contrary even had passed into a proverb, while she was in her teens; but, to counterbalance this defect in external qualities, nature had endowed her with great benevolence, while she was renowned for her probity. One day the Laird of Combie, who piqued himself on his *bon-mots*, was, as frequently happened, a guest of Miss MacNabb's, and after dinner several toasts had gone round as usual, Combie addressed his hostess, and requested an especial bumper, insisting on all the guests to fill to the brim. He then rose, and said, addressing himself to Miss MacNabb, "I propose the old Scottish toast of 'Honest men and *bonnie* lassies,'" and bowing to the hostess, he resumed his seat. The lady returned his bow with her usual amiable smile, and taking up her glass, replied, "Weel, Combie, I am sure *we* may drink that, for it will neither apply to *you* nor *me*."

An amusing example of a quiet cool view of a pecuniary transaction happened to my father whilst doing the business of the rent day. He was receiving sums of money from the tenants in succession. After looking over a bundle of notes which he had just received from one of them, a well-known character, he said in banter, "James, the notes are not correct." To which the farmer, who was much of a humorist, dryly answered, "I dinna ken what they may be *noo;* but they were a' richt afore ye had your fingers in amang 'em." An English farmer would hardly have spoken thus to his landlord. The Duke of Buccleuch told me an answer very quaintly Scotch, given to his grandmother by a farmer of the old school. A dinner was given to some tenantry of the vast estates of the family, in the time of Duke Henry. His Duchess (the last descendant of the Dukes of Montague) always appeared at table on such occasion, and did the honours with that mixture of dignity and of affable kindness for which she was so remarkable. Abundant hospitality was shown to all the guests. The Duchess, having observed one of the tenants supplied with boiled beef from a noble round, proposed that he should add a supply of cabbage; on his declining, the Duchess good humouredly remarked, "Why, boiled beef and greens seem so naturally to go together, I wonder you don't take it." To which the honest farmer objected, "Ah, but your Grace maun alloo it's a vary *windy* vegetable," in delicate allusion to the flatulent quality of the esculent. Similar to this was the naïve answer of a farmer on the occasion of a rent day. The lady of the house asked him if he would take some *rhubarb* tart: "Mony thanks, mem, I dinna need it."

Amongst the lower orders, humour is found, occasionally, very rich in mere children, and I recollect a remarkable illustration of this early native humour occurring in a family in Forfarshire, where I used, in former days, to be very intimate. A wretched woman, who used to traverse the country as a beggar or tramp, left a poor, half starved little girl by the road-side, near the house of my friends. Always ready to assist the unfortunate, they took charge of the child, and as she grew a little older, they began to give her some education, and taught her to read. She soon made some progress in reading the Bible, and the native odd humour, of which we speak, began soon to show itself. On reading the passage, which began, "Then David rose," etc., the child stopped, and looking up knowingly, to say, "I ken wha that was," and, on being asked what she could mean, she confidently said, "That's David Rowse the pleuchman." And again reading the passage where the words occur, "He took Paul's girdle," the child said, with much confidence, "I ken what he took that for," and on being asked to explain, replied at once, "To bake's bannocks on;" "girdle" being, in the north, the name for the iron plate hung over the fire, for making oat cakes or bannocks.

To a distinguished member of the Church of Scotland I am indebted for an excellent story of quaint child humour, which he had from the lips of an old woman who related the story of herself:—When a girl of eight years of age, she was taken by her grandmother to church. The parish minister was not only a long preacher, but, as the custom was, delivered two sermons on the Sabbath day without any interval, and thus saved the parishioners the two journeys to church. Elizabeth was sufficiently wearied before the close of the first discourse; but when, after singing and prayer, the good minister opened the Bible, read a second text, and prepared to give a second sermon, the young girl, being both tired and hungry, lost all patience, and cried out to her grandmother, to the no small amusement of those who were so near as to hear her, "Come awa, granny, and gang hame; this is a lang grace, and nae meat."

A most amusing account of child humour used to be narrated by an old Mr. Campbell of Jura, who told the story of his own son. It seems the boy was much spoilt by indulgence. In fact, the parents were scarce able to refuse him anything he demanded. He was in the drawing-room on one occasion when dinner was announced, and on being ordered up to the nursery, he insisted on going down to dinner with the company. His mother was for refusal, but the child persevered, and kept saying, "If I dinna gang, I'll tell thon." His father then, for peace sake, let him go. So he went and sat at table by his mother. When he found every one getting soup and himself omitted, he demanded soup, and repeated, "If I dinna get it, I'll tell thon." Well, soup was given, and various other things yielded to his importunities, to which he always added the usual threat of "telling thon." At last, when it came to wine, his mother stood firm, and positively refused, as "a bad thing for little boys," and so on. He then became more vociferous than ever about "telling thon;" and as still he was refused, he declared, "Now I will tell thon," and at last roared out, "*Ma new breeks were made oot' o' the auld curtains!*"

A facetious and acute friend who rather leans to the Sydney Smith view of Scottish wit, declares that all our humorous stories are about lairds, and about lairds who are drunk. Of such stories there are certainly not a few; one of the best belonging to my part of the country, and to many persons I should perhaps apologise for introducing it at all. The story has been told of various parties and localities, but no doubt the genuine laird was a laird of Balnamoon (pronounced in the country Bonnymoon), and that the locality was a wild tract of land, not far from his place, called Munrimmon Moor. Balnamoon had been dining out in the neighbourhood, where, by mistake, they had put down to him after dinner cherry brandy, instead of port wine, his usual beverage. The rich flavour and strength so pleased him, that having tasted it, he would have nothing else. On rising from table, therefore, the laird would be more affected by his drink than if he had taken his ordinary allowance of port. His servant Harry, or Hairy,* was to drive him home in a gig or whisky, as it was called, the usual open carriage of the time. On crossing the moor, however, whether from greater exposure to the blast, or from the laird's unsteadiness of head, his hat and wig came off and fell upon the ground. Harry got out to pick them up and restore them to his master. The laird was satisfied with the hat, but demurred at the wig. "It's no my wig, Hairy, lad; it's no my wig," and refused to have anything to do with it. Hairy lost his patience, and, anxious to get home, remonstrated with his master, "Ye'd better tak it, sir, for there's nae waile o' wigs on Munrimmon Moor." The humour of the argument is exquisite, putting to the laird, in his unreasonable objection, the sly insinuation that in such a locality, if he did not take *this* wig, he was not likely to find another. Then, what a rich expression, "waile o' wigs." In English what is it? "A choice of perukes;" which is nothing comparable to the "waile o' wigs." I ought to mention also an amusing sequel to the story, viz., in what happened after the affair of the wig had been settled, and the laird had consented to return home. When the whisky drove up to the door, Hairy, sitting in front, told the servant who came to "tak out the laird." No laird was to be seen; and it appeared that he had fallen out on the moor without Hairy observing it. Of course, they went back, and, pick-

---

* In corroboration of the genuineness and authenticity of the story, I am assured by a correspondent that he knows the name of the servant was *not* Hairy; but I have mislaid the reference.

ing him up, brought him safe home. A neighbouring laird having called a few days after, and having referred to the accident, Balnamoon quietly added, "Indeed, I maun hae a lume* that'll *had in*."

The laird of Balnamoon was a truly eccentric character. He joined with his drinking propensities a great zeal for the Episcopal Church, the service of which he read to his own family with much solemnity and earnestness of manner. Two gentlemen, one of them a stranger to the country, having called pretty early one Sunday morning, Balnamoon invited them to dinner, and as they accepted the invitation, they remained and joined in the forenoon devotional exercises conducted by Balnamoon himself. The stranger was much impressed with the laird's performance of the service, and during a walk which they took before dinner mentioned to his friend how highly he esteemed the religious deportment of their host. The gentleman said nothing, but smiled to himself at the scene which he anticipated was to follow. After dinner Balnamoon set himself, according to the custom of old hospitable Scottish hosts, to make his guests as drunk as possible. The result was, that the party spent the evening in a riotous debauch, and were carried to bed by the servants at a late hour. Next day, when they had taken leave and left the house, the gentleman who had introduced his friend asked him what he thought of their entertainer—"Why, really," he replied, with evident astonishment, "sic a speat o' praying, and sic a speat o' drinking, I never knew in the whole course of my life."

Lady Dalhousie, mother, I mean, of the late distinguished Marquis of Dalhousie, used to tell a characteristic anecdote of her day. But here, on mention of the name Christian, Countess of Dalhousie, may I pause a moment to recal the memory of one who was a very remarkable person. She was, for many years, to me and mine, a sincere and true and valuable friend. By an awful dispensation of God's

---

* A vessel.

providence, her death happened *instantaneously* under my roof in 1839. Lady Dalhousie was eminently distinguished for a fund of the most varied knowledge, for a clear and powerful judgment, for acute observation, a kind heart, a brilliant wit. Her story was thus:—A Scottish judge, somewhat in the predicament of the Laird of Balnamoon, had dined at Coalstoun with her father Charles Brown, an advocate, and son of George Brown, who sat in the Supreme Court as a judge with the title of Lord Coalstoun. The party had been convivial, as we know parties of the highest legal characters often were in those days. When breaking up and going to the drawing-room, one of them, not seeing his way very clearly, stepped out of the dining-room window, which was open to the summer air. The ground at Coalstoun sloping off from the house behind, the worthy judge got a great fall, and rolled down the bank. He contrived, however, as tipsy men generally do, to regain his legs, and was able to reach the drawing-room. The first remark he made was an innocent remonstrance with his friend the host, "Od, Charlie Brown, what gars ye hae sic lang steps to your *front* door?"

On Deeside, where many original stories had their origin, I recollect hearing several of an excellent and worthy, but very simple-minded man, the Laird of Craigmyle. On one occasion, when the beautiful and clever Jane, Duchess of Gordon, was scouring through the country, intent upon some of those electioneering schemes which often occupied her fertile imagination and active energies, she came to call at Craigmyle, and having heard that the laird was making bricks on the property, for the purpose of building a new garden wall, with her usual tact she opened the subject, and kindly asked, "Well, Mr. Gordon, and how do your bricks come on?" Good Craigmyle's thoughts were much occupied with a new leather portion of his dress, which had been lately constructed, so, looking down on his nether garments, he said in pure Aberdeen dialect, "Muckle obleeged to yer Grace, the breeks war sum ticht at first, but they are deeing weel eneuch noo." The last Laird of Macnab, before the clan finally broke up and emigrated to Canada, was a well-known character in the country, and being poor, used to ride about on a most wretched horse, which gave occasion to many jibes at his expense. The laird was in the constant habit of riding up from the country to attend the Musselburgh races. A young wit, by way of playing him off on the race-course, asked him, in a contemptuous tone, "Is that the same horse you had last year, laird?" "Na," said the laird, brandishing his whip in the interrogator's face in so emphatic a manner as to preclude further questioning, "Na; but it's the same *whup*." In those days, as might be expected, people were not nice in expressions of their dislike of persons and measures. If there be not more charity in society than of old, there is certainly more courtesy. I have, from a friend, an anecdote illustrative of this remark, in regard to feelings exercised towards an unpopular laird. In the neighbourhood of Banff, in Forfarshire, the seat of a very ancient branch of the Ramsays, lived a proprietor who bore the appellation of Corb, from the name of his estate. The family has passed away, and its property merged in Banff. This laird was intensely disliked in the neighbourhood. Sir George Ramsay was, on the other hand, universally popular and respected. On one occasion, Sir George, in passing a morass in his own neighbourhood, had missed the road and fallen into a bog to an alarming depth. To his great relief, he saw a passenger coming along the path, which was at no great distance. He called loudly for his help, but the man took no notice. Poor Sir George felt himself sinking, and redoubled his cries for assistance; all at once the passenger rushed forward, carefully extricated him from his perilous position, and politely apologised for his first neglect of his appeal, adding, as his reason, "Indeed, Sir George, I thought it was Corb!" evidently meaning that *had* it been Corb, he must have taken his chance for him.

In Lanarkshire, there lived a sma' sma' laird named Hamilton, who was noted for his eccentricity. On one occasion, a neighbour waited on him, and requested his name as an accommodation to a bit bill for twenty pounds at three months' date, which led to the following characteristic and truly Scottish colloquy :—" Na, na, I canna do that." " What for no, laird, ye hae dune the same thing for ithers." " Aye, aye, Tammas, but there's wheels within wheels ye ken naething about ; I canna do't." " It's a sma' affair to refuse me, laird." " Weel ye see, Tammas, if I was to pit my name till't, ye wad get the siller frae the bank, and when the time came round, ye wadna be ready, and I wad hae to pay't ; sae then you and me wad quarrel ; sae we mae just as weel quarrel *the noo*, as lang's the siller's in ma pouch." On one occasion, Hamilton having business with the late Duke of Hamilton at Hamilton Palace, the Duke politely asked him to lunch. A liveried servant waited upon them, and was most assiduous in his attentions to the Duke and his guest. At last our eccentric friend lost patience, and looking at the servant, addressed him thus, " What the deil for are ye dance, dancing, about the room that gait ; can ye no draw in your chair and sit down ? I'm sure there's *plenty on the table for three*."

Of another laird whom I heard often spoken of in old times, an anecdote was told strongly Scotch. Our friend had much difficulty (as many worthy lairds have had) in meeting the claims of those two woful periods of the year called with us in Scotland the " tarmes." He had been employing for some time as workman a stranger from the south on some house repairs, of the not uncommon name in England of Christmas. His servant early one morning called out at the laird's door in great excitement that " Christmas had run away, and nobody knew where he had gone." He turned in his bed with the earnest ejaculation, " I only wish he had taken Whitsunday and Martinmas along with him." I do not know a better illustration of quiet, shrewd, and acute Scottish humour than the following little story, which an esteemed correspondent mentions having heard from his father when a boy, relating to a former Duke of Athole, who had *no family of his own*, and whom he mentions as having remembered very well :—He met, one morning, one of his cottars or gardeners, whose wife he knew to be in the *hopeful way*. Asking him "how Marget was the day," the man replied, that she had that morning given him twins. Upon which the Duke said,—"Weel, Donald ; ye ken the Almighty never sends bairns without the meat." "That may be, your Grace," said Donald ; "but whiles I think that Providence maks a mistak in thae matters, and sends the bairns to ae hoose and the meat to anither !" The Duke took the hint, and sent him a cow with calf the following morning.

I have heard of an amusing scene between a laird celebrated for his saving propensities, and a wandering sort of Edie Ochiltree, a well-known itinerant who lived by his wits and what he could pick up in his rounds amongst the houses of lairds and farmers. One thrifty laird having seen him sit down near his own gate to examine the contents of his poke or wallet, conjectured that he had come from the house, and so he drew near to see what he had carried off. As he was keenly investigating the mendicant's spoils, his quick eye detected some bones on which there remained more meat than should have been allowed to leave his kitchen. Accordingly he pounced upon the bones, and declared he had been robbed, and insisted on his returning to the house and giving back the spoil. The beggar was, however, prepared for the attack, and sturdily defended his property, boldy asserting, "Na, na, laird, thae are no Todbrae banes ; thae are Inch-Byre banes, and nane o' your honour's"—meaning that he had received these bones at the house of a neighbour of a more liberal character. But the beggar's professional discrimination between the bones of the two mansions, and his pertinacious defence of his own property, would have been most amusing to a bystander.

I have, however, a reverse story, in which the beggar is quietly silenced by the proprietor. A noble lord, some generations back, well known for his frugal habits, had just picked up a small copper coin in his own avenue, and had been observed by one of the itinerating mendicant race, who, grudging the transfer of the piece into the peer's pocket, exclaimed, "O, gie't to me, my lord;" to which the quiet answer was, "Na, na; fin' a fardin for yersell, puir body."

There are always pointed anecdotes against houses wanting in a liberal and hospitable expenditure in Scotland. Thus, we have heard of a master leaving such a mansion, and taxing his servant with being drunk, which he had too often been after country visits. On this occasion, however, he was innocent of the charge, for he had not the *opportunity* to transgress. So, when his master asserted, "Jemmy, you are drunk!" Jemmy very quietly answered, "Indeed, sir, I wish I wur." At another mansion, notorious for scanty fare, a gentleman was inquiring of the gardener about a dog which some time ago he had given to the laird. The gardener showed him a lank greyhound, on which the gentleman said, "No, no; the dog I gave your master was a mastiff, not a greyhound;" to which the gardener quietly answered, "Indeed, ony dog micht sune become a greyhound by stopping here."

From a friend and near relative, a minister of the Established Church of Scotland, I used to hear many characteristic stories. He had a curious vein of this sort of humour in himself, besides what he brought out of others. One of his peculiarities was a mortal antipathy to the whole French nation, whom he frequently abused in no measured terms. At the same time he had great relish of a glass of claret, which he considered the prince of all social beverages. So he usually finished off his antigallican tirades with the reservation, "But the bodies brew the braw drink." He lived amongst his own people, and knew well the habits and peculiarities of a race gone by. He had many stories connected with the pastoral relation between minister and people, and all such stories are curious, not merely for their amusement, but from the illustration they afford us of that peculiar Scottish humour which we are now describing. He had himself, when a very young boy, before he came up to the Edinburgh High School, been at the parochial school where he resided, and which, like many others, at that period, had a considerable reputation for the skill and scholarship of the master. He used to describe school scenes rather different, I suspect, from school scenes in our day. One boy, on coming late, exclaimed that the cause had been a regular pitched battle between his parents, with the details of which he amused his school-fellows ; and he described the battle in vivid and Scottish Homeric terms, "And eh, as they faucht and they faucht," adding, however, with much complacency, "but my minnie dang, she did tho'."

There was a style of conversation and quaint modes of communication between ministers and their people at that time, which, I suppose, would seem strange to the present generation ; as, for example, I recollect a conversation between this relative and one of his parishioners of this description. It had been a very wet and unpromising autumn. The minister met a certain Janet of his flock, and accosted her very kindly. He remarked, "Bad prospect for the har'st (harvest), Janet, this wet." Janet—"Indeed, sir, I've seen as muckle as that there'll be nae har'st the year." Minister—"Na, Janet, deil as muckle as that't ever ye saw."

As I have said, he was a clergyman of the Established Church, and had many stories about ministers and people, arising out of his own pastoral experience, or the experience of friends and neighbours. He was much delighted with the not very refined rebuke which one of his own farmers had given to a young minister who had for some Sundays occupied his pulpit. The young man had dined with the farmer in the afternoon when services were over, and his appetite was so sharp, that he thought it necessary to apologise to his host for eating so substantial a dinner. —"You see," he said, "I am always very hungry after preaching." The old gentleman, not much admiring the youth's pulpit ministrations, having heard this apology two or three times, at last replied sarcastically, "Indeed, sir, I'm no surprised at it, considering the trash that comes aff your stomach in the morning."

What I wish to keep in view is, to distinguish anecdotes which are amusing on account merely of the expressions used, from those which have real wit and humour *combined*, with the purely Scottish vehicle in which they are conveyed.

Of this class I could not have a better specimen to commence with than the defence of the liturgy of his church, by John Skinner of Langside, of whom previous mention has been made. It is witty and clever.

Being present at a party [I think at Lord Forbes's], where were also several ministers of the Establishment, the conversation over their wine turned, among other things, on the Prayer-book. Skinner took no part in it, till one minister remarked to him, "The great faut I hae to your prayer-book is that ye use the Lord's Prayer sae aften,—ye juist mak a dishclout o't."

Skinner's rejoinder was, "Verra true! Ay, man, we mak a dishclout o't, an' we wring't, an we wring't, an' we wring't, an' the bree* o't washes a' the lave o' our prayers."

No one, I think, could deny the wit of the two following rejoinders.

A ruling elder of a country parish in the west of Scotland was well known in the district as a shrewd and ready-witted man. He got many a visit by persons who liked a banter, or to hear a good joke. Three young students gave him a call in order to have a little amusement at the elder's expense. On approaching him, one of them saluted him, "Well, Father Abraham, how are you to-day?" "You are wrong," said the other, "this is old Father Isaac." "Tuts," said the third, "you are both mistaken; this is old Father Jacob." David looked at the young men, and in his own way replied, "I am neither old Father Abraham, nor old Father Isaac, nor old Father Jacob; but I am Saul,

* Juice.

the son of Kish, seeking his father's asses, and lo! I've found three o' them."

For many years the Baptist community of Dunfermline was presided over by brothers David Dewar and James Inglis, the latter of whom has just recently gone to his reward. Brother David was a plain, honest, straightforward man, who never hesitated to express his convictions, however unpalatable they might be to others. Being elected a member of the Prison Board, he was called upon to give his vote in the choice of a chaplain from the licentiates of the Established Kirk. The party who had gained the confidence of the Board had proved rather an indifferent preacher in a charge to which he had previously been appointed; and on David being asked to signify his assent to the choice of the Board, he said, "Weel, I've no objections to the man, for I understand he has preached a kirk toom (empty) already, and if he be as successful in the jail, he'll maybe preach it vawcant as weel."

From Mr. Inglis, clerk of the Court of Session, I have the following Scottish rejoinder:—

"I recollect my father giving a conversation between a Perthshire laird and one of his tenants. The laird's eldest son was rather a simpleton. Laird says, "I am going to send the young laird abroad." "What for?" asks the tenant; answered, "To see the world;" tenant replies, "But, lordsake, laird, will no the world see *him?*"

An admirably humorous reply is recorded of a Scotch officer, well known and esteemed in his day for mirth and humour. Captain Innes of the Guards (usually called Jock Innes by his contemporaries) was with others getting ready for Flushing or some of those expeditions of the beginning of the great war. His commanding officer (Lord Huntly, my correspondent thinks) remonstrated about the badness of his hat, and recommended a new one.—"Na, na! bide a wee," said Jock; "where we're gain', faith there'll soon be mair hats nor *heads.*"

There is an odd and original way of putting a matter

sometimes in Scotch people, which is irresistibly comic, although by the persons nothing comic is intended ; as for example, when in 1786 Edinburgh was illuminated on account of the recovery of George III. from severe illness —in a house where great preparation was going on for the occasion, by getting the candles fixed in tin sconces, an old nurse of the family looking on, exclaimed, " Ay, it's a braw time for the cannel-makers when the king is sick, honest man !"

Scottish farmers of the old school were a shrewd and humorous race, sometimes not indisposed to look with a little jealousy upon their younger brethren, who on their part, perhaps, showed their contempt for the old-fashioned ways. I take the following example from the columns of the *Peterhead Sentinel*, just as it appeared—June 14, 1861 :—

" An Anecdote for Dean Ramsay.—The following characteristic and amusing anecdote was communicated to us the other day by a gentleman who happened to be a party to the conversation detailed below. This gentleman was passing along a road not a hundred miles from Peterhead one day this week. Two different farms skirt the separate sides of the turnpike, one of which is rented by a a farmer who cultivates his land according to the most advanced system of agriculture, and the other of which is farmed by a gentleman of the old school. Our informant met the latter worthy at the side of the turnpike opposite his neighbour's farm, and seeing a fine crop of wheat upon what appeared to be [and really was] very thin and poor land, asked, 'When was that wheat sown ?' 'O, I dinna ken,' replied the gentleman of the old school, with a sort of half-indifference, half-contempt. 'But isn't it strange that such a fine crop should be reared on such bad land ?' asked our informant. 'O, na—nae at a'—devil thank it ; a gravesteen wad gie guid bree gin ye geed it plenty o' butter !'"

But perhaps the best anecdote illustrative of the keen

shrewdness of the Scottish farmer is related by Mr. Boyd in one of his charming series of papers reprinted from *Fraser's Magazine.* "A friend of mine, a country parson, on first going to his parish, resolved to farm his glebe for himself. A neighbouring farmer kindly offered the parson to plough one of his fields. The farmer said that he would send his man John with a plough and a pair of horses on a certain day. 'If ye're goin' about,' said the farmer to the clergyman, 'John will be unco' weel pleased if you speak to him, and say it's a fine day, or the like o' that; but dinna,' said the farmer, with much solemnity, 'dinna say onything to him about ploughin' and sawin'; for John,' he added, 'is a stupid body, but he has been ploughin' and sawin' all his life, and he'll see in a minute that *ye* ken naething aboot ploughin' and sawin'. And then,' said the sagacious old farmer, with extreme earnestness, 'if he comes to think that ye ken naething aboot ploughin' and sawin', he'll think that ye ken naething about onything!'"

The following is rather an original commentary, by a layman, upon clerical incomes :—A relative of mine going to church with a Forfarshire farmer, one of the old school, asked him the amount of the minister's stipend. He said, "Od, it's a gude ane—the maist part of £300 a year." "Well," said my relative, "many of these Scotch ministers are but poorly off." "They've eneuch, sir; they have eneuch; if they'd mair, it would want a' their time to the spending o't."

Scotch gamekeepers had often much dry quiet humour. I was much amused by the answer of one of those under the following circumstances :—An Ayrshire gentleman, who was from the first a very bad shot, or rather no shot at all, when out on 1st of September, having failed, time after time, in bringing down a single bird, had at last pointed out to him by his attendant bag-carrier a large covey, thick and close on the stubbles. "Noo, Mr. Jeems, let drive at them, just as they are!" Mr. Jeems did let drive, as advised, but not a feather remained to testify the shot. All flew off, safe and sound—"Hech, sir (remarks his friend), but ye've made thae yins shift their quarters."

The two following anecdotes of rejoinders from Scottish gudewives, and for which I am indebted, as for many other kind communications, to the Rev. Mr. Blair of Dunblane, appear to me as good examples of the peculiar Scottish pithy phraseology which we now refer to, as any that I have met with.

An old lady who lived not far from Abbotsford, and from whom the "Great Unknown" had derived many an ancient tale, was waited upon one day by the author of "Waverley." On endeavouring to give the authorship the go-by, the old dame protested, "D'ye think, sir, I dinna ken my ain groats in ither folk's kail?"

A conceited packman called at a farm-house in the west of Scotland, in order to dispose of some of his wares. The goodwife was startled by his southern accent, and his high talk about York, London, and other big places. "An' whaur come ye frae yersell?" was the question of the gudewife. "Ou, I am from the Border." "The Border—Oh! I thocht that; for we aye think the *selvidge* is the wakest bit o' the wab!"

The following was a good specimen of ready Scotch humorous reply, by a master to his discontented workman, and in which he turned the tables upon him, in his reference to Scripture. In a town of one of the central counties a Mr. J— carried on, about a century ago, a very extensive business in the linen manufacture. Although *strikes* were then unknown among the labouring classes, the spirit from which these take their rise has no doubt at all times existed. Among Mr. J—'s many workmen, one had given him constant annoyance for years, from his discontented and argumentative spirit. Insisting one day on getting something or other which his master thought most unreasonable, and refused to give in to, he at last submitted, with a bad grace, saying, "You're nae better than *Pharaoh*, sir. forcin puir folk to mak' bricks without straw." "Well, Saunders," quietly rejoined his master, "if I'm nae better than Pharaoh in one respect, I'll be better in another, for *I'll no hinder ye going to the wilderness whenever ye choose."*

. Persons who are curious in Scottish stories of wit and humour, speak much of the sayings of a certain "Laird of Logan," who was a well-known character of the west of Scotland. This same Laird of Logan was at a meeting of the heritors of Cumnock, where a proposal was made to erect a new churchyard wall. He met the proposition with the dry remark, "I never big dykes till the *tenants* complain."

The laird sold a horse to an Englishman, saying, "You buy him as you see him; but he's an *honest* beast." The purchaser took him home. In a few days he stumbled and fell, to the damage of his own knees and his rider's head. On this the angry purchaser remonstrated with the laird, whose reply was, "Well, sir, I told you he was an honest beast; many a time has he threatened to come down with me, and I kenned he would keep his word some day."

At the time of the threatened invasion, the laird had been taunted at a meeting at Ayr with want of loyal spirit at Cumnock, as at that place no volunteer corps had been raised to meet the coming danger; Cumnock, it should be recollected, being on a high situation, and ten or twelve miles from the coast. "What sort of people are you, up at Cumnock?" said an Ayr gentleman; "you have not a single volunteer!" "Never you heed," says Logan, very quietly; "if the French land at Ayr, there will soon be plenty of volunteers up at Cumnock."

A pendant to the story of candid admission on the part of the minister, that the people might be *weary* after his sermon, has been given on the authority of the narrator, a Fife gentleman, ninety years of age when he told it. He had been to church at Elie, and listening to a young and perhaps bombastic preacher, who happened to be officiating for the Rev. Dr. Milligan, who was in church. After service, meeting the Doctor in the passage, he introduced the young clergyman, who, on being asked by the old man how he did, elevated his shirt collar, and complained of fatigue, and being very much "*tired.*" "Tired, did ye say, my man?" said the old satirist, who was slightly deaf; "Lord, man! if you're *half* as tired as I am I pity ye!"

I have been much pleased with an offering from Carluke, containing two very pithy anecdotes. Mr. Rankin very kindly writes,—"Your 'Reminiscences' are most refreshing. I am very little of a story collector, but I have recorded some of an old schoolmaster, who was a story-teller. As a sort of payment for the amusement I have derived from your book, I shall give one or two."

He sends the two following:—

"Shortly after Mr. Kay had been inducted schoolmaster of Carluke (1790) the bederal called at the school, verbally announcing, proclamation-ways, that Mrs. So-and-So's funeral would be on Fuirsday. 'At what hour?' asked the dominie. 'Ou, ony time atween ten and twa. At two o'clock of the day fixed, Mr. Kay—quite a stranger to the customs of the district—arrived at the place, and was astonished to find a crowd of men and lads, standing here and there, some smoking, and all *arglebargling*,* as if at the end of a fair. He was instantly, but mysteriously, approached, and touched on the arm by a red-faced bareheaded man, who seemed to be in authority, and was beckoned to follow. On entering the barn, which was seated all round, he found numbers sitting, each with the head bent down, and each with his hat between his knees —all gravity and silence. Anon a voice was heard issuing from the far end, and a long prayer was uttered. They had worked at this—what was called '*a service*' during three previous hours, one party succeeding another, and many taking advantage of every service, which consisted of

* Disputing or bandying words backwards and forwards.

a prayer by way of grace, a glass of *white* wine, a glass of *red* wine, a glass of *rum*, and a prayer, by way of thanksgiving. After the long invocation, bread and wine passed round. Silence prevailed. Most partook of both *rounds* of wine, but when the rum came, many nodded refusal, and by-and-by the nodding seemed to be universal, and the trays passed on so much the more quickly. A sumphish weather-beaten man, with a large flat blue bonnet on his knee, who had nodded unwittingly, and was about to lose the last chance of a glass of rum, raised his head, saying, amid the deep silence, 'Od, I daursay I *wull* tak anither gless,' and in a sort of vengeful, yet apologetic tone, added, 'the auld jaud yince cheated me wi' a cauve' (calf)."

At a farmer's funeral in the country, an undertaker was in charge of the ceremonial, and directing how it was to proceed, when he noticed a little man giving orders, and, as he thought, rather encroaching upon the duties and privileges of his own office. He asked him, "And wha are ye, mi' man, that tak sae muckle on ye?" "Oh, dinna ye ken?" said the man, under a strong sense of his own importance, "I'm the corp's brither?"*

Curious scenes took place at funerals where there was, in times gone by, an unfortunate tendency to join with such solemnities more attention to festal entertainment than was becoming. A farmer, at the interment of his second wife, exercised a liberal hospitality to his friends at the inn near the church. On looking over the bill, the master defended the charge as moderate. But he reminded him, "Ye forget, man, that it's no ilka ane that brings a *second* funeral to your house."

"Dr. Scott, minister of Carluke (1770), was a fine graceful kindly man, always stepping about in his bag wig and cane in hand, with a kind or ready word to every one. He was officiating at a bridal in his parish, where there was a goodly company, had partaken of the good cheer, and

* In Scotland the remains of the deceased person is called the "corp."

waited till the young people were fairly warmed in the dance. A dissenting body had sprung up in the parish, which he tried to think was beneath him even to notice, when he could help it, yet never seemed to feel at all keenly when the dissenters were alluded to. One of the chief leaders of this body was at the bridal, and felt it to be his bounden duty to call upon the minister for his reasons for sanctioning by his presence so sinful an enjoyment. 'Weel, minister, what think ye o' this dancin'?' 'Why, John,' said the minister, blithely, 'I think it an excellent exercise for young people, and I dare say, so do you.' 'Ah, sir, I'm no sure about it; I see nae authority for't in the Scriptures.' 'Umph, indeed, John; you cannot forget David.' 'Ah, sir, Dauvid; gif they were a' to dance as Dauvid did, it would be a different thing a' thegither.' 'Hoot o fie, hoot o fie, John; would you have the young folk strip to the sark?'"

Reference has been made to the eccentric laird of Balnamoon, his wig, and his "speats o' drinking and praying." A story of this laird is recorded, which I do think is well named, by a correspondent who communicates it, as a "quintessential phasis of dry Scotch humour," and the explanation of which would perhaps be thrown away upon any one who *needed* the explanation. The story is this:—The laird riding past a high steep bank, stopped opposite a hole in it, and said, "John, I saw a brock gang in there." "Did ye?" said John; "wull ye haud my horse, sir?" "Certainly," said the laird, and away rushed John for a spade. After digging for half an hour, he came back, nigh speechless, to the laird, who had regarded him musingly. "I canna find him, sir," said John. "Deed," said the laird, very coolly, "I wad ha' wondered if ye had, for it's ten years sin' I saw him gang in there."

Amongst many humorous colloquies between Balnamoon and his servant, the following must have been very racy and very original. The laird, accompanied by John, after a dinner party, was riding, on his way home, through a ford, when he fell off into the water. "Whae's that faun," he inquired. "Deed," quoth John, "I witna an it be no your honour."

We have more than once had occasion to mention the late Rev. Walter Dunlop of the U.P. Church, Dumfries. To a kind clerical correspondent in that neighbourhood, I am indebted for the following. He was very much esteemed by his congregation as a faithful and affectionate minister. Few men equalled him for racy humour and originality. Many anecdotes are recorded of him in connection with his ministerial visitations. He was firmly persuaded that the workman was worthy of his meat, and he did not hesitate occasionally to intimate how agreeable certain "*presents*" would be to him and his better-half. He was widely respected by all denominations, and his death was greatly lamented.

One evening, while making his pastoral visitations among some of the country members of his flock, he came to a farm-house where he was expected; and the mistress, thinking that he would be in need of refreshment, proposed that he should take his tea before engaging in *exercises*, and said she would soon have it ready. Mr. Dunlop replied, "I aye tak' my tea better when my wark's dune. I'll just be gaun on. Ye can hing the pan on, an' lea' the door ajar, an' I'll draw to a close in the prayer when I hear the haam fizzin'."

Another day, while engaged in the same duty of visitation, and while offering up prayer, a peculiar sound was heard to issue from his great-coat pocket, which was afterwards discovered to have proceeded from a half-choked duck, which he "had gotten in a *present*," and whose neck he had been squeezing all the time to prevent its crying.

On another occasion, after a hard day's labour, and while at a "denner-tea," as he called it, he kept incessantly praising the "haam," and stating that "Mrs. Dunlop at hame was as fond o' haam like that as he was," when the mistress kindly offered to send her the present of a ham.

"It's unco kin' o' ye, unco kin', but I'll no pit ye to the trouble ; I'll just tak' it hame on the horse afore me." When, on leaving, he mounted, and the ham was put into a sack, some difficulty was experienced in getting it to lie properly. His inventive genius soon cut the Gordian-knot. "I think, mistress, a cheese in the ither en' wad mak' a gran' balance." The hint was immediately acted on, and, like another John Gilpin, he moved away with his "balance true."

One day, returning from a short visit to the country, he met two ladies in Buccleuch Street, who stopped him to inquire after his welfare, and that of his wife. Lifting his hat politely, to the consternation of all three, out tumbled to his feet his handkerchief, followed by a large lump of potted-head, which he had received in a "present," and was thus carrying home, but which, at the moment, he had entirely forgotten.

One Sunday, after sermon, just before pronouncing the blessing, he made the following intimation :—"My freens, I hae a baaptism at Locharbriggs the nicht, an' maybe some o' ye wad be sae kin' as to gie me a cast oot in a dandy-cart." On descending from the pulpit, several vehicles of the description were placed at his service.

He would not allow any of his congregation to sleep in church, if his eye caught them. One day he suddenly stopped in his sermon, and said, "I doot some o' ye hae taen ower mony whey porridge the day ; sit up, or I'll name ye oot."

Some four-and-twenty years ago, when Mr. Dunlop lost his excellent and amiable wife, to whom it was well known he was strongly attached, Dr. Wightman, parish minister of Kirkmahoe, in the immediate neighbourhood of Dumfries, then upwards of seventy years of age and a bachelor, was invited to the funeral. On entering the house, he was surprised to observe that Mr. Dunlop, now a widower for a second time, did not appear to be so much affected as he would have expected, and indeed seemed wonderfully composed and cheerful. His peculiar humour could not be repressed even on this occasion, for he said, "Come awa, Dr. Wightman, come awa'; it will be lang to the day when ye hae onything o' this kind to do."

It is more common in Scotland than in England to find national feeling breaking out in national humour upon great events connected with national *history*. The following is, perhaps, as good as any:—The Rev. Robert Scott, a Scotchman who forgets not Scotland in his southern vicarage, and whom I have named before as having sent me some good reminiscences, tells me that, at Inverary, some thirty years ago, he could not help overhearing the conversation of some Lowland cattle-dealers in the public room in which he was. The subject of the bravery of our navy being started, one of the interlocutors expressed his surprise that Nelson should have issued his signal at Trafalgar in the terms, "*England expects*," etc. He was met with the answer (which seemed highly satisfactory to the rest), "Ay, Nelson only said '*expects*' of the English; he said naething of Scotland, for he *kent* the *Scotch* would do theirs."

I am assured the following manifestation of national feeling against the memory of a Scottish public character actually took place within a few years:—Williamson (the Duke of Buccleuch's huntsman) was one afternoon riding home from hunting through Haddington; and as he passed the old abbey, he saw an ancient woman looking through the iron grating in front of the burial-place of the Lauderdale family, holding by the bars, and grinning and dancing with rage. "Eh, gudewife," said Williamson, "what ails ye?" "It's the Duke o' Lauderdale," cried she. "Eh, if I could win at him, I wud rax the banes o' him."

To this class belongs the following complacent Scottish remark upon Bannockburn. A splenetic Englishman said to a Scottish countryman, something of a wag, that no man of taste would think of remaining any time in such a country as Scotland. To which the canny Scott replied,

"Tastes differ; I'se tak ye to a place, no far frae Stirling, whaur thretty thousand o' yer countrymen ha' been for five hunder years, an' they've nae thocht o' leavin' yet."

In a similar spirit, an honest Scotch farmer, who had sent some sheep to compete at a great English agricultural cattle-show, consoled himself for the disappointment by insinuating that the judges could hardly act quite impartially by a Scottish competitor, complacently remarking, "It's aye been the same since Bannockburn."

A north-country drover had, however, a more *tangible* opportunity of gratifying his national animosity against the Southron, and of which he availed himself. Returning homewards, after a somewhat unsuccessful journey, and not in very good humour with the Englishers, when passing through Carlisle, he saw a notice stuck up, offering a reward of £50 for any one who would do a piece of service to the community, by officiating as executioner of the law on a noted criminal then under sentence of death. Seeing a chance to make up for his bad market, and comforted with the assurance that he was unknown there, he undertook the office, hanged the rogue, and got the fee. When moving off with the money, he was twitted as a mean beggarly Scot, doing for money what no *Englishman* would; he replied with a grin and quiet glee, "I'll hang ye a' at the price."

Some Scotchmen no doubt have a very complacent feeling regarding the superiority of their countrymen, and make no hesitation in proclaiming their opinion. I have always admired the quaint expression of such belief in a case which has recently been reported to me. A young Englishman had taken a Scottish shooting-ground, and enjoyed his mountain sport so much as to imbibe a strong partiality for his northern residence and all its accompaniments. At a German watering-place he encountered, next year, an original character, a Scotchman of the old school, very national and somewhat bigoted in his nationality: he determined to pass himself off to him as a genuine Scottish native ; and, accordingly, he talked of Scotland and haggis, and sheep's head and whisky ; he boasted of Bannockburn, and admired Queen Mary ; looked upon Scott and Burns as superior to all English writers ; and staggered, although he did not convince, the old gentleman. On going away he took leave of his Scottish friend, and said, "Well, sir, next time we meet, I hope you will receive me as a real countryman." "Weel," he said, "I'm jest thinkin', my lad, ye're nae Scotchman ; but I'll tell ye what ye are—ye're jest an *impruived* Englishman."

We find in the conversation of old people frequent mention of parochial functionaries, now either become commonplace, like the rest of the world, or removed altogether, and shut up in poor-houses or mad-houses—I mean parish idiots—eccentric, or somewhat crazy, useless, idle creatures, who used to wander about from house to house, and sometimes made very shrewd, sarcastic remarks upon what was going on in the parish. They used to take great liberty of speech regarding the conduct and disposition of those with whom they came in contact; and many odd sayings which emanated from the parish idiots were traditionary in country localities. I have a kindly feeling towards these imperfectly intelligent, but often perfectly cunning beings; partly I believe from recollections of early associations in boyish days with some of those Davy Gellatleys. I have therefore preserved several anecdotes with which I have been favoured, where their odd sayings and indications of a degree of mental activity have been recorded. Parish idiots seem to have had a partiality for getting near the pulpit in church, and their presence there was accordingly sometimes annoying to the preacher and the congregation ; as at Maybole, when Dr. Paul, now of St. Cuthbert's, was minister in 1823, the idiot John McLymont had been in the habit of standing so close to the pulpit door as to overlook the Bible and pulpit board. When required, however, by the clergyman to keep at a greater distance, and not *look in upon the minister*, he got intensely angry and violent. He threatened the minister, —"Sir, bæby (maybe) I'll come further;" meaning to intimate that perhaps he would, if much provoked, come into the pulpit altogether. This, indeed, actually took place on another occasion, and the tenure of the ministerial position was justified by an argument of a most amusing nature. The circumstance, I am assured, happened in a parish of the north. The clergyman, on coming into church, found the pulpit occupied by the parish idiot. The authorities had been unable to remove him without more violence than was seemly, and therefore waited for the minister to dispossess Tam of the place he had assumed. "Come down, sir, immediately!" was the peremptory and indignant call; and on Tam being unmoved, it was repeated with still greater energy. Tam, however, replied looking down confidentially from his elevation, "Na, na, minister! juist ye come up wi' me. This is a perverse generation, and faith they need us baith." It is curious to mark the sort of glimmering of sense, and even of discriminating thought displayed by persons of this class; as an example, take a conversation held by this same idiot, John McLymont, with Dr. Paul, whom he met some time after. He seemed to have recovered his good humour, as he stopped him, and said, "Sir, I would like to speer a question at ye on a subject that's troubling me." "Well, Johnnie, what is the question?" To which he replied, "Sir, is it lawful at ony time to tell a lee?" The minister desired to know what Johnnie himself thought upon the point. "Weel, sir," said he, "I'll no say but in every case it's wrang to tell a lee; but," added he, looking archly and giving a knowing wink, "I think there are *waur lees than ithers.*" 'How, Johnnie?" and then he instantly replied with all the simplicity of a fool, "to *keep down a din for instance.* I'll no say but a man does wrang in telling a lee to keep down a din, but I'm sure he does not do half sae muckle wrang as a man who tells a lee to kick up a deevilment o' a din." This opened a question not likely to occur to such a mind. Mr.

Asher, minister of Inveraven, in Morayshire, narrated to Dr. Paul a curious example of want of intelligence combined with a power of cunning to redress a fancied wrong, shown by a poor natural of the parish, who had been seized with a violent inflammatory attack, and was in great danger. The medical attendant saw it necessary to bleed him, but he resisted, and would not submit to it. At last the case became so hopeless that they were obliged to use force, and, holding his hands and feet, the doctor opened a vein and drew blood, upon which the poor creature, struggling violently, bawled out, "O doctor, doctor! you'll kill me! you'll kill me! and depend upon it, the first thing I'll do when I get to the other world will be to *report you to the Board of Supervision there, and get you dismissed.*" A most extraordinary sensation was once produced on a congregation by Rab Hamilton, a well-remembered idiot of the west country, on the occasion of his attendance at the parish-kirk of "Auld Ayr, wham ne'er a toun surpasses." Miss Kirkwood, Bothwell, relates the story from the recollection of her aunt, who was present. Rab had put his head between some iron rails, the first intimation of which to the congregation was a stentorian voice crying out, "Murder! my head'll hae to be cutit aff! Holy minister! congregation! O my head maun be cutit aff. It's a judgment for leaving my godlie Mr. Peebles at the Newton." After he had been extricated and quieted, when asked why he put his head there? he said, "It was jeest to look on* wi' *anither woman.*"

The pathetic complaint of one of this class, residing at a farm-house, has often been narrated, and forms a good illustration of idiot life and feelings. He was living in the greatest comfort, and every want provided. But, like the rest of mankind, he had his own trials, and his own cause for anxiety and annoyance. In this poor fellow's case it was the *great turkey-cock* at the farm, of whom he stood so

* Read from the same book.

terribly in awe, that he was afraid to come within a great distance of his enemy. Some of his friends coming to visit him, reminded him how comfortable he was, and how grateful he ought to be for the great care taken of him; he admitted the truth of the remark generally, but still, like others, he had his unknown grief which sorely beset his path in life. There was a secret grievance which embittered his lot; and to his friend he thus opened his heart:—"Ae, ae, but oh, I'm sare hadden doun wi' the bubbly jock." *

I have received two anecdotes illustrative both of the occasional acuteness of mind, and of the sensitiveness of feeling occasionally indicated by persons thus situated. A well-known idiot, Jamie Fraser, belonging to the parish of Lunan, in Forfarshire, quite surprised people sometimes by his replies. The congregation of his parish-church had for sometime distressed the minister by their habit of sleeping in church. He had often endeavoured to impress them with a sense of the impropriety of such conduct, and one day when Jamie was sitting in the front gallery wide awake, when many were slumbering round him, the clergyman endeavoured to awaken the attention of his hearers by stating the fact, saying, "You see even Jamie Fraser, the idiot, does not fall asleep, as so many of you are doing." Jamie, not liking, perhaps, to be thus designated, coolly replied, "An' I hadna been an idiot, I micht ha' been sleepin' too." Another of these imbeciles, belonging to Peebles, had been sitting at church for some time listening attentively to a strong representation from the pulpit of the guilt of deceit and falsehood in Christian characters. He was observed to turn red, and grow very uneasy, until at last, as if wincing under the supposed attack upon himself personally, he roared out, "Indeed, minister, there's mair leears in Peebles than me." As examples of idiots possessing much of the dry humour of

* Sorely kept under by the turkey-cock.

their more sane countrymen, and of their facility to utter sly and ready-witted sayings, I have received the two following from Mr. W. Chambers :—Daft Jock Gray, the supposed original of David Gellatley, was one day assailed by the minister of a south-country parish, on the subject of his idleness. "John," said the minister, rather pompously, "you are a very idle fellow ; you might surely herd a few cows." "Me hird !" replied Jock, "I dinna ken corn frae gerse."

In the Memorials of the Montgomeries, Earls of Eglinton, vol. i. p. 134, occurs an anecdote of an idiot illustrative of the peculiar acuteness and quaint humour which occasionally mark the sayings of this class. There was a certain "Daft Will Speir," who was a privileged haunter of Eglinton Castle and grounds. He was discovered by the Earl one day taking a near cut, and crossing a fence in the demesne. The Earl called out, "Come back, sir, that's not the road." "Do you ken," said Will, "whaur I'm gaun ?" "No," replied his lordship. "Weel, hoo the deil do ye ken whether this be the road or no ?"

The following anecdote is told regarding the late Lord Dundrennan :—A half silly basket-woman passing down his avenue at Compstone one day, he met her, and said, "My good woman, there's no road this way." "Na, sir," she said, "I think ye're wrang there ; I think it's a most beautifu' road."

These poor creatures have invariably a great delight in attending funerals. In many country places, hardly a funeral ever took place without the attendance of the parochial idiot. It seemed almost a necessary association ; and such attendance seemed to constitute the great delight of those creatures. I have myself witnessed again and again the sort of funeral scene portrayed by Sir Walter Scott, who no doubt took his description from what was common in his day. "The funeral pomp set forth—saulies with their batons and gumphions of tarnished white crape. Six starved horses, themselves the very emblems of mortality, well cloaked and plumed, lugging along the hearse with its dismal emblazonry, crept in slow pace towards the place of interment, preceded by Jamie Duff, an idiot, who, with weepers and cravat made of white paper, *attended on every funeral*, and followed by six mourning coaches filled with the company."—*Guy Mannering.*

The following anecdote, supplied by Mr. Blair, is an amusing illustration, both of the funeral propensity, and of the working of a defective brain, in a half-witted carle, who used to range the county of Galloway, armed with a huge pike-staff, and who one day met a funeral procession a few miles from Wigtown. A long train of carriages, and farmers riding on horseback, suggested the propriety of his bestriding his staff, and following after the funeral. The procession marched at a brisk pace, and on reaching the kirkyard style, as each rider dismounted, "Daft Jock" descended from his wooden steed, besmeared with mire and perspiration, exclaiming, "Hech, sirs, had it no been for the fashion o' the thing, I micht as well hae been on my ain feet."

The withdrawal of these characters from public view, and the loss of importance which they once enjoyed in Scottish society, seem to me inexplicable. Have they ceased to exist, or are they removed from our sight to different scenes? The fool was, in early times, a very important personage in most Scottish households of any distinction. Indeed, this had been so common as to be a public nuisance.

It seemed that persons *assumed* the character, for we find a Scottish Act of Parliament, dated 19th January 1449, with this title:—"Act for the way-putting of *Fenyent* Fules," etc. (Thomson's Acts of Parliament of Scotland, vol. i.); and it enacts very stringent measures against such persons. They seem to have formed a link between the helpless idiot and the boisterous madman, sharing the eccentricity of the latter and the stupidity of the former, generally adding, however, a good deal of the sharp-wittedness of the *knave*. Up to the middle of the eighteenth century, this appears to have been still an appendage to some families. I have before me a little publication with the title, "The Life and Death of Jamie Fleeman, the Laird of Udny's Fool. Tenth edition. Aberdeen, 1810." With Portrait. Also twenty-sixth edition, of 1829. I should suppose this account of a family fool was a fair representation of a good specimen of the class. He was evidently of defective intellect, but at times showed the odd humour and quick conclusion which so often mark the disordered brain. I can only now give two examples taken from his history:—Having found a horse-shoe on the road, he met Mr. Craigie, the minister of St. Fergus, and showed it to him, asking, in pretended ignorance, what it was. "Why, Jamie," said Mr. Craigie, good-humouredly, "anybody that was not a fool would know that it is a horse shoe." "Ah!" said Jamie, with affected simplicity, "what it is to be wise—to ken it's no a meer's shoe!"

On another occasion, when all the country-side were hastening to the Perth races, Jamie had cut across the fields and reached a bridge near the town, and sat down upon the parapet. He commenced munching away at a large portion of a leg of mutton which he had somehow become possessed of, and of which he was amazingly proud. The laird came riding past, and seeing Jamie sitting on the bridge, accosted him:—"Ay, Fleeman, are ye here already?" "Ou ay," quoth Fleeman, with an air of assumed dignity and archness not easy to describe, while his eye glanced significantly towards the mutton, "Ou ay, ye ken a body when he *has onything*."

Of witty retorts by half-witted creatures of this class, I do not know of one more pointed than what is recorded of such a character, who used to hang about the residence of a late Lord Fife. It would appear that some parts of his lordship's estates were barren, and in a very unproductive condition. Under the improved system of agriculture and of draining, great preparations had been made for securing a good crop in a certain field, where Lord Fife, his factor, and others interested in the subject, were collected together. There was much discussion, and some difference of opinion as to the crop with which the field had best be sown. The idiot retainer, who had been listening unnoticed to all that was said, at last cried out, "Saw't wi' factors, ma lord ; they are sure to thrive everywhere."

"Daft Will Speir" (mentioned page 192) was passing the minister's glebe, where haymaking was in progress. The minister asked Will if he thought the weather would keep up, as it looked rather like rain. "Weel," said Will, "I canna be very sure, but I'll be passin' this way the nicht, an' I'll ca' in and tell ye." "Well, Will," said his master one day to him, seeing that he had just finished his dinner, "have you had a good dinner to-day?" (Will had been grumbling some time before). "Ou, vera gude," answered Will ; "but gin onybody asks if I got a dram after't, what will I say?" This poor creature had a high sense of duty. It appears he had been given the charge of the coal stores at the Earl of Eglinton's. Having on one occasion been reprimanded for allowing the supplies to run out before further supplies were ordered, he was ever afterwards most careful to fulfil his duty. In course of time poor Will became "sick unto death," and the minister came to see him. Thinking him in really a good frame of mind, the minister asked him, in presence of the laird and others, if there were not *one great* thought which was ever to him the highest consolation in his hour of trouble? "Ou ay," gasped the sufferer, "Lord be thankit, a' the bunkers are fu'."

There was an idiot who lived long in Lauder, and seems to have had a great resemblance to the jester of old times. He was a staunch supporter of the Established Church. One day, some one gave him a bad shilling. On Sunday he went to the Seceders' meeting-house, and when the ladle was taken round he put in his bad shilling and took out elevenpence halfpenny. Afterwards he went in high glee to the late Lord Lauderdale, calling out, "I've cheated the Seceders the day, my lord ; I've cheated the Seceders."

Jemmy had long harboured a dislike to the steward on the property, which he paid off in the following manner : Lord Lauderdale and Sir Anthony Maitland used to take him out shooting ; and one day Lord Maitland (he was then) on having to cross the Leader, said, "Now, Jemmy, you shall carry me through the water," which Jemmy duly did. Lord Lauderdale's steward, to whom he had taken a great dislike, and who was shooting with them, said, "Now, Jemmy, you must carry *me* over." "Vera weel," said Jemmy. He took the steward on his back, and when he had carefully carried him half way across the river, he dropped him quietly into the water.

I have recorded an anecdote received from Mr. W. Chambers, of a half-idiot, Rab Hamilton, whose name was familiar to most persons who knew Ayr in former days. He certainly was a natural ; but the following anecdote of him from a kind correspondent at Ayr sanctions the opinion that he must have occasionally said such clever things as made some think him more rogue than fool. Dr. Auld often showed him kindness, but being once addressed by him when in a hurry and out of humour, he said, "Get away, Rab ; I have nothing for you to-day." "Whaw, whew," cried Rab, in a half howl, half whining tone, "I dinna want onything the day, Mister Auld ; I wanted to tell you an awsome dream I hae had. I dreamt I was deed." "Weel, what then?" said Dr. Auld. "Ou, I was carried far, far, and up, up, up, till I cam to heeven's yett, where I chappit, and chappit, and chappit, till at last an angel keekit out, and said, 'Wha are ye?' 'A'm puir Rab Hamilton.' 'Whaur are ye frae?' 'Frae the wicked toun o' Ayr.' 'I dinna ken ony sic place,' said the angel. 'Oh, but A'm joost frae there.' Weel, the angel sends for the Apostle Peter, and Peter comes wi' his key and opens the yett, and says to me, 'Honest man, do you come frae the auld toun o' Ayr,' 'Deed do I,' says I. 'Weel,' says

Peter, 'I ken the place, but naebody's cam frae the toun o' Ayr, no since the year'" so and so—mentioning the year when Dr. Auld was inducted into the parish. Dr. Auld could not resist giving him his answer, and telling him to go about his business.

A daft individual used to frequent the same district, about whom a variety of opinions were entertained,—some people thinking him not so foolish as he sometimes seemed. On one occasion, a person, wishing to test whether he knew the value of money, held out a sixpence and a penny, and offered him his choice. "I'll tak the wee ane," he says, giving as his modest reason, "I'se no be greedy." At another time, a miller laughing at him for his witlessness, he said, "Some things I ken, and some I dinna ken." On being asked what he knew, he said, "I ken a miller has aye a gey fat sou." "An' what d'ye no ken?" said the miller. "Ou," he returned, "I dinna ken wha's expense she's fed at."

A very amusing collision of one of these penurious lairds already referred to, a certain Mr. Gordon of Rothy, with a half-daft beggar wanderer of the name of Jock Muilton, has been recorded. The laird was very shabby, as usual, and, meeting Jock, began to banter him on the subject of his dress:—"Ye're very grand, Jock. That's fine claes ye hae gotten; whaur did ye get that coat?" Jock told him who had given him his coat, and then, looking slily at the laird, he inquired, as with great simplicity, "And where did ye get *yours*, laird?"

Another example of shrewd and ready humour in one of that class is the following. In this case the idiot was musical, and earned a few stray pence by playing Scottish airs on a flute. He resided at Stirling, and used to hang about the door of the inn to watch the arrival and departure of travellers. A lady who used to give him something occasionally, was just starting, and said to Jamie that she had only a fourpenny piece, and that he must be content with that, for she could not stay to get more. Jamie was not satisfied, and, as the lady drove out, expressed his feelings by playing with all his might, "O weerie o' the *toom pouch.*"*

The spirit in Jamie Fraser before mentioned, and which had kept him awake, shows itself in idiots occasionally by making them restless and troublesome. One of this character had annoyed the clergyman where he attended church by fidgetting and by uncouth sounds, which he uttered during divine service. Accordingly, one day before church began, he was cautioned against moving or "making a whisht," under the penalty of being turned out. The poor creature sat quite still and silent till, in a very important part of the sermon, he felt an inclination to cough. So he shouted out, "Minister, may a puir body like me noo gie a hoast?"†

I have two anecdotes of two peers, who might be said to come under the description of half-witted. In their case, the same sort of dry Scottish humour came out under the cloak of mental disease. The first is of a Scottish nobleman of the last century who had been a soldier the greater part of his life, but was obliged to come home on account of aberration of mind, superinduced by hereditary propensity. Desirous of putting him under due restraint, and, at the same time, of engaging his mind in his favourite pursuit, his friends secured a Serjeant Briggs to be his companion and overseer; and to render the serjeant acceptable as a companion, they introduced him to the old earl as *Colonel* Briggs. Being asked how he liked "the colonel," the earl showed how acute he still was by his answer, "Oh, very well; he is a sensible man, and a good soldier, but he *smells damnably of the halbert.*"

The second anecdote is of a *mad* Scottish nobleman, and I believe is a traditionary one. In Scotland, some hundred years ago, madhouses did not exist, or were on a very limited scale; and there was often great difficulty in procuring suitable accommodation for patients who required

---

* Empty pocket. † A cough.

special treatment and seclusion from the world. The nobleman in question had been consigned to the Canongate prison, and his position there was far from comfortable. An old friend called to see him, and asked how it had happened that he was placed in so unpleasant a situation. His reply was, "Sir, it was more the kind interest and patronage of my friends than my own merits that have placed me here." "But have you not remonstrated or complained?" asked his visitor. "I told them," said his lordship, "that they were a pack of infernal villains." "Did you?" said his friend; "that was bold language; and what did they say to that?" "Oh," said the peer, "I took care not to tell them till they were fairly out of the place, and weel up the Canongate."

In Peebles there was a crazy being of this kind called "Daft Yedie." On one occasion he saw a gentleman, a stranger in the town, who had a club foot. Yedie contemplated this phenomenon with some interest, and addressing the gentleman, said compassionately, "It's a great pity—it spoils the boot." There is a story of one of those half-witted creatures of a different character from the humorous ones already recorded; I think it is exceedingly affecting, and with it I will conclude my collection. The story is traditionary in a country district, and I am not aware of its being ever printed. A poor boy, of this class, who had evidently manifested a tendency towards religious and devotional feelings, asked permission from the clergyman to attend the Lord's Table and partake of the holy communion with the other members of the congregation (whether Episcopalian or Presbyterian I do not know). The clergyman demurred for some time, under the impression of his mind being incapable of a right and due understanding of the sacred ordinance. But observing the extreme earnestness of the poor boy, at last give consent, and he was allowed to come. He was much affected, and all the way home was heard to exclaim, "Oh! I hae seen the pretty man." This referred to his seeing the Lord

Jesus, whom he had approached in the sacrament. He kept repeating the words, and went with them on his lips to rest for the night. Not appearing at the usual hour for breakfast, when they went to his bedside they found him dead! The excitement had been too much—mind and body had given way—and the half-idiot of earth awoke to the glories and the bliss of his Redeemer's presence.

Analogous with the language of the *defective* intellect is the language of the imperfectly-formed intellect, and I have often thought there was something very touching and very fresh in the expression of feelings and notions by children. I have given an example before, but the following is, to my taste, a charming specimen:—A little boy had lived for some time with a very penurious uncle, who took good care that the child's health should not be injured by over-feeding. The uncle was one day walking out, the child at his side, when a friend accosted him, accompanied by a greyhound. While the elders were talking, the little fellow, never having seen a dog of so slim and slight a texture, clasped the creature round the neck with the impassioned cry, "Oh, doggie, doggie, and div ye live wi' your uncle tae, that ye are so thin!"

In connection with funerals, I am indebted to the kindness of Lord Kinloch for a characteristic anecdote of cautious Scottish character in the west country. It was the old fashion, still practised in some districts, to carry the coffin to the grave on long poles or "spokes," as they were commonly termed. There were usually two bearers abreast on each side. On a certain occasion, one of the two said to his companion, "I'm awfu' tired wi' carryin'." "Do you *carry?*" was the interrogatory in reply. "Yes; what do you do?" "Oh," said the other, "I aye *lean.*" His friend's fatigue was at once accounted for.

I am strongly tempted to give the following account of a parish functionary in the words of a kind correspondent from Kilmarnock, although communicated in the following very flattering terms :—" In common with every Scottish man worthy of the name, I have been delighted with your book, and have the ambition to add a pebble to the cairn, and accordingly send you a *bellman story ;* it has, at least, the merit of being unprinted and unedited."

The incumbent of Craigie parish, in this district of Ayrshire, had asked a Mr. Wood, tutor in the Cairnhill family, to officiate for him on a particular Sunday. Mr. Wood, however, between the time of being asked and the appointed day, got intimation of the dangerous illness of his father ; in the hurry of setting out to see him, he forgot to arrange for the pulpit being filled. The bellman of Craigie parish, by name Matthew Sinning, and at this time about eighty years of age, was a very little "crined"* old man, and always wore a broad Scottish blue bonnet, with a red "bob" on the top. The parish is a small rural one, so that Matthew knew every inhabitant in it, and had seen the most of them grow up. On this particular day, after the congregation had waited for some time, Matthew was seen to walk very slowly up the middle of the church with the large Bible and psalm-book under his arm, to mount the pulpit stair ; and after taking his bonnet off, and smoothing down his forehead with his "loof," thus addressed the audience :—

"My freens, there was ane Wuds tae hae preached here the day, but he has nayther comed himsel', nor had the ceevility tae sen' us the scart o' a pen. Ye'll bide here for ten meenonts, and gin naebody comes forrit in that time, ye can gang awa' hame. Some say his feyther's dead, as for that I kenna."

The following is another illustration of the character of the old Scottish betheral. One of those worthies, who was parochial grave-digger, had been missing for two days or so, and the minister had in vain sent to discover him at most likely places. He bethought, at last, to make inquiry at a

* Shrivelled.

"public" at some distance from the village, and on entering the door he met his man in the trance, quite fou, staggering out, supporting himself with a hand on each wa'. To the minister's sharp rebuke and rising wrath for his indecent and shameful behaviour, John, a wag in his way, and emboldened by liquor, made answer, "Deed, sir, sin' I ca'd at the manse, I hae buried an auld wife, and I've just drucken her, hough and horn." Such was his candid admission of the manner in which he had disposed of the church fees paid for the interment.

An encounter of wits between a laird and an elder :—A certain laird in Fife, well known for his parsimonious habits, whilst his substance largely increased did not increase his liberality, and his weekly contribution to the church collection never exceeded the sum of one penny. One day, however, by mistake he dropped into the plate at the door a five-shilling-piece, but discovering his error before he was seated in his pew, hurried back, and was about to replace the dollar by his customary penny, when the elder in attendance cried out, "Stop, laird ; ye may put *in* what ye like, but ye maun tak naething *out!*" The laird, finding his explanations went for nothing, at last said, "Aweel, I suppose I'll get credit for it in heaven." "Na, na, laird," said the elder, "ye'll only get credit for the *penny*."

The following is not a bad specimen of sly *piper* wit :—

The Rev. Mr. Johnstone of Monquhitter, a very grandiloquent pulpit orator in his day, accosting a travelling piper, well known in the district, with the question, "Well, John, how does the wind pay ?" received from John, with a low bow, the answer, "Your Reverence has the advantage of me."

Of *table* stories there is an anecdote which may be placed along with those of the two worthy farmers, p. 164, and which has occurred to my recollection as a Deeside story. My aunt, Mrs. Forbes, receiving a farmer at Banchory Lodge, offered him a draught of ale, which was accepted, and a large glass of it quickly drunk off. My aunt observing no froth or head, said she was afraid it was not a good bottle. "Oh, vera good, mem ; it's just some strong o' the apple" (a common country expression for beer which is rather tart or sharp). The fact turned out that a bottle of *vinegar* had been decanted by mistake.

And further, upon the subject of tenants at table. It was a most pungent remark of an honest farmer to the servant who put down beside him a dessert-spoon, when he had been helped to pudding, "Tak it awa, mi man ; mi mou's as big for puddin' as it is for kail."

I have received from Rev. William Blair, A.M., U.P. minister at Dunblane, many kind communications. I have made a selection, which I now group together, and they have this character in common, that they are all anecdotes of ministers :—

Rev. Walter Dunlop of Dumfries was accompanying a funeral one day, when he met a man driving a flock of geese. The wayward disposition of the bipeds at the moment was too much for the driver's temper, and he indignantly cried out, "Deevil choke them !" Mr. Dunlop walked a little further on, and passed a farm-stead, where a servant was driving out a number of swine, and banning them with "Deevil tak them !" Upon which, Mr. Dunlop stepped up to him, and said, "Ay, ay, my man, your gentleman'll be wi' ye i' the noo ; he's just back the road there a bit, choking some geese till a man."

Shortly after the disruption, Dr. Cook of St. Andrews was introduced to Mr. Dunlop, upon which occasion Mr. Dunlop said, "Weel, sir, ye've been lang Cook, Cooking them, but ye've dished them at last."

Mr. Clark of Dalreoch, whose head was vastly disproportioned to his body, met Mr. Dunlop one day. "Weel, Mr. Clark, that's a great head o' yours." "Indeed it is, Mr. Dunlop ; I could contain yours inside of my own." "Just sae," echoed Mr. Dunlop, "I was e'en thinkin' it was geyan *toom*."

Mr. Dunlop happened one day to be present in a Church

Court of a neighbouring presbytery. A Rev. Dr. was asked to pray, and declined. On the meeting adjourning, Mr. Dunlop stepped up to the Doctor, and asked how he did. The Doctor never having been introduced, did not reply. Mr. Dunlop withdrew, and said to his friend, "Eh! but is'na he a queer man, that Doctor, he'll neither speak to God nor man."

The Rev. John Brown of Whitburn was riding out one day on an old pony, when he was accosted by a rude youth: "I say, Mr. Broon, what gars your horse's tail wag that way." "Oo, jest what gars your tongue wag; it's fashed wi' a *wakeness*."

About sixty years ago there were two ministers in Sanquhar of the name of Thomson, one of whom was father of the late Dr. Andrew Thomson of Edinburgh, the other was father of Dr. Thomson of Balfron. The domestic in the family of the latter was rather obtrusive with her secret devotions, sometimes kneeling on the stairs at night, and talking loud enough to be heard. On a communion season she was praying devoutly for her minister, "Remember Mr. Tamson, no him at the Green, but oor ain Mr. Tamson."

Rev. Mr. Leslie of Morayshire combined the duties of justice of peace with those of parochial clergyman. One day he was taken into confidence by a culprit who had been caught in the act of smuggling, and was threatened with a heavy fine. The culprit was a staunch Seceder, and owned a small farm. Mr. Leslie said to him, "The king will come in the cadger's road some day. Ye wadna come to the parish kirk though it were to save your life, wad ye? Come noo, an' I'se mak ye a' richt!" Next Sabbath the seceding smuggler appeared in the parish kirk, and as the paupers were receiving parochial allowance, Mr. Leslie slipt a shilling into the smuggler's hand. When the J. P. Court was held, Mr. Leslie was present, when a fine was proposed to be exacted from the smuggler. "Fine!" said Mr. Leslie, "he's mair need o' something to get duds to his back

He's ane o' my *poor roll;* I gie'd him a shilling just last Sabbath."

A worthy old Seceder used to ride from Gargunnock to Bucklyvie every Sabbath to attend the Burgher kirk. One day as he rode past the parish kirk of Kippen, the elder at the plate accosted him, "I'm sure, John, it's no like the thing to see you ridin' in sic a doon-pour o' rain sae far by to thae Seceders. Ye ken the mercifu' man is mercifu' to his beast. Could ye no step in by." "Weel," said John, "I wadna care sae muckle about stablin' my beast inside, but it's anither thing mysel' gain' in."

The Rev. Dr. George Lawson of Selkirk acted for many years as theological tutor to the Secession Church. One day on entering the Divinity Hall he overheard a student remark that the professor's wig was uncombed. That same student, on that very day, had occasion to preach a sermon before the doctor, for which he received a bit of severe criticism, the sting of which was in its tail, "You said my wig wasna kaimed this mornin', my lad, but I think I've redd your head to you."

The Rev. John Heugh of Stirling was one day admonishing one of his people of the sin of intemperance: "Man, John, you should never drink except when you're dry." "Weel, sir," quoth John, "that's what I'm aye doin', for I am never slockin'd."

The Rev. Mr. M—— of Bathgate came up to a street-paviour one day, and addressed him, "Eh, John, what's this you're at?" "Oh! I'm mending the ways of Bathgate!" "Ah, John, I've long been tryin' to mend the ways o' Bathgate, an' they're no weel yet." "Weel, Mr. M., if you had tried my plan, and come doon to your *knees,* ye wad maybe hae come mair speed!"

There once lived in Cupar a merchant whose store contained supplies of every character and description, so that he was commonly known by the soubriquet of Robbie A'Thing. One day a minister who was well known for making a free use of his notes in the pulpit, called at the store asking for a rope and pin to tether a young calf in the glebe. Robbie at once informed him that he could not furnish such articles to him. But the minister being somewhat importunate, said, "Oh! I thought you were named Robbie A'Thing from the fact of your keeping all kinds of goods." "Weel a weel," said Robbie, "I keep a'thing in my shop but calf's tether-pins and paper sermons for ministers to read."

It was a somewhat whimsical advice, supported by whimsical argument, which used to be given by a Scottish minister to young preachers, on going abroad among people, "to sup well at the kail, for if they were good they were worth the supping, and if not they might be sure there was not much worth coming after them."

A good many families in and around Dunblane rejoice in the patronymic of Dochart. This name, which sounds somewhat Irish, is derived from Loch Dochart, in Argyleshire. The M'Gregors having been proscribed, were subjected to severe penalties, and a group of the clan having been hunted by their superiors, swam the stream which issues from Loch Dochart, and in gratitude to the river they afterwards assumed the family name of Dochart. A young lad of this name, on being sent to Glasgow College, presented a letter from his minister to Reverend Dr. Heugh of Glasgow. He gave his name as Dochart, and the name in the letter was M'Gregor: "Oh," said the Doctor, "I fear there is some mistake about your identity, the names don't agree." "Weel, sir, that's the way they spell the name in our country."

The relative whom I have mentioned as supplying so many Scottish anecdotes had many stories of a parochial functionary whose eccentricities have, in a great measure, given way before the assimilating spirit of the times. I mean the old Scottish beadle, or betheral, as he used to be called. Some classes of men are found to have that nameless but distinguishing characteristic of figure and aspect which marks out particular occupations and professions of mankind. This was so much the case in the betheral class, that an old lady observing a well-known judge and advocate walking together in the street, remarked to a friend as they passed by, "Dear me, Lucy, wha are they twa *beddle-looking* bodies?" They were often great originals, and, I suspect, must have been in past times somewhat given to convivial habits, from a remark I recollect of the late Baron Clerk Rattray, viz., that in his younger days he had hardly ever known a perfectly sober betheral. However this may have been, they were, as a class, remarkable for quaint humour, and for being shrewd observers of what was going on. I have heard of an occasion where the betheral made his wit furnish an apology for his want of sobriety. He had been sent round the parish by the minister to deliver notices at all the houses of the catechising which was to precede the preparation for receiving the communion. On his return it was quite evident that he had partaken too largely of refreshment since he had been on his expedition. The minister reproached him for this improper conduct. The betheral pleaded the pressing *hospitality* of the parishioners. The clergyman did not admit the plea, and added, "Now, John, I go through the parish, and you don't see me return fou as you have done." "Ay, minister," rejoined the betheral, with much complacency, "but then aiblins ye're no sae popular i' the parish as me." My relative used to tell of one of these officials receiving, with much ceremony, a brother betheral from a neighbouring parish, who had come with the minister thereof about to preach for some special occasion. After service, the betheral of the stranger clergyman felt proud of the performance of the appointed duty, and said, in a triumphant tone, to his friend, "I think our minister did weel; ay, he gars the stour flee out o' the cushion." To which the other rejoined, with a calm feeling of superiority, "Stour oot o' the cushicn! hout, our minister, sin' he cam wi' us has dung the guts oot o' twa Bibles."

Another description I have heard of an energetic preacher more forcible than delicate—" Eh, our minister had a great power o' watter, for he grat, and spat, and swat like mischeef." An obliging anonymous correspondent has sent me a story of a functionary of this class whose pride was centred not so much in the performance of the minister as of the precentor. He states that he remembers an old beadle of the church which was called "Haddo's Hole," and sometimes the Little Kirk," in Edinburgh, whose son occasionally officiated as precentor. He was not very well qualified for the duty, but the father had a high opinion of his son's vocal powers. In those days there was always service in the church on the Tuesday evenings; and when the father was asked on such occasions, "Who's to preach to-night?" his self-complacent reply used to be, "I divna ken wha's till preach, but my son's for till precent." This class of functionaries were very free in their remarks upon the preaching of strangers, who used occasionally to occupy the pulpit of their church—the city betherals speaking sometimes in a most condescending manner of clergy from the provincial parishes. As, for example, a betheral of one of the large churches in Glasgow, criticising the sermon of a minister from the country who had been preaching in the city church, characterised it as "gude coorse country wark." A betheral of one of the churches of St. Giles, Edinburgh, used to call on the family of Mr. Robert Stevenson, engineer, who was one of the elders. On one occasion they asked him what had been the text on such a night, when none of the family had been present. The man of office, confused at the question, and unwilling to show anything like ignorance, poured forth, "Weel, ye see, the text last day, was just entirely, sirs—yes—the text, sirs—what was it again—ou ay, just entirely, ye see it was 'What profiteth a man if he lose the world, and gain his own soul.'" Most of such stories are usually of an old standing. A more recent one has been told me of a betheral of a royal burgh much decayed from former importance, and governed by a feeble municipality of old men who continued in office, and in fact constituted rather the shadow than the substance of a corporation. A clergyman from a distance having come to officiate in the parish church, the betheral, knowing the terms on which it was usual for the minister officiating to pray for the efficiency of the local magistracy, quietly cautioned the clergyman before service that, in regard to the town council there, it would be quite out of place for him to pray that they should be a "terror to evil doers," because, as he said, the "poor auld bodies could be nae terror to onybody." Another functionary of a country parish is usually called the *minister's man*, and to one of these who had gone through a long course of such parish official life, a gentleman one day remarked—"John, ye hae been sae lang about the minister's hand that I dare say ye could preach a sermon yersell now." To which John modestly replied, "O na, sir, I couldna preach a sermon, but maybe I could draw an inference." "Well, John," said the gentleman, humouring the quiet vanity of the beadle, "what inference could ye draw frae this text, 'A wild ass snuffeth up the wind at her pleasure?'" (Jer. ii. 24). "Weel, sir, I wad draw this inference, he wad snuff a lang time afore he would fatten upon't." I had an anecdote from a friend of a reply from a betheral to the minister in church, which was quaint and amusing from the shrewd self-importance it indicated in his own acuteness. The clergyman had been annoyed during the course of his sermon by the restlessness and occasional whining of a dog, which at last began to bark outright. He looked out for the beadle, and directed him very peremptorily, "John, carry that dog out." John looked up to the pulpit, and with a very knowing expression said, "Na, na, sir; I'se just mak him gae out on his ain four legs." I have another story of canine misbehaviour in church. A dog was present during the service, and in the sermon the worthy minister was in the habit of speaking very loud, and, in fact, when he got warmed with his subject, of shouting almost to the top of his voice. The dog who, in the early part, had been very quiet, became quite excited, as is not uncommon with some dogs when hearing a noise, and from whinging and whining, as the speaker's voice rose loud and strong, at last began to bark and howl. The minister, naturally much annoyed at the interruption, called upon the betheral to put out the dog, who at once expressed his readiness to obey the order, but could not resist the temptation to look up to the pulpit, and to say very significantly, "Ay, ay, sir ; but indeed it was yoursell began it." There is a dog story connected with Reminiscences of Glasgow (See Chambers's Journal, March 1855), which is full of meaning. The bowls of rum punch which so remarkably characterised the Glasgow dinners of last century and the early part of the present, it is to be feared made some of the congregation given to somnolency on the Sundays following. The members of the town council often adopted Saturday for such meetings ; accordingly, the Rev. Mr. Thom, an excellent clergyman, took occasion to mark this propensity with some acerbity. A dog had been very troublesome, and disturbed the congregation for some time, when the minister at last gave orders to the beadle, "Take out that dog ; he'd wauken a Glasgow magistrate."

The parochial grave-diggers had sometimes a very familiar professional style of dealing with the solemn subjects connected with their office. Thus I have heard of a grave-digger pointing out a large human bone to a lady who was looking at his work, of digging a grave, and asking her—"D'ye ken wha's bane that is, mem ?—that's Jenny Fraser's hench-bane ;" adding with a serious aspect —"a weel-baned family thae Frasers !"

The "minister's man" was a functionary now less often to be met with. He was the minister's own servant and *factotum*. Amongst this class there was generally much Scottish humour and original character. They were (like the betheral) great critics of sermons and often severe upon strangers. sometimes with a sly hit at their own minister. One of these, David, a well known character, complimenting a young minister who had preached, told him, "Your introduction, sir, is aye grand; it's worth a' the rest o' the sermon,—could ye no mak it a' introduction?"

David's criticisms of his master's sermons were sometimes sharp enough and shrewd. On one occasion, driving the minister home from a neighbouring church where he had been preaching, and who, as he thought, had acquitted himself pretty well, inquired of David what *he* thought of it. The subject of discourse had been the escape of the Israelites from Egypt. So David opened his criticism—"Thocht o't, sir? deed I thocht nocht o't ava. It was a vara imperfect discourse, in ma opinion; ye did weel eneuch till ye took them through, but where did ye leave them? just daunerin' o' the sea-shore without a place to gang till. Had it no been for Pharaoh they had been better on the other side where they were comfortably encampit than daunerin' where ye left them. It's painful to hear a sermon stoppit afore it is richt ended, just as it is to hear ane streeket out lang after it's dune. That's my opinion o' the sermon ye geid us to-day." "Very freely given, David, very freely given; drive on a little faster, for I think ye're daunerin' noo yersell."

It would be impossible in these reminiscences to omit the well-known and often repeated anecdote connected with an eminent divine of our own country, whose works take a high place in our theological literature. The story to which I allude was rendered popular throughout the kingdom some years ago, by the inimitable mode in which it was told, or rather acted, by the late Charles Matthews. But Matthews was wrong in the person of whom he related the humorous address. I have assurance of the parties from a friend, whose father, a distinguished clergyman in the Scottish Church at the time, had accurate knowledge of the whole circumstances. The late celebrated Dr. Macknight, a learned and profound scholar and commentator, was nevertheless, as a preacher, to a great degree, heavy, unrelieved by fancy or imagination; an able writer, but a dull speaker. His colleague, Dr. Henry, well known as the author of a history of England, was, on the other hand, a man of great humour, and could not resist a joke when the temptation came upon him. On one occasion when coming to church, Dr. Macknight had been caught in a shower of rain, and entered the vestry soaked with wet. Every means were used to relieve him from his discomfort; but as the time drew on for divine service he became much distressed, and ejaculated over and over, "Oh, I wush that I was dry; do you think I'm dry? do you think I'm dry eneuch noo?" His jocose colleague could resist no longer, but, patting him on the shoulder, comforted him with the sly assurance, "Bide a wee, Doctor, and ye'se be dry eneuch when ye get into the pu'pit." Another quaint remark of the facetious Doctor to his more formal colleague has been preserved by friends of the family. Dr. Henry, who, with all his pleasantry and abilities, had himself as little popularity in the pulpit as his coadjutor, had been remarking to Dr. Macknight what a blessing it was that they were two colleagues in one charge, and continued dwelling on the subject so long, that Dr. Macknight, not quite pleased at the frequent reiteration of the remark, said that it certainly was a great pleasure to himself, but he did not see what great benefit it might be to the world. "Ah," said Dr. Henry, "an it hadna been for that, there wad hae been *twa* toom* kirks this day." I am indebted to a gentleman, himself also a distinguished member of the Scottish Church, for an authentic anecdote of this learned divine, and which occurred whilst Dr. Macknight was the minister of Maybole. One of his parishioners, a well-known humorous blacksmith of the parish, who, no doubt, thought that the Doctor's learned books were rather a waste of time and labour for a country

---

* Empty.

pastor, was asked if his minister was at home. The Doctor was then busy bringing out his laborious and valuable work, his "Harmony of the Four Gospels." "Na, he's gane to Edinburgh on a verra useless job." On being asked what this useless work might be which engaged his pastor's time and attention, he answered, "He's gane to mak four men agree wha ne'er cast out." The good-humoured and candid answer of a learned and rather long-winded preacher of the old school, always appeared to me quite charming. The good man was far from being a popular preacher, and yet he could not reduce his discourses below the hour and a half. On being asked, as a gentle hint of their possibly needless length, if he did not feel *tired* after preaching so long, he replied, "Na, na, I'm no tired;" adding, however, with much naïveté, "But, Lord, hoo tired the fowk whiles are."

The late good, kind-hearted Dr. David Dickson was fond of telling a story of a Scottish termagant of the days before kirk-session discipline had passed away. A couple were brought before the court, and Janet, the wife, was charged with violent and undutiful conduct, and with wounding her husband, by throwing a three-legged stool at his head. The minister rebuked her conduct, and pointed out its grievous character, by explaining that just as Christ was head of his church, so the husband was head of the wife; and therefore in assaulting *him*, she had in fact injured her own body. "Weel," she replied, "it's come to a fine pass gin a wife canna kame her ain head;" "Aye, but Janet," rejoined the minister, "a three-legged stool is a thief-like bane-kame to scart yer ain head wi'!"

The following is a dry Scottish case, of a minister's wife quietly "kaming her husband's head." Mr. Mair, a Scotch minister, was rather short-tempered, and had a wife named Rebecca, whom for brevity's sake he addressed as "Becky." He kept a diary, and among other entries this one was very frequent—"Becky and I had a rippet, for which I desire to be humble." A gentleman who had been on a visit to the minister went to Edinburgh, and told the story to a minister and his wife there, when the lady replied, "Weel, he must have been an excellent man, Mr. Mair. My husband and I sometimes too have 'rippets,' but catch him if he's ever humble."

Our object in bringing up and recording anecdotes of this kind is to elucidate the sort of humour we refer to, and to show it as a humour of *past* times. A modern clergyman could hardly adopt the tone and manner of the older class of ministers—men not less useful and beloved, on account of their odd Scottish humour, which indeed suited their time. Could a clergyman, for instance, now come off from the trying position in which we have heard of a northern minister being placed, and by the same way through which he extricated himself with much good nature and quiet sarcasm? A young man sitting opposite to him in the front of the gallery, had been up late on the previous night, and had stuffed the cards with which he had been occupied into his coat-pocket. Forgetting the circumstance, he pulled out his handkerchief, and the cards all flew about. The minister simply looked at him, and remarked, "Eh man, your psalm-buik has been ill bund."

Many anecdotes of pithy and facetious replies are recorded of a minister of the south, usually distinguished as "Our Watty Dunlop." On one occasion two irreverent young fellows determined, as they said, to "taigle"* the minister. Coming up to him in the High Street of Dumfries, they accosted him with much solemnity— "Maister Dunlop, dae ye hear the news?" "What news?" "Oh, the deil's deed." "Is he?" said Mr. Dunlop, "then I maun pray for twa faitherless bairns." On another occasion Maister Dunlop met, with characteristic humour, an attempt to play off a trick against him. It was known that he was to dine with a minister whose house was close to the church.

* Confound.

so that his return back must be through the churchyard. Accordingly some idle and mischievous youths waited for him in the dark night, and one of them came up to him, dressed as a ghost, in hopes of putting him in a fright. Watty's cool accost speedily upset the plan:—"Weel, Maister Ghaist, is this a general rising, or are ye juist taking a daunder frae yer grave by yersell?" I have received from a correspondent another specimen of Watty's acute rejoinders. Some years ago the celebrated Edward Irving had been lecturing at Dumfries, and a man who passed as a wag in that locality had been to hear him. He met Watty Dunlop the following day, who said, "Weel, Willie, man, an' what do ye think of Mr. Irving?" "Oh," said Willie, contemptuously, "the man's crack't." Dunlop patted him on the shoulder, with a quiet remark, "Willie, ye'll aften see a light peeping through a crack!"

An admirable story of a quiet pulpit rebuke is traditionary in Fife, and is told of Mr. Shirra, a seceding minister of Kirkcaldy, a man still well remembered by some of the older generation for many excellent and some eccentric qualities. A young officer of a volunteer corps on duty in the place, very proud of his fresh uniform, had come to Mr. Shirra's church, and walked about as if looking for a seat, but in fact to show off his dress, which he saw was attracting attention from some of the less grave members of the congregation. He came to his place, however, rather quickly, on Mr. Shirra quietly remonstrating, "O man, will ye sit doun, and we'll see your new breeks when the kirk's dune." This same Mr. Shirra was well known from his quaint, and, as it were, parenthetical comments which he introduced in his reading of Scripture; as, for example, on reading from the 116th Psalm, "I said in my haste all men are liars," he quietly observed, "Indeed, Dauvid, an' ye had been i' this parish ye might hae said it at your leesure."

There was something even still more pungent in the incidental remark of a good man, in the course of his sermon, who had in a country place taken to preaching out of doors in the summer afternoons. He used to collect the people as they were taking air by the side of a stream outside the village. On one occasion he had unfortunately taken his place on a bank, and fixed himself on an *ants' nest.* The active habits of those little creatures soon made the position of the intruder upon their domain very uncomfortable ; and afraid that his audience might observe something of this discomfort in his manner, he apologised by the remark—"Brethren, though I hope I have the word of God in my mouth, I think the deil himself has gotten into my breeks."

There was often no doubt a sharp conflict of wits when some of these humorist ministers came into collision with members of their flocks who were *also* humorists. Of this nature is the following anecdote, which I am assured is genuine :—A minister in the north was taking to task one of his hearers who was a frequent defaulter, and was reproaching him as an habitual absentee from public worship. The accused vindicated himself on the plea of a dislike to long sermons. "'Deed, man," said his reverend monitor, a little nettled at the insinuation thrown out against himself, "if ye dinna mend, ye may land yersell where ye'll no be troubled wi' mony sermons either lang or short." "Weel, aiblins sae," retorted John, "but it mayna be for want o' ministers." An *answer* to Mr. Shirra himself, strongly illustrative of Scottish ready and really clever wit, and which I am assured is quite authentic, must, I think, have struck the fancy of that excellent humorist himself. When Mr. Shirra was parish minister of St. Ninian's, one of the members of the church was John Henderson or Anderson—a very decent douce shoemaker—and who left the church and joined the Independents, who had a meeting in Stirling. Some time afterwards, when Mr. Shirra met John on the road, he said, "And so, John, I understand you have become an Independent ?" "'Deed, sir," replied John, "that's true." "Oh, John," said the minister, "I'm sure you ken that a rowin' (rolling) stane gathers nae fog" (moss). "Aye," said John, "that's true too; but can ye tell me what guid the fog does to the stane?" Mr. Shirra himself afterwards became a Baptist. The wit, however, was all in favour of the minister in the following:—

Dr. Gilchrist, formerly of the East Parish of Greenock, and who died minister of the Canongate, Edinburgh, received an intimation of one of his hearers, who had been exceedingly irregular in his attendance, that he had taken seats in an Episcopal chapel. One day soon after, he met his former parishioner, who told him candidly that he had "changed his religion." "Indeed," said the Doctor quietly, "how's that? I ne'er heard ye had ony." It was this same Dr. Gilchrist who gave the well-known quiet but forcible rebuke to a young minister whom he considered rather conceited and fond of putting forward his own doings, and who was to officiate in the Doctor's church. He explained to him the mode in which he usually conducted the service, and stated that he always finished the prayer before the sermon with the Lord's Prayer. The young minister demurred at this, and asked if he "might not introduce any other short prayer?" "Ou aye," was the Doctor's quiet reply, "gif ye can gie us onything *better*."

At Banchory, on Deeside, some of the criticisms and remarks on sermons were very quaint and characteristic. My cousin had asked the Ley's grieve what he thought of a young man's preaching, who had been more successful in appropriating the words than the ideas of Dr. Chalmers. He drily answered, "Ou, Sir Thomas, just a floorish o' the surface." But the same hearer bore this unequivocal testimony to another preacher whom he really admired. He was asked if he did not think the sermon long; "Na, I shuld nae hae thocht it lang an' I'd been sitting on thorns."

I think the following is about as good a sample of what we call Scotch "pawky" as any I know: A countryman had lost his wife and a favourite cow on the same day His friends consoled him for the loss of the wife; and being highly respectable, several hints and offers were made towards getting another for him. "Ou ay," he at length replied, "you're a' keen aneuch to get me anither wife, but no yin o' ye offers to gie me anither coo."

The following anecdotes, collected from different contributors, are fair samples of the quaint and original character of Scottish ways and expressions now becoming more and more matters of reminiscence:—A poor man came to his minister for the purpose of intimating his intention of being married. As he expressed, however, some doubts on the subject, and seemed to hesitate, the minister asked him if there were any doubts about his being accepted. No, that was not the difficulty; but he expressed a fear that it might not be altogether suitable, and he asked whether, if he were once married, he could not (in case of unsuitability and unhappiness) get *un*married? The clergyman assured him that it was impossible; if he married, it must be for better and worse; that he could not go back upon the step. So thus instructed he went away. After a time he returned, and said he had made up his mind to try the experiment, and he came and was married. Ere long he came back very disconsolate, and declared it would not do at all; that he was quite miserable, and begged to be unmarried. The minister assured him that was out of the question, and urged him to put away the notion of anything so absurd. The man insisted that the marriage could not hold good, for the wife was waur than the deevil. The minister demurred, saying that it was quite impossible. "'Deed, sir," said the poor man, "the Bible tells ye that if ye resist the deil he flees frae ye, but if ye resist her she flees *at* ye."

A faithful minister of the gospel being one day engaged in visiting some members of his flock, came to the door of a house where his gentle tapping could not be heard for the noise of contention within. After waiting a little he opened the door, and walked in, saying, with an authoritative voice, "I should like to know who is the head of this house." "Weel, sir," said the husband and father, "if ye sit doon a wee, we'll maybe be able to tell ye, for we're just trying to settle that point."

A minister in the north returning thanks in his prayers one Sabbath for the excellent harvest, began as usual, "O Lord, we thank thee," etc., and went on to mention its abundance, and its safe ingathering; but feeling anxious to be quite candid and scrupulously truthful, added, "all except a few fields between this and Stonehaven, not worth mentioning."

A Scotch preacher being sent to officiate one Sunday at a country parish, was accommodated at night in the manse, in a very diminutive closet, instead of the usual best bed-room appropriated to strangers.

"Is this the bed-room?" he said, starting back in amazement.

"Deed aye, sir, this is the prophets' chalmer."

"It maun be for the *minor* prophets, then," was the quiet reply.

Elders of the kirk, no doubt, frequently partook of the original and humorous character of ministers and others, their contemporaries; and amusing scenes must have passed, and good Scotch sayings been said, where they were concerned. Dr. Chalmers used to repeat one of these sayings of an elder with great delight. The Doctor associated with the anecdote the name of Lady Glenorchy and the church which she endowed; but I am assured that the person was Lady Elizabeth Cunninghame, sister of Archibald eleventh Earl of Eglinton, and wife of Sir John Cunninghame, Bart. of Caprington, near Kilmarnock. It seems her ladyship had, for some reason, taken offence at the proceedings of the Caprington parochial authorities, and a result of which was that she ceased putting her usual liberal offering into the plate at the door. This had gone on for some time, till one of the elders, of less forbearing character than the others, took his turn at the plate. Lady Elizabeth, as usual, passed by without a contribution, but made a formal courtesy to the elder as she passed, and sailed up the aisle. The good man was determined not to let her pass so easily. He quickly followed her up the passage, and urged the remonstrance, "My Lady, gie us less o' your mainers and mair o' your siller." *

Of an eccentric and eloquent professor and divine of a northern Scottish university, there are numerous and extraordinary traditionary anecdotes. I have received an account of some of these anecdotes from the kind communication of an eminent Scottish clergyman, who was himself, in early days, his frequent hearer. The stories told of the strange observations and allusions which he introduced

---

* Although the name of Lady Glenorchy has been erroneously associated with the above story, and with a demeanour which was quite foreign to her general character, still it is very suitable, I think, to retain my former reference to the history of this noble lady *since* her death, as forming a striking illustration of the uncertainty of all earthly concerns, and as supplying a Scottish reminiscence belonging to the last seventy years. Wilhelmina Viscountess Glenorchy, during her lifetime, built and endowed a church for two ministers, who were provided with very handsome incomes. She died 17th July 1786, and was buried on the 24th July, aged 44. Her interment took place, by her own direction, in the church she had founded, immediately in front of the pulpit; and she fixed upon that spot as a place of security and safety, where her mortal remains might rest in peace till the morning of the resurrection. But alas for the uncertainty of all earthly plans and projects for the future!—the iron road came on its reckless course, and swept the church away. The site was required for the North British Railway, which passed directly over the spot where Lady Glenorchy had been buried. Her remains were accordingly disinterred 24th December 1844; and the trustees of the church, not having yet erected a new one, deposited the body of their foundress in the vaults beneath St. John's Episcopal Church, and after resting there for fifteen years, they were, in 1859, removed to the building which is now Lady Glenorchy's Church.

into his pulpit discourses, almost surpass belief. For many reasons, they are not suitable to the nature of this publication, still less could they be tolerated in any pulpit administration now, although familiar with his contemporaries. The remarkable circumstance, however, connected with these eccentricities was, that he introduced them with the utmost gravity, and oftentimes after he had delivered them, pursued his subject with great earnestness and eloquence, as if he had said nothing uncommon. One saying of the professor, however, *out* of the pulpit, is too good to be omitted, and may be recorded without violation of propriety. He happened to meet at the house of a lawyer, whom he considered rather a man of *sharp* practice, and for whom he had no great favour, two of his own parishioners. The lawyer jocularly and ungraciously put the question : "Doctor, these are members of your flock ; may I ask, do you look upon them as white sheep or as black sheep ?" "I don't know," answered the professor drily, "whether they are black or white sheep, but I know that if they are long here they are pretty sure to be fleeced."

It was a pungent answer given by a Free Kirk member who had deserted his colours and returned to the old faith. A short time after the Disruption, the Free Church minister chanced to meet him who had then left him and returned to the Established Church. The minister bluntly accosted him—"Ay, man, John, an' ye've left us ; what micht be your reason for that ? Did ye think it wasna a guid road we was gaun ?" "Ou, I darsay it was a guid eneuch road and a braw road ; but, O minister, the tolls were unco high."

The following story I received from a member of the Penicuik family :—Dr. Ritchie, who died minister of St. Andrew's, Edinburgh, was, when a young man, tutor to Sir G. Clerk and his brothers. Whilst with them, the clergyman of the parish became unable, from infirmity and illness, to do his duty, and Mr. Ritchie was appointed interim assistant. He was an active young man, and during his residence in the country had become fond of fishing and was a good shot. When the grouse-shooting came round, his pupils happened to be laid up with a fever, so Mr. Ritchie had all the shooting to himself. One day he walked over the moor so far that he became quite weary and footsore. On returning home he went into a cottage, where the good woman received him kindly, gave him water for his feet, and refreshment. In the course of conversation, he told her he was acting as assistant minister of the parish, and he explained how far he had travelled in pursuit of game, how weary he was, and how completely knocked up he was. "Weel, sir, I dinna doubt ye maun be sair travelled and tired wi' your walk." And then she added, with sly reference to his profession, "Deed, sir, I'm thinking ye micht hae travelled frae Genesis to Revelation and no been sae footsore."

I cannot do better in regard to the three following anecdotes of the late Professor Gillespie of St. Andrews, than give them to my readers in the words with which Dr. Lindsay Alexander kindly communicated them to me.

"In the *Cornhill Magazine* for March 1860, in an article on Student Life in Scotland, there is an anecdote of the late Professor Gillespie of St. Andrews, which is told in such a way as to miss the point and humour of the story. The correct version, as I have heard it from the professor himself, is this: Having employed the village carpenter to put a frame round a dial at the manse of Cults, where he was a minister, he received from the man a bill, to the following effect—'To fencing the *deil*, 5s. 6d.' 'When I paid him,' said the professor, 'I could not help saying, John, this is rather more than I counted on; but I haven't a word to say. I get somewhere about two hundred a year for fencing the *deil*, and I'm afraid I don't do it half so effectually as you've done.'

"Whilst I am writing, another of the many stories of the learned and facetious professor rises in my mind. There was a worthy old woman at Cults whose place in church was what is commonly called the Lateran; a kind of small gallery at the top of the pulpit steps. She was a most regular attender, but as regularly fell asleep during sermon, of which fault the preacher had sometimes audible intimation. It was observed, however, that though Janet always slept during her own pastor's discourse, she could be attentive enough when she pleased, and especially was she alert when some young preacher occupied the pulpit. A little piqued, perhaps, at this, Mr. Gillespie said to her one day, 'Janet, I think you hardly behave very respectfully to your own minister in one respect.' 'Me, sir,' exclaimed Janet, 'I wad like to see ony man, no to say woman, by yoursel say that o' me! what can you mean, sir?' 'Weel, Janet, ye ken when I preach, you're almost always fast asleep before I've well given out my text; but when any of these young men from St. Andrews preach for me, I see you never sleep a wink. Now, that's what I call no using me as you should do.' 'Hoot, sir,' was the reply, 'is that a'? I'll soon tell you the reason o' that. When you preach, we a' ken the word o' God's safe in your hands; but when thae young birkies tak' it in haun, my certie, but it tak's us a' to look after them.' *

"I am tempted to subjoin another. In the Humanity Class, one day, a youth who was rather fond of showing off his powers of language, translated Hor. Od. iii., 3, 61, 62, somewhat thus—'The fortunes of Troy renascent under sorrowful omen shall be repeated with sad catastrophe.' 'Catastrophe!' cried the professor. 'Catastrophe, Mr.——, that's Greek. Give us it in plain English, if you please.' Thus suddenly pulled down from his high horse, the student effected his retreat with a rather lame and impotent version. 'Now,' said the professor, his little

* I have abundant evidence to prove that a similar answer to that which Dr. Alexander records to have been made to Mr. Gillespie has been given on similar occasions by others.—*E. B. R.*

sharp eyes twinkling with fun, 'that brings to my recollection what once happened to a friend of mine, a minister in the country. Being a scholarly man, he was sometimes betrayed into the use of words in the pulpit which the people were not likely to understand; but being very conscientious, he never detected himself in this, without pausing to give the meaning of the word he had used, and sometimes his extempore explanations of very fine words were a little like what we have just had from Mr. ——, rather too flat and commonplace. On one occasion, he allowed this very word 'catastrophe' to drop from him, on which he immediately added, 'that, you know my friends, means the *end* of a thing.' Next day, as he was riding through his parish, some mischievous youth succeeded in fastening a bunch of furze to his horse's tail—a trick which, had the animal been skittish, might have exposed the worthy pastor's horsemanship to too severe a trial, but which happily had no effect whatever on the sober-minded and respectable quadruped which he bestrode. On, therefore, he quietly jogged, utterly unconscious of the addition that had been made to his horse's caudal region, until, as he was passing some cottages, he was arrested by the shrill voice of an old woman, exclaiming, 'Heh, sir! Heh, sir! there's a whun-buss at your horse's catawstrophe!'"

I have brought in the following anecdote, exactly as it appeared in the *Scotsman* of October 4, 1859, because it introduces the name of Rev. John Skinner, of Langside, author of "Tullochgorum,"* "The Ewie wi' the Crooked Horn," and other excellent Scottish songs. Skinner was also a learned divine, and wrote theological works in Latin and English. He was a correspondent of Burns, and his name was "familiar as household words" to the old people of Aberdeenshire and Forfar.

"The late Rev. John Skinner, author of "Annals of

* Hence frequently spoken of under the sobriquet of "Tullochgorum."

Scottish Episcopacy," was his grandson. He was first appointed to a charge in Montrose, from whence he was removed to Banff, and ultimately to Forfar. After he had left Montrose, it reached his ears that an ill-natured insinuation was circulating in Montrose that he had been induced to leave this town by the temptation of a better income and of fat pork, which, it would appear, was plentiful in the locality of his new incumbency. Indignant at such an aspersion, he wrote a letter, directed to his maligners, vindicating himself sharply from it, which he showed to his grandfather, John Skinner of Langside, for his approval. The old gentleman objected to it as too lengthy, and proposed the following pithy substitute :—

" 'Had Skinner been of carnal mind,
As strangely ye suppose,
Or had he even been fond of swine,
He'd ne'er have left Montrose.' "

But there is an anecdote of John Skinner which should endear his memory to every generous and loving heart. On one occasion he was passing a small dissenting place of worship at the time when the congregation were engaged in singing ; on passing the door—old-fashioned Scottish Episcopalian as he was—he reverently took off his hat. His companion said to him, "What ! do you feel so much sympathy with this Anti-Burgher congregation ?" "No," said Mr. Skinner, "but I respect and love any of my fellow-Christians who are engaged in singing to the glory of the Lord Jesus Christ." Well done, old Tullochgorum ! thy name shall be loved and honoured by every true liberal-minded Scotsman.

On the subject of epigrams, I have received a clever impromptu of a judge's lady, produced in reply to one made by the witty Henry Erskine. At a dinner party at Lord Armadale's, when a bottle of claret was called for, port was brought in by mistake. A second time claret was sent for, and a second time the same mistake occurred.

Henry Erskine addressed the host in an impromptu, which was meant as a parody on the well-known Scottish song, "My jo, Janet"—

> "Kind sir, it's for your courtesie
> When I come here to dine, sir,
> For the love ye bear to me,
> Gie me the claret wine, sir."

To which Mrs. Honeyman retorted—

> "Drink the port, the claret's dear,
> Erskine, Erskine;
> Ye'll get fou on't, never fear,
> My jo, Erskine."

Some of my younger readers may not be familiar with the epigram of John Home, author of the tragedy of "Douglas." The lines were great favourites with Sir Walter Scott, who delighted in repeating them. Home was very partial to claret, and could not bear port. He was exceedingly indignant when the government laid a tax upon claret, having previously long connived at its introduction into Scotland under very mitigated duties. He embodied his anger in the following epigram—

> "Firm and erect the Caledonian stood,
> Old was his mutton, and his claret good;
> 'Let him drink port,' an English statesman cried—
> He drank the poison, and his spirit died."

There is a curious story traditionary in some families connected with the nobleman who is the subject of it, which I am assured is true, and farther, that it has never yet appeared in print. The story is, therefore, a "Scottish reminiscence," and, as such, deserves a place here. The Earl of Lauderdale was so ill as to cause great alarm to his friends, and perplexity to his physicians. One distressing symptom was a total absence of sleep, and the medical men declared their opinion, that without sleep being induced, he could not recover. His son, a queer eccentric-looking boy, who was considered not entirely right in his mind, but somewhat "*daft*," and who accordingly had had little attention paid to his education, was sitting under the table, and cried out, "Sen' for that preaching man frae Livingstone, for faither aye sleeps in the kirk." One of the doctors thought this hint worth attending to. The experiment of "getting a minister till him" succeeded, and sleep coming on, he recovered. The Earl, out of gratitude for this benefit, took more notice of his son, paid attention to his education, and that boy became the Duke of Lauderdale, afterwards so famous or infamous in his country's history.

The following very amusing anecdote, although it belongs more properly to the division on peculiarities of Scottish phraseology, I give in the words of a correspondent who received it from the parties with whom it originated. About twenty years ago, he was paying a visit to a cousin, married to a Liverpool merchant of some standing. The husband had lately had a visit from his aged father, who formerly followed the occupation of farming in Stirlingshire, and who had probably never been out of Scotland before in his life. The son, finding his father rather *de trop* in his office, one day persuaded him to cross the ferry over the Mersey, and inspect the harvesting, then in full operation, on the Cheshire side. On landing he approached a young woman reaping with the sickle in a field of oats, when the following dialogue ensued :—

Farmer.—Lassie, are yer aits muckle bookit th' year?

Reaper.—Sir?

Farmer.—I was speiring gif yer aits are muckle bookit th' year?

Reaper (in amazement).—I really don't know what you are saying, sir.

Farmer (in equal astonishment).—Gude—safe—us,—do ye no understaan gude plain English?—are—yer—aits—muckle—bookit?

Reaper decamps to her nearest companion, saying that was a madman, while he shouted in great wrath, "They were naething else than a set o' ignorant pock-puddings."

An English tourist visited Arran, and being a keen disciple of Izaak Walton, was arranging to have a day's good sport. Being told that the cleg, or horse-fly, would suit his purpose admirably for lure, he addressed himself to Christy, the Highland servant-girl :—"I say, my girl, can you get me some horse-flies?" Christy looked stupid, and he repeated his question. Finding that she did not yet comprehend him, he exclaimed, "Why, girl, did you never see a horse-fly?" "Naa, sir," said the girl, "but a wanse saw a coo jump ower a preshipice."

The following anecdote is highly illustrative of the thoroughly attached old family serving-man. A correspondent sends it as told to him by an old schoolfellow of Sir Walter Scott's at Fraser and Adam's class, High School :—

One of the lairds of Abercairnie proposed to *go out*, on the occasion of one of the risings for the Stuarts, in the '15 or '45—but this was not with the will of his old serving-man, who, when Abercairnie was pulling on his boots, preparing to go, overturned a kettle of boiling water upon his legs, so as to disable him from joining his friends—saying, "Tak that—let them fecht wha like, stay ye at hame and be Laird o' Abercairnie."

A story illustrative of a union of polite courtesy with rough and violent ebullition of temper common in the old Scottish character, is well known in the Lothian family. William Henry, fourth Marquis of Lothian, had for his guest at dinner an old countess to whom he wished to show particular respect and attention.* After a very compli-

* This Marquis of Lothian was aid-de-camp to the Duke of Cumberland at the battle of Culloden, and sullied his character as a soldier and a nobleman by the cruelties which he exercised on the vanquished.

mentary reception, he put on his white gloves to hand her down stairs, led her to the upper end of the table, bowed and retired to his own place. This I am assured was the usual custom with the chief lady guest by persons who themselves remember it. After all were seated, the Marquis addressed the lady, "Madam, may I have the honour and happiness of helping your ladyship to some fish?" But he got no answer, for the poor woman was deaf as a post, and did not hear him; after a pause, but still in the most courteous accents, "Madam, have I your ladyship's permission to send you some fish!" Then a little quicker, "Is your ladyship inclined to take fish?" Very quick, and rather peremptory, "Madam, do ye choice fish?" At last the thunder burst, to everybody's consternation, with a loud thump on the table and stamp on the floor: "Con—found ye, will ye have any fish?" I am afraid the exclamation might have been even of a more pungent character.

A correspondent has kindly enabled me to add a reminiscence and anecdote of a type of Scottish character now nearly extinct,—I mean the old Scottish *military* officer of the wars of Holland, and the Low Countries. I give them in his own words: "My father, the late Rev. Dr. Bethune, minister of Dornoch, was on friendly terms with a fine old soldier, the late Colonel Alexander Sutherland of Calmaly and Braegrudy, in Sutherlandshire, who was lieutenant-colonel of the '*Local Militia*,' and who used occasionally, in his word of command, to break out with a Gaelic phrase to the men, much to the amusement of bystanders. He called his charger, a high boned not overfed animal, Cadăver—a play upon accents, for he was a good classical scholar, and fond of quoting the Latin poets. But he had no relish nor respect for the '*modern languages*,' particularly for that of our neighbours, whom he looked upon as '*hereditary*' enemies! My father and the colonel were both politicians, as well as scholars. Reading a newspaper article in his presence one day, my father stopped short, handing the paper to him, and said, 'Colonel, here is a *French* quotation, which you can translate better than I can.' 'No, sir!' said the colonel, 'I never learnt the language of the scoundrels!!!' The colonel was known as 'Col. Sandy Sutherland,' and the men always called him *Colonel Sandy*. He was a splendid specimen of the hale veteran, with a stentorian voice, and the last queue I remember to have seen."

A correspondent kindly sends me from Aberdeenshire a humorous story, very much of the same sort as that of Colonel Erskine's servant, who considerately suggested to his master that "maybe an aith might relieve him."* My correspondent heard the story from the late Bishop Skinner.

It was among the experiences of his father, Bishop *John* Skinner, while making some pastoral visits in the neighbourhood of the town (Aberdeen), the Bishop took occasion to step into the cottage of two humble parishioners, a man and his wife, who cultivated a little croft. No one was within; but as the door was only on the latch, the Bishop knew that the worthy couple could not be far distant. He therefore stepped in the direction of the outhouses, and found them both in the barn winnowing corn, in the primitive way, with "riddles," betwixt two open doors. On the Bishop making his appearance, the honest man ceased his winnowing operations, and in the gladness of his heart stepped briskly forward to welcome his pastor; but in his haste he trod upon the rim of the riddle, which rebounded with great force against one of his shins. The accident made him suddenly pull up; and, instead of completing the reception, he stood vigorously rubbing the injured limb; and, not daring in such a venerable presence to give vent to the customary strong ejaculations, kept twisting his face into all sorts of grimaces. As was natural, the Bishop went forward, uttering the usual formulas of condolence and sympathy, the patient,

---

* Sir H. Moncreiff's Life of Dr. J. Erskine.

meanwhile, continuing his rubbings and his silent but expressive contortions. At last Janet came to the rescue; and, clapping the Bishop coaxingly on the back, said, "Noo, Bishop, jist gang ye yir waas in to the hoose, an' we'll follow fan he's had time to curse a fyllie, an' I'se warran' he'll seen be weel eneuch!"

The following might have been added as examples of the dry humorous manner in which our countrymen and countrywomen sometimes treat matters with which they have to deal, even when serious ones:—

An itinerant vender of wood in Aberdeen having been asked how his wife was, replied, "O she's fine, I hae ta'en her to Banchory;" and on it being innocently remarked that the change of air would do her good, he looked up, and, with a half smile, said, "Hoot, she's i' the kirkyard."

The well-known aversion of the Scotch to hearing *read* sermons has often led to amusing occurrences. One indulged pastor in a country district was permitted so far to transgress the rule, as to be allowed notes, which never in number exceeded three, and which of course were—"1st, 2d, thirdly and lastly." One Sabbath afternoon, having exhausted both firstly and secondly, he came to the termination of his discourse; but, unfortunately the manuscript was awanting. In vain efforts to seek the missing paper, he repeated "thirdly and lastly" *ad nauseam* to his hearers. At last one, cooler than the others, rose, and nodding to the minister, observed, "Deed, sir, if I'm no mista'en, I saw 'thirdly and lastly' fa' ower the poopit stairs."

A man who had had four wives, and who meditated a fifth time entering the marriage state, was conversing with his friend on the subject, who was rather disposed to banter him a little upon his past matrimonial schemes, as having made a good deal of *money* by his wives,—"Na, na," he replied, "they cam' t' me wi' auld kists,* and I sent them hame i' new anes."

* Chests.

The two following are from a correspondent who heard them told by the late Dr. Barclay the anatomist, well known for his own dry Scottish humour.

A country laird, at his death, left his property in equal shares to his two sons, who continued to live very amicably together for many years. At length one said to the other, "Tam, we're getting auld now, you'll tak' a wife, and when I dee you'll get my share o' the grund." "Na, John, you're the youngest and maist active, you'll tak' a wife, and when I dee you'll get my share." "Od," says John, "Tam, that's just the way wi' you when there's ony *fash or trouble.* The deevil a thing you'll do at a'."

A country clergyman, who was not on the most friendly terms with one of his heritors who resided in Stirling, and who had annoyed the minister by delay in paying him his teinds (or tythe), found it necessary to make the laird understand that his proportion of stipend must be paid so soon as it became due. The payment came next term punctual to the time. When the messenger was introduced to the minister, he asked who he was, remarking, that he thought he had seen him before. "I am the hangman of Stirling, sir." "Oh, just so, take a seat till I write you a receipt." It was evident that the laird had chosen this medium of communication with the minister as an affront, and to show his spite. The minister, however, turned the tables upon him, sending back an acknowledgment for the payment in these terms :—"Received from Mr ——, by the hands of the hangman of Stirling, *his doer*,* the sum of," etc. etc.

The following story of pulpit criticism by a beadle, used to be told, I am assured, by the late Rev. Dr. Andrew Thomson :—

A clergyman in the country had a stranger preaching for him one day, and meeting his beadle, he said to him,

* In Scotland it is usual to term the law-agent or man of business of any party his "doer."

"Well, Saunders, how did you like the sermon to-day?" "I watna', sir; it was rather ower plain and simple for me. I like thae sermons best that jumbles the joodgment and confoonds the sense; Od, sir, I never saw ane that could come up to yoursel' at that."

The epithet "canny" has frequently been applied to our countrymen, not in a severe or invidious spirit, but as indicating a due regard to personal interest and safety. In the larger edition of Jamieson (see edition of 1840) I find there are no fewer than eighteen meanings given of this word. The following extract from a provincial paper, which has been sent me, will furnish a good illustration. It is headed, the "PROPERTY QUALIFICATION," and goes on—"Give a Chartist a large estate, and a copious supply of ready money, and you make a Conservative of him. He can then see the other side of the moon, which he could never see before. Once, a determined Radical in Scotland, named Davy Armstrong, left his native village; and many years afterwards, an old fellow-grumbler met him, and commenced the old song. Davy shook his head. His friend was astonished, and soon perceived that Davy was no longer a grumbler, but a rank Tory. Wondering at the change, he was desirous of knowing the reason. Davy quietly and laconically replied—'I've a coo (cow) noo.'"

But even still more "canny" was the eye to the main chance in an Aberdonian fellow-countryman, communicated in the following pleasant terms from a Nairn correspondent:—"I have just been reading your delightful 'Reminiscences,' which has brought to my recollection a story I used to hear my father tell. It was thus:—A countryman in a remote part of Aberdeenshire having got a newly-coined sovereign, in the days when such a thing was seldom seen in his part of the country, went about showing it to his friends and neighbours for the charge of 1d. each sight. Evil days, however, unfortunately overtook him, and he was obliged to part with his loved coin.

Soon after, a neighbour called on him, and asked a sight of his sovereign, at the same time tendering a penny 'Ah, man,' says he, 'I'ts gane; but I'll lat ye see *the cloutie it was row't in* for a bawbee.'"

I have often been amused with the wonderful coolness with which a parishioner announced his canny care for his supposed interests when he became an elder of the kirk. The story is told of a man who had got himself installed in the eldership, and, in consequence, had for some time carried round the ladle for the collections. He had accepted the office of elder because some wag had made him believe that the remuneration was sixpence each Sunday, with a boll of meal at New Year's Day. When the time arrived he claimed his meal, but was told he had been hoaxed. "It may be sae wi' the meal," he said coolly, "but I took care o' the saxpence mysel'."

There was a good deal both of the *pawky* and the *canny* in the following anecdote, which I have from an honoured lady of the south of Scotland:—"There was an old man who always rode a donkey to his work, and tethered him while he worked on the roads, or wherever else it might be. It was suggested to him by my grandfather that he was suspected of putting it in to feed in the fields at other people's expense. 'Eh, laird, I could never be tempted to do that; for my cuddy winna eat onything but nettles and thristles.' One day my grandfather was riding along the road, when he saw Andrew Leslie at work, and his donkey up to the knees in one of his clover fields, feeding luxuriously. 'Hollo, Andrew!' said he; 'I thought you told me your cuddy would eat nothing but nettles and thistles.' 'Ay,' said he, 'but he misbehaved the day; he nearly kicket me ower his head, sae I pat him in there just to *punish* him.'"

The following from a provincial paper, contains a very amusing recognition of a return which one of the itinerant race considered himself conscientiously bound to make to his clerical patron for an alms:—"A beggar while on his rounds one day this week, called on a clergyman (within two and a half miles of the Cross of Kilmarnock), who, obeying the biblical injunction of clothing the naked, offered the beggar an old top-coat. It was immediately rolled up, and the beggar, in going away with it under his arm, thoughtfully (!) remarked, 'I'll hae tae gie ye a day's *hearin'* for this na.'"

The natural and self-complacent manner in which the following anecdote brings out in the Highlander an innate sense of the superiority of Celtic blood is highly characteristic :—A few years ago, when an English family were visiting in the Highlands, their attention was directed to a child crying ; on their observing to the mother it was *cross*, she exclaimed, "Na, na, it's nae cross, for we're baith true Hieland."

The late Mr. Grame of Garsock, in Strathearn, whose grandson already "is laird himsel," used to tell, with great *unction*, some thirty years ago, a story of a neighbour of his own of a still earlier generation, Drummond of Keltie, who, as it seems, had employed an itinerant tailor instead of a metropolitan artist. On one occasion a new pair of inexpressibles had been made for the laird ; they were so tight that, after waxing hot and red in the attempt to try them on, he *let out* rather savagely at the tailor, who calmly assured him, "It's the fash'n ; it's jist the fash'n." "Eh ? ye haveril, is it the fashion for them *no to go on ?*"

An English gentleman writes to me :—"We have all heard much of Scotch caution, and I met once with an instance of it which I think is worth recording, and which I tell as strictly original. About 1827, I fell into conversation, on board of a Stirling steamer, with a well-dressed middle-aged man, who told me he was a soldier of the 42d, going on leave. He began to relate the campaigns he had gone through, and mentioned having been at the siege of St. Sebastian.—'Ah ! under Sir Thomas Graham ?' 'Yes, sir ; he commanded there.' 'Well,' I said, merely by way of carrying on the *crack*, 'and what do you think of *him?*' Instead of answering, he scanned me several times from head to foot, and from foot to head, and then said in a tone of the most diplomatic caution, 'Ye'll perhaps be of the name of Grah'm yersell, sir.' There could hardly be a better example, either of the circumspection of a real canny Scot, or of the lingering influence of the old patriarchal feeling, by which 'A name, a word, makes clansmen vassals to their lord.'"

Colonel Erskine, the father of the celebrated lawyer, and the grandfather of Dr. John Erskine of this city, no less celebrated as a divine, was quite a character in his day. He was of a very choleric temper, of which some racy anecdotes are told in Sir Henry Moncreiff's life of Dr. J. Erskine. He had an old servant of the true caste. On one occasion he had done something that very much displeased his master. The colonel's wrath became quite uncontrollable, his utterance was choked, and his countenance became pale as death. The servant grew somewhat uneasy, and at last said, "Eh, sir! maybe an aith would relieve you."

Now when we linger over these old stories, we seem to live at another period, and in such reminiscences we converse with a generation different from our own. Changes are still going on around us. They have been going on for some time past. The changes are less striking as society advances, and our later years have less and less alterations to remark. Probably each generation will have fewer changes to record than the generation that preceded; still every one who is tolerably advanced in life must feel that, comparing its beginning and its close, he has witnessed two epochs, and that he looks on a different world from one which he can remember. To elucidate this fact has been my present object, and in attempting this task I cannot but feel how trifling and unsatisfactory my remarks must seem to many who have a more enlarged and minute acquaintance wth Scottish life and manners than I have. But I shall be encouraged to hope for a favourable, or at least an indulgent sentence upon these Reminiscences, if to any of my readers I shall have opened a fresh insight into the subject of social changes amongst us. Many causes have their effect upon the habits and customs of mankind, and of late years such causes have been greatly multiplied in number and activity. In many persons, and in some who have not altogether lost their national partialities, there is a general tendency to merge Scottish usages and Scottish expressions into the English forms, as being more correct and genteel. The facilities for moving, not merely from place to place in our own country, but from one country to another; the spread of knowledge and information by means of periodical publications and newspapers; and the incredibly low prices at which literary works are produced, must have great effects. Then there is the improved taste in art, which, together with literature, has been taken up by young men who, fifty, sixty, seventy years ago, or more, would have known no such sources of interest, or indeed, who would have looked upon them as unmanly and effeminate. When first these pursuits were taken up by our Scottish young men, they excited in the north much amazement, and, I fear, contempt, as was evinced by a laird of the old school, who, the first time he saw a young man at the pianoforte, asked, with evident disgust, "Can the creature *sew* ony?" evidently putting the accomplishment of playing the pianoforte and the accomplishment of the needle in the same category. The greater facility of producing books, prints, and other articles which tend to the comfort and embellishment of domestic life, must have considerable influence upon the habits and tastes of a people. I have often thought how much effect might be traced to the single circumstance of the cheap production of pianofortes. An increased facility of procuring the means of acquaintance with good works of art and literature, acts both as cause and effect. A growing and improved taste tends to stimulate the *production* of the best works of art. These, in return, foster and advance the power of forming a due *estimate* of art. In the higher department of music, for example, the cheap rate not only of *hearing* compositions of the first class, but of *possessing* the works of the most eminent composers, must have had influence upon thousands. The principal oratories of Handel may be purchased for as many shillings each as they cost pounds years ago. Indeed, at that time the very names of those immortal works were known only to a few who were skilled to appreciate their high beauties. Now associations are formed for practising and studying the choral works of the great masters. In connection, however, with this subject, I may notice here, that a taste for that most interesting style of music, the pure Scottish, is in some quarters becoming a matter of reminiscence. Of reminiscence I mean so far as concerns the enthusiasm with which it was once esteemed and cultivated amongst us. I do not speak so much of the *songs* of Scotland, which can never lose their charm, although of them even some are growing fast out of the acquaintance of the younger members of society: but I refer more particularly to the reels and strathspeys, which with many Scotch persons have become nearly quite obsolete. When properly performed, it is a most animating and delightful strain—not of a refined or scientific class, but joyous and inspiriting. It has a peculiar character of its own, and requires to be performed with a particular and *spicy* dexterity of hand, whether for the bow or keys. Accordingly, young ladies used to take lessons in it as a finish to their musical education. Such teaching would now, I fear, be treated with contempt by many of our modern fair ones. I recollect at the beginning of the present century, my eldest sister, who was a good musician of the school of Pleyel, Kozeluch, Clementi, etc., having such lessons from Nathaniel Gow, a celebrated reel and strathspey performer. Nathaniel was the son of Neil Gow, who was the most eminent performer and composer of the pure Scottish dance music. A correspondent who knew Neil Gow, and was inquiring after him at his cottage the day of his death, in 1807, has kindly communicated a characteristic anecdote :—Neil was rather addicted to the whisky bottle. On walking home to Dunkeld, one night, from *Perth*, where he had been engaged, as usual, to play the violin at some ball, upon being asked, next day, how he had got home, for it was a long walk, and he was very tipsy, replied 'that he didna mind the length o' the road; it was the *breadth* o' it that he cast oot wi' !"—under the recollection of his having knocked about from side to side. At the close of the last century Gow's celebrity might be said to rival that of Burns ; and Neil's strathspeys were on a par with the songs of Robby. But alas ! that celebrity and popularity are becoming matters of reminiscence with the few. With the rising generation the name has passed away. It is a pity. Even still, let a good strathspey performer begin to play such tunes, for example, as "Up an' Waur them a', Willie," "Brig o' Dee," "Reel o' Tulloch," "Loch Eric Side," or "Monimusk," and every countenance brightens with animation.

We must acknowledge that the love of Scottish music used to be with some of the older generation a very *exclusive* taste, and that they had as little sympathy with the admirers of Italian strains as such admirers could have with theirs. I have been supplied with an amusing illustration of this intolerance :—A family belonging to the Scottish Border, after spending some time at Florence, had returned home, and proud of the progress they had made in music, the young ladies were anxious to show off their accomplishments before an old confidential servant of the family, and accordingly sung to her some of their finest Italian songs which they had learned abroad. Instead, however, of paying them a compliment on their performance, she showed what she thought of it by asking with much naïveté, "Eh, mem, do they ca' skirling like yon *singing* in foreign pairts ?"

There are many causes in operation to produce changes in taste, habits, and associations, amongst us. Families do not vegetate for years in one retired spot as they used to do ; young men are encouraged to attain accomplishments, and to have other sources of interest than the field or the bottle. Every one knows, or may know, everything that is going on through the whole world. There is a tendency in mankind to lose all that is peculiar, and in nations to part with all that distinguishes them from each other. We hear of wonderful changes in habits and customs where change seemed impossible. In India and Turkey even, peculiarities and prejudices are fading away under the influence of time. Amongst ourselves, no doubt, one circumstance tended greatly to call forth, and, as we may say, to *devolope*, the peculiar Scotch humour of which we speak—and that was the familiarity of intercourse which took place between persons in different positions of life. This extended even to an occasional interchange of words between the minister and the members of his flock during time of service. I have two anecdotes in illustration of this fact, which I have reason to believe are quite authentic. In the church of Banchory on Deeside, to which I have referred, a former minister always preached without book, and being of an absent disposition, he sometimes forgot the head of discourse on which he was engaged, and got involved in confusion. On one occasion, being desirous of recalling to his memory the division of his subject, he called out to one of his elders, a farmer on the estate of Ley, "Bush (the name of his farm), Bush, ye're sleeping." "Na, sir, I'm no sleeping—I'm listening." "Weel then, what had I begun to say?" "O, ye were saying so and so." This was enough, and supplied the minister with the thread of his discourse ; and he went on. The other anecdote related to the parish of Cumbernauld, the minister of which was, at the time referred to, noted for a very disjointed and rambling style of preaching, without method or connection. His principal heritor was the Lord Elphinstone of the time, and unfortunately the minister and the peer were not on good terms, and always ready to annoy each other by sharp sayings or otherwise. The minister on one occasion had somewhat in this spirit called upon the beadle to "wauken my Lord Elphinstone," upon which Lord E said, "I'm no sleeping, minister." "Indeed you were, my lord." He again disclaimed the sleeping. So as a test the preacher asked him, "What had I been saying last then ?" "Oh, just wauken Lord Elphinstone." "Ay, but what did I say before that ?" "Indeed," retorted Lord Elphinstone, "I'll gie ye a guinea if ye'll tell that yersell, minister" We cannot imagine the *possibility* of such scenes taking place amongst us in church now. It seems as if all men were gradually approximating to a common type or form in their manners and views of life ; oddities are sunk, prominences are rounded off, sharp features are polished, and all is becoming amongst us smooth and conventional. The remark, like the effect, is general, and extends to other countries as well as to our own. But as we have more recently parted with our peculiarities of dialect, oddity, and eccentricity, it becomes the more amusing to mark *our* participation in this change, because a period of fifty years shows here a greater contrast than the same period would show in many other localities.

I have already referred to a custom which prevailed in all the rural parish churches, and which I remember in my early days at Fettercairn ; the custom I mean, now quite obsolete, of the minister, after pronouncing the blessing, turning to the heritors, who always occupied the front seats of the gallery, and making low bows to each family. Another custom I recollect :—When the text had been given out, it was usual for the elder branches of the congregation to hand about their Bibles amongst the younger members, marking the place, and calling their attention to the passage. During service another handing about was frequent amongst the seniors, and that was a circulation of the sneeshin mull or snuff-box. Indeed, I have heard of the same practice in an Episcopal church, and particularly in one case of an ordination, where the bishop took his pinch of snuff, and handed the mull to go round amongst the clergy assembled for the solemn occasion within the altar rails.

Amongst "reminiscences" which do not extend beyond our own recollection, we may mention the disappearance of Trinity Church in Edinburgh, which has taken place within the last quarter of a century. It was founded by Mary of Gueldres, queen of James II. of Scotland, in 1446, and liberally endowed for a provost, prebendaries, choristers, etc. It was never completed, but the portions built—viz., choir, transept, and central tower—were amongst the finest specimens of later Gothic work in Scotland. The pious founder had placed it at the east end of what was then the North Loch. Like Lady Glenorchy, she chose her own church for the resting-place of her remains as a sanctuary of safety and repose. A railway parliamentary bill, however, overrides founders' intentions and Episcopal consecrations. Where once stood the beautiful church of the Holy Trinity, where once the "pealing organ" and the "full-voiced choir" were daily heard "in service high and anthems clear"—where for 400 years slept the ashes of a Scottish Queen—now resound the noise and turmoil of a railway station.

In our reminiscences of many *changes*, which have taken place during fifty years in Scottish manners, it might form an interesting section to record some of the peculiarities which *remain*. I mean such peculiarities as yet linger amongst us, and still mark a difference in some of our social habits from those of England. Some Scottish usages die hard, and are found here and there for the amusement of southern visitors. To give a few examples, persons still persist among us in calling the head of the family, or the host, the *landlord*, although he never charged his guests a halfpenny for the hospitality he exercises. In games, golf and curling still continue to mark the national character—cricket was long an exotic amongst us. In many of our educational institutions, however, it seems now fairly to have taken root. We continue to call our reception rooms "*public* rooms," although never used for any but domestic purposes. Military rank is attached to ladies, as we speak of Mrs. Lieutenant Fraser, Mrs. Captain Scott, Mrs. Major Smith. On the occasion of a death, we persist in sending circular notices to all the relatives, whether they know of it or not—a custom which, together with men wearing weepers at funeral solemnities, is unknown in England. Announcing a married lady's death under her maiden name must seem strange to English ears—as, for example, we read of the demise of Jane Dixon, spouse of Thomas Morison. Scottish cookery retains its ground, and hotch-potch, minced collops, sheep's head singed, and occasionally haggis, are still marked peculiarities of the Scottish table. These social differences linger amongst us. But stronger points are worn away; eccentricities and oddities such as existed once will not do now. One does not see why eccentricity should be more developed in one age than in another, but we cannot avoid the conclusion that the day for real oddities is no more. Professors of colleges are those in whom one least expects it—grave and learned characters; and yet such *have* been in former times. We can scarcely now imagine such professors as we read of in a past generation. Take the case of no less distinguished a person than Adam Smith, author of the "Wealth of Nations," who went about the streets talking and laughing to himself in such a manner as to make the market women think he was deranged; and he told of one himself who ejaculated, as he passed, "Hech, sirs, and he is weel pat on, too!" expressing surprise that a decided lunatic, who from his dress appeared to be a gentleman, should be permitted to walk abroad unattended. Professors still have their crotchets like other people; but we can scarcely conceive a professor of our day coming out like Adam Smith and making fishwives pass such observations on his demeanour. There are changes which the dignified muse of history will scarcely condescend to record or notice; and are perhaps better described in idle gossip like this than by the historic page; and this made me remark, as an introduction to the record of these anecdotes, that personal recollections and reminiscences might be extremely valuable in describing those lighter variations of society which do not come properly within the scope of history. For example, how could that prevalence of drinking habits, so commonly recognised in *all* classes and varieties of a past generation, be so keenly illustrated as by the description of a townsman, a small shopkeeper, given by a gentleman noted for his quiet sarcastic humour, "O, he's just a fine religious drucken body." Then again take the story told in Lockhart's life of Sir W. Scott, of the blacksmith whom Sir Walter had formerly known as a horse doctor, and whom he found at a small country town south of the Border, practising medicine with a reckless use of "laudamy and calomy," apologizing at the same time for the mischief he might do, by the assurance that it "would be lang before it made up for Flodden." How graphically it describes the interest felt by Scotchmen of his rank in the incidents of their national history. A similar example has been recorded in connection with Bannockburn. Two English gentlemen visited the field of that great battle, and a country blacksmith pointed out with much intelligence the positions of the two armies, the stone on which was fixed the Bruce's standard, etc. The gentlemen, on leaving, pressed his acceptance of a crown-piece. "Na, na," replied the Scotsman, with much pride, "it has cost ye eneuch already." Such an example of self-denial on the part of a Scottish cicerone is, we fear, now rather a "reminiscence."

In further illustration of these remarks, we may refer to the bearing of some old-fashioned language upon past national historical connections. Thus, from some words which are quite domesticated throughout Scotland, we learn how close, at one time, must have been our alliance with France, and how much influence must have been exercised upon general society by French intercourse.

Scoto-Gallic words were quite differently situated from French words and phrases adopted in England. With us they proceeded from a real admixture of the two *peoples.* With us they were of the ordinary common language of the country, that was from a distant period moulded by French. In England, the educated and upper classes of late years *adopted* French words and phrases. With us, some of our French derivatives are growing obsolete as vulgar, and nearly all are passing from fashionable society. In England, we find the French-adopted words rather receiving accessions than going out of use.

Examples of words such as we have referred to, as showing a French influence and admixture, are familiar to many of my readers. I recollect some of them in constant use amongst old-fashioned Scottish people, and those terms, let it be remembered, are unknown in England.

A leg of mutton was always, with old-fashioned Scotch people, a gigot (Fr. gigot).

The crystal jug or decanter in which water is placed upon the table, was a caraff (Fr. carafe).

Gooseberries were groserts, or grossarts (Fr. groseille).

Partridges were pertricks,—a word much more formed upon the French perdrix than the English partridge.

The plate on which a joint or side-dish was placed upon the table was an ashet (Fr. assiette).

In the old streets of Edinburgh, where the houses are very high, and where the inhabitants all live in flats, before the introduction of soil-pipes there was no method of disposing of the foul water of the household, except by throwing it out of the window into the street. This operation, dangerous to those outside, was limited to certain hours, and the well-known cry which preceded the missile and warned the passenger, was gardeloo! or, as Smollet writes it, gardy loo (Fr. garde de l'eau).

Anything troublesome or irksome used to be called, Scotticé, fashious (Fr. facheux, facheuse); to fash one's-self (Fr. se facher).

The small cherry, both black and red, common in gardens, is in Scotland, never in England, termed gean (Fr. guigne), from Guigne, in Picardy.

The term dambrod, which has already supplied materials for a good story, arises from adopting French terms into Scottish language, as dams were the pieces with which the game of draughts was played (Fr. dammes).

A bedgown, or loose female upper garment, is still in many parts of Scotland termed a jupe (Fr. jupe).

In Kincardineshire the ashes of a blacksmith's furnace had the peculiar name of smiddy-coom (Fr. écume, *i.e.*, dross).

Oil, in common Scotch, used always to be ule,—as the uley pot, or uley cruse (Fr. huile).

Many of my readers are no doubt familiar with the notice taken of these words by Lord Cockburn, and with the account which he gives of these Scottish words derived from the French, probably during the time of Queen Mary's minority, when French troops were quartered in Scotland. I subjoin a more full list, for which I am indebted to a correspondent, because the words of it still lingering amongst us are in themselves the best REMINISCENCES of former days.

Scotch.	English.	French.
Serviter	Napkin	From Serviette.
Gigot (of mutton)	...	,, Gigot.
Reeforts	Radishes	,, Raiforts.
Grosserts	Gooseberries	,, Groseilles.
Gardyveen	Case for holding wine	,, Garde-vin.
Jupe	Part of a woman's dress	,, Jupe.
Bonnaille	A parting glass with a friend going on a journey	,, Bon aller.
Gysart	Person in a fancy dress	,, Guise.
Dambrod	Draught-board	,, Dammes.
Pantufles	Slippers	,, Pantoufles.
Haggis	Hashed meat	,, Hachis.

Scotch.	English.	French.
Gou	Taste, smell	From Gout
Hogue	Tainted	,, Haut gout.
Grange	Granary	,, Grange.
Mouter	Miller's perquisite	,, Mouture.
Dour	Obstinate	,, Dur.
Douce	Mild	,, Doux.
Dorty	Sulky	,, Dureté.
Braw	Fine	,, Brave
Kimmer	Gossip	,, Commère.
Jalouse	Suspect	,, Jalouser.
Vizzy	To aim at, to examine	,, Viser.
Ruckle	Heap (of stones)	,, Recueil.
Gardy-loo	(Notice well known in Edinburgh)	,, Gardez l'eau.
Dementit	Out of patience, deranged	,, Dementir.
On my verity	Assertion of truth	,, Verité.
By my certy	Assertion of truth	,, Certes.
Aumrie	Cupboard	,, Almoire, in old French.
Walise	Portmanteau	,, Valise.
Sucker	Sugar	,, Sucre.

Edinburgh street cry :—" Neeps like sucker. Whae'll buy neeps ?" (turnips).

Petticoat-tails	Cakes of triangular shapes	,, Petits gatelles (gateaux).
Ashet	Meat-dish	,, Assiette.
Fashious	Troublesome	,, Facheux.
Prush, Madame*	Call to a cow to come forward	,, Approchez, Madame.

* This expression was adopted apparently in ridicule of the French applying the word "Madame" to a cow.

CONCLUSION.

In all these details regarding the changes which many now living have noticed to have taken place in our customs and habits of society in Scotland, this question must always occur to the thoughtful and serious mind, Are the changes which have been observed for *good?* Is the world a better world than that which we can remember? On some important points changes have been noticed in the upper classes of Scottish society, which unquestionably are improvements. For example, the greater attention paid to attendance upon public worship,—the disappearance of profane swearing and of excess in drinking. But then the painful questions arise, Are such beneficial changes *general* through the whole body of our countrymen? may not the vices and follies of one grade of society have found a refuge in those that are of a lower class? may not new faults have taken their place where older faults have been abandoned? Of this we are quite sure,—no lover of his country can fail to entertain the anxious wish, that the change we noticed in regard to drinking and swearing were universal, and that we had some evidence of its being extended through all classes of society. We ought certainly to feel grateful when we reflect that in many instances which we have noticed, the ways and customs of society are much improved in common sense, in decency, in delicacy, and refinement. There are certain modes of life, certain expressions, eccentricity of conduct, coarseness of speech, books, and plays, which were in vogue amongst us, even fifty or sixty years ago, which would not be tolerated in society at the present time. We cannot illustrate this in a more satisfactory manner than by reference to the acknowledgment of a very interesting and charming old lady, who died so lately as 1823. In 1821, Mrs. Keith of Ravelstone, grand-aunt of Sir Walter Scott, thus writes, in returning to him the work of a female novelist which she had borrowed from him out of curiosity, and to remind her of "auld lang syne:"—"Is it not a very odd thing that I, an old woman of eighty and upwards, sitting alone, feel myself ashamed to read a book which, sixty years ago, I have heard read aloud for the amusement of large circles, consisting of the first and most creditable society in London!" There can be no doubt that at the time referred to by Mrs. Keith, Tristram Shandy,* Tom Jones, Humphrey Clinker, etc., were on the drawing-room tables of ladies whose grandchildren or great-grandchildren never saw them, or would not acknowledge it if they *had* seen them. But authors not inferior to Sterne, Fielding, or Smollet, are now popular, and who can describe the scenes of human life with as much force and humour, and yet there is nothing in their pages which need offend the taste of the most refined, or shock the feelings of the most pure. This is a change where there is also great improvement. It indicates not merely a better moral perception in authors themselves, but it is itself a homage to the improved spirit of the age. We will hope that, with an improved exterior, there is improvement in society within. If the feelings shrink from what is coarse in expression, we may hope that vice has, in some sort, lost attraction. At any rate, from what we discern

* Sterne, in one of his letters, describes his reading Tristram Shandy to his wife and daughter—his daughter copying from his dictation, and Mrs. Sterne sitting by and listening whilst she worked. In the life of Sterne, it is recorded that he used to carry about in his pocket a volume of this same work, and read it aloud when he went into company. Admirable reading for the church dignitary, the prebendary of York! How well adapted to the hours of social intercourse with friends! How fitted for domestic seclusion with his family!

around us, we hope favourably for the general improvement of mankind, and of our own beloved country in particular. If Scotland, in parting with her rich and racy dialect, her odd and eccentric characters, is to lose something in quaint humour and good stories, we will hope she may grow and strengthen in *better* things—good as those are which she loses. However this may be, I feel quite assured that the examples which I have now given of Scottish expressions, Scottish modes and habits of life, and Scottish anecdotes, which belong in a great measure to the past, and yet which are remembered as having a place in the present century, must carry conviction that great changes have taken place in the Scottish social circle. There were some things belonging to our country which we must all have desired should be changed. There were others which we could only see changed with regret and sorrow. The hardy and simple habits of Scotsmen of many past generations,—their industry, economy, and integrity, which made them take so high a place in the estimation and the confidence of the people amongst whom they dwelt in all countries of the world. The intelligence and superior education of her mechanics and her peasantry, combined with a strict moral and religious demeanour, fully justified the praise of Burns when he described the humble, though sublime piety of the "Cottar's Saturday Night," and we can well appreciate the testimony which he bore to the hallowed power and sacred influences of the devotional exercises of his boyhood's home, when he penned the immortal words :—

> "From scenes like these old Scotia's grandeur springs,
> That makes her loved at home, revered abroad."

These things, we hope and trust, under the Divine blessing, will never change, except to increase, and will never become a question of reminiscences for the past. If Scotland has lost much of the quaint and original character of former lawyers, lairds and old ladies, much of the pungent wit and dry humour of sayings in her native dialect, she can afford to sustain the loss if she gain in refinement, and lose not the more solid qualities and more valuable characteristics by which she has been distinguished. If peculiarities of former days are partially becoming obsolete, let them at least be preserved. Let our younger contemporaries, let those who are to come, know something of them from history, as we elders have known something of them from experience. The humour and the point cannot all be lost in their being recorded, although they may lose much. I still hope to see this carried on further by others, as I am convinced great additions could be made to these reminiscences, which I have endeavoured to preserve. Changes of this nature in the habits and language of a nation are extremely interesting, and it is most desirable that we should have them recorded as well as those greater changes and revolutions which it is the more immediate object of history to enrol amongst her annals. And, whether the changes of which we are now treating mark the deterioration or improvement of manners, useful lessons and important moral conclusions may be drawn from these narratives of the past. Causes are at work which must ere long produce still greater changes, and it is impossible to foresee what will be the future picture of Scottish life, as it will probably be now becoming every year less and less distinguished from the rest of the world. But if there shall be little to mark our national peculiarities in the time to come, we cannot be deprived of our reminiscences of the *past.* I am interested in everything which is Scottish. I consider it an honour to have been born a Scotchman. And I make no secret in acknowledging that I take pride in my family and ancestral Scottish associations. One fair excuse I have to offer for entertaining a proud feeling on the subject, one proof I can adduce, that a Scottish lineage is considered a legitimate source of self-congratulation, and that is the fact that I never in my life knew an English or Irish family with Scottish relations, where the members did not refer with much complacency to such connection.

I seem to linger over these Reminiscences as if unwilling to part for ever with the remnants of our past national social history. But I will crave permission to add in parting the following anecdotes :—The first of them I had received long ago, but I delayed its introduction till this time, because some reasons existed against bringing it forward, which have only lately been removed. It should be preserved—as I know many competent judges consider it as *the* choice specimen of our past Scottish wit and humour. The story is this : The late Sir William Maxwell of Monreith, grandfather of the present baronet, and brother of Jane Duchess of Gordon, was a remarkable specimen of the old Scottish laird—shrewd, humorous, and somewhat rough. The Earl of Galloway of the time had just been appointed Lord-Lieutenant of the county, and Sir William, rather against the grain, had consented to pay his respects to him, and he went over on a Monday morning. The visit passed off smoothly ; but as Sir William was coming away, the Earl said, in a rather patronising tone, "I am very glad to see you, Sir William ; but you are not perhaps aware that I have a day *of my own* for receiving. I set apart Fridays for seeing my county friends, and shall be glad always to see you on that day, whenever you will honour me with a call." Sir William was a good deal nettled at this, as he thought it a hint against his present visit, and answered with some asperity, "My lord, I ken but ae Lord wha has a day o' his ain, and, God forgie me, I dinna keep that day ; but d—— me if I keep yours." The other two I received since these sheets were committed to the press. They were sent to me from Golspie, and are original, as they occurred to my correspondent's own experience. The one is a capital illustration of thrift ; the other of kind feeling for the friendless in the Highland character. I give the anecdotes in my correspondent's own words :—A little boy, some twelve years of age, came to me one day with the following message, "My mother wants a vomit from you, sir; and she bade me say if it will not be strong enough, she will send it back." "O Mr. Begg," said a woman to me, for whom I was weighing two grains of calomel for a child, "dinna be so mean wi' it; it is for a poor faitherless bairn."

In this volume I finally take my leave of "Reminiscences of Scottish Life and Character," not because I think the subject has been exhausted, or that fresh fields of inquiry might not be opened; but having accomplished the particular object I had in view, I would now leave to others to collect further materials for elucidating the manners and habits of our grandfathers. To one at all advanced in years, the retrospect of life is but a melancholy office, and suggests many painful topics for his reflection. The changes which he marks in the world around him, the sad blanks which time has made in his own social circle, remind him very forcibly of the marked uncertainties of an earthly condition; and when, during the same period, he is called upon to notice how greatly manners, customs, and language have themselves been altered, the world in which he now lives seems scarcely the *same* world as that which he can remember. We have been retracing footprints of the past, and I can truly say it is the love of my country which has induced me to dwell so long and so minutely upon certain peculiarities by which I can myself remember it to have been more marked and more distinguished than it is at present. The task, perhaps, will be called a useless one,—the labour to no good end. Why, it may be asked, retain any longer a memory of these national peculiarities? Scotland has become a portion of a great empire; she is not now a separate nation, but has become *part* of a nation more powerful and distinguished than anything recorded in her own past history. She has lost her individuality, and must be satisfied to take that integral position for evermore. It may be so; but this I humbly think offers no reason why we should forget our former national greatness and independence. Scotland *once* formed a distinct kingdom from England, and as we can still point to a remnant of a Regalia which belonged to a separate and independent CROWN, memory will cling to peculiarities which still tell of a separate and independent PEOPLE.

Scotchmen (at least such as are worthy of the name) have always been noted for their love of country. When sojourning in distant lands, recollections of Scotland bring with them something of that *maladie du pays* to Scotchmen, which is said so often to visit the hardy Swiss when in exile—thoughts of his mountain home are brought back to his recollection.

There is something quite touching in the attachment of Scotchmen to the old Scottish ways and remembrances of their early days. No example of this feeling has ever struck me more than the story told of old Lord Balmerino, which is amongst the many touching anecdotes which are traditionary of his unfortunate period. On his return from the trial at Westminster Hall, where he had been condemned to death for his adherence to the Stuart cause, he saw out of the coach window a woman selling the sweet yellow gooseberries which recalled the associations of youth in his native country. "Stop a minute," cried the old scoffer, who knew his days on earth were numbered; "stop a minute, and gie me a ha'porth of *honey blobs*," as if he had gone back in fond recollection to his schoolboy days in the High Street of Edinburgh, when honey blobs had been amongst the pet luxuries of his young life.

Independent of personal feelings, it must always be interesting to mark the features which distinguish one people from another, or to note the causes which are rendering those distinctions less prominent and less striking than they *once* were; and if we are destined soon to lose all indications of a national existence, let us note, ere they vanish, the lingering traces of our past individuality.

We do no wrong surely in cherishing our love for Scotland, or in retaining a deep interest in all that is still left to Scotland. A Scotchman may have his pride and boast in being the countryman of those who won the fields of Agincourt and Cressy, but without losing the deeper recollection of being a descendant of those who fought at Bannockburn and Flodden. His heart will swell when he sees the great and noble of the land pass before him decorated with the blue ribbon and the garter of that ancient order of knighthood, the St. George of England. But does there not spring up a warmer interest when his eye rests upon the green ribbon and the thistle badge of poor Scotland's order of St. Andrew? A Scotchman may pay all due homage to the genius of a Shakspeare, a Milton, a Gibbon, and yet indulge a more home and heartfelt pride in the literary achievements of a Buchanan, a Walter Scott, and a Macaulay. Religious differences cannot quench the national feelings of a Scotchman towards the piety and the stern sincerity of Presbyterian Scotland. Nor will any Scottish Episcopalian—even the most attached to his own form of polity and worship—ever fail to pay his tribute of respect and admiration to the old Scottish elder of a simpler creed, or ever cease to feel a Scotchman's national pride in the stern and unbending piety of men who maintained, at the hazard of life and property, the COVENANT which they had signed with their blood. We feel assured that such feelings and such emotions are, in their tendencies, favourable to the human character.

We have at least the authority of our own Walter Scott in favour of such a sentiment. In the often-quoted passage from the "Lay," how indignantly he makes his aged minstrel spurn the thought of any one with right feelings being utterly indifferent to the name and sympathy of COUNTRY; —in whom are awakened no emotions of pride at a remembrance of its former triumph and its past glories—in whom is no sense of indignation for its wrongs, and no sorrow for its humiliation :—

" Breathes there the man with soul so dead,
Who never to himself hath said,
This is my own, my native land!
Whose heart hath ne'er within him burn'd,
As home his footsteps he hath turn'd,
From wandering on a foreign strand!"

With what deep indignation does he mark this character, in whomsoever it may be found, and with whatever rank or fortune allied !—

" If such there breathe, go, mark him well;
For him no minstrel raptures swell;
High though his titles, proud his name,
Boundless his wealth as wish can claim;
Despite those titles, power, and pelf,
The wretch, concentered all in self,
Living, shall forfeit fair renown,
And, doubly dying, shall go down
To the vile dust, from whence he sprung,
Unwept, unhonour'd, and unsung."

Such language as this, it may perhaps be said, is to be judged of rather as an effusion of poetical enthusiasm than as a deliberate judgment, or as belonging to the business of real life. It should be remembered, however, that genuine poetry will ever draw its best appeals and noblest inspirations from the *realities* of human existence. Scott was a true poet; but no man took more sagacious views of life and character. He holds up patriotism as a virtue and excellence of our nature, and as leading men to right feelings and lofty sentiments. And he was right.

Love of country *must* draw forth good feeling in men's minds, as it will tend to make them cherish a desire for its welfare and improvement. To claim kindred with the honourable and high-minded, as in some degree allied with them, must imply at least an *appreciation* of great and good qualities. Whatever, then, supplies men with a motive for following upright and noble conduct

—whatever advances in them a kindly benevolence towards fellow-countrymen in distress, *must* have a beneficial effect upon the hearts and intellects of a Christian people —and these objects are, I think, all more or less fostered and encouraged under the influence of that patriotic spirit which identifies national honour and national happiness with its own.

This is surely a spirit to be cultivated in a world like this;—in a world where we find so many causes arising that produce bitter animosities and violent contentions: —in a world where we find even the stronger ties of natural affection broken amidst the jealousies and alienations of men's hearts.

The love of country, then, we would advocate, not as a matter of pride or as a mere sentiment, but as a *principle*, of which the tendencies are decidedly favourable to benevolent and virtuous emotions. We have no hesitation in advocating the cause, even at the risk of incurring thereby the charge of being "*national*," which this declaration may bring upon us. Feelings connected with such national predilections towards our countrymen may be, I think, more fully called forth when Scotchmen meet Scotchmen in places far separate from their own homes. In distant lands, and in colonial settlements, Scotchmen will naturally draw together. Natives of the same glen or of the same town must, in every quarter of the world, have a bond to bring them into friendly relations, as they would have common objects of kindly retrospection and of tender memories. Even at school, I recollect it was always reckoned a cause for boys being friends, that they "*knew each other at home*." I should indeed be rejoiced to think that these "Reminiscences" had, in any circumstances, fostered and encouraged such mutual good feelings, and such healthful mutual considerations amongst Scotchmen, when they had met far from their Fatherland. It would be a full reward were the author to be assured that in any case his representations of "Scottish Life and Cha racter" had helped to procure for a poor, a suffering, or a sorrowful Scotchman, one act of kindness, one visit of sympathy or consolation, from a countryman.

There is one point connected with the publication of these Reminiscences, on which, although of an entirely personal nature, I am desirous, before closing the volume, of saying a few words. There may be persons who do *not* sympathise with my great desire to preserve and to record these specimens of Scottish humour; indeed, I have reason to suspect that some have been disposed to consider the time and attention which I have given to the subject as ill-bestowed, and perhaps even as somewhat unsuitable to one of my advanced age and sacred profession. If any persons really think so, all I would say is, I cannot agree with them. National peculiarities must ever form an interesting and improving study, inasmuch as it is a study of human nature; and the anecdotes of this volume not only illustrate features of the Scottish mind, which, as moral and religious traits of nature, are deeply interesting, but are marks of character which are fast fading from our view. I desire to preserve peculiarities which I think should be recorded because they are national, and because they are Reminiscences of genuine Scottish Life and Character. No doubt these peculiarities have been deeply tinged with the quaint and quiet humour which is more strictly characteristic of our countrymen than their wit. And, as exponents of that *humour*, our stories may often have excited some harmless merriment in those who have appreciated the real fun of the dry Scottish character. That, I trust, is no offence. I should never be sorry to think that, within the "limits of becoming mirth," I had contributed, in however small a degree, to the entertainment and recreation of my countrymen. I am convinced that every one, whether Clergyman or Layman, who adds something to the innocent enjoyment of human life, has joined in a good work, inasmuch as he has diminished the inducement to *vicious* indulgence. God knows there is enough of sin and of sorrow in the world to make sad the heart of every Christian man. No one, I think, need be ashamed of having sought to cheer the darker hours of his fellow travellers' steps through life, or to beguile their hearts, when weary and heavy-laden, into cheerful and amusing trains of thought. So far as my experience of life goes, I have never found that the cause of morality and religion was promoted by sternly checking all tendencies of our nature to relaxation and amusement. If mankind be too ready to enter upon pleasures which are dangerous or questionable, it is the part of wisdom and of benevolence to supply them with sources of interest, the enjoyment of which is innocent and permissible.

It would be affectation to disclaim having been deeply gratified by the favourable reception which has for so long a time been given to these Reminiscences both at home and in all countries where Scotchmen are to be found. It has been very pleasant for the author to think that there were times in which this little work may have cheered the hour of depression or of sickness—that even for a few moments it may have beguiled the pressure of corroding care and worldly anxiety. He has been desirous of saying a word in favour of old Scottish life; and with some minds, perhaps, the book may have promoted a more kindly feeling towards hearts and heads of bygone days. And certainly the author of this work can truly say that his highest reward—his greatest honour and gratification —would spring from the feeling that it had become a standard volume in Scottish cottage libraries, and that by the firesides of Scotland his pages had become as "household words."

INDEX.

88 Princes Street,
Edinburgh, March 15, 1871.

EDMONSTON & DOUGLAS'
LIST OF WORKS

——oOo——

The Culture and Discipline of the Mind, and other Essays
By JOHN ABERCROMBIE, M.D. New Edition. Fcap. 8vo, cloth, 3s. 6d.

Wanderings of a Naturalist in India,
The Western Himalayas, and Cashmere. By Dr. A. L. ADAMS of the 22d Regiment. 8vo, with Illustrations, price 10s. 6d.

"The author need be under no apprehension of wearying his readers. . . He prominently combines the sportsman with the naturalist."—*Sporting Review.*

Notes of a Naturalist in the Nile Valley and Malta.
By ANDREW LEITH ADAMS. Author of "Wanderings of a Naturalist in India." Crown 8vo, with Illustrations, price 15s.

"Most attractively instructive to the general reader."—*Bell's Messenger.*

Alexandra Feodorowna, late Empress of Russia.
By A. TH. VON GRIMM, translated by Lady Wallace. 2 vols. 8vo, with Portraits, price 21s.

"Contains an amount of information concerning Russian affairs and Russian society."—*Morning Post.*

Always in the Way.
By the author of 'The Tommiebeg Shootings.' 12mo, price 1s. 6d.

The Malformations, Diseases, and Injuries of the Fingers
and Toes, and their Surgical Treatment. By THOMAS ANNANDALE, F.R.C.S., 8vo, with Illustrations, price 10s. 6d.

Odal Rights and Feudal Wrongs.
A Memorial for Orkney. By DAVID BALFOUR of Balfour and Trenaby. 8vo, price 6s.

Sermons by the late James Bannerman, D.D., Professor of
Apologetics and Pastoral Theology, New College, Edinburgh. In 1 vol., extra fcap. 8vo, price 5s.

The Life, Character, and Writings of Benjamin Bell,
F.R.C.S.E., F.R.S.E. Author of a 'System of Surgery,' and other Works. By his Grandson, BENJAMIN BELL, F.R.C.S.E. Fcap. 8vo, price 3s. 6d.

The Holy Grail. An Inquiry into the Origin and Signifi-
cation of the Romances of the San Grëal. By Dr. F. G. BERGMANN. Fcap. 8vo, price 1s. 6d.

"Contains, in a short space, a carefully-expressed account of "the romances of chivalry, which compose what has been called the Epic cycle of the San Greal."—*Athenæum.*

Homer and the Iliad.
In Three Parts. By JOHN STUART BLACKIE, Professor of Greek in the University of Edinburgh. 4 vols. demy 8vo, price 42s.

By the same Author.

On Democracy.
Sixth Edition, price 1s.

Musa Burschicosa.
A Book of Songs for Students and University Men. Fcap. 8vo, price 2s. 6d.

War Songs of the Germans, translated, with the Music, and
Historical Illustrations of the Liberation War and the Rhine Boundary Question. Fcap. 8vo, price 2s. 6d. cloth, 2s. paper. *Dedicated to Thomas Carlyle.*

On Greek Pronunciation.
Demy 8vo, 3s. 6d.

Political Tracts.
No. 1. GOVERNMENT. No. 2. EDUCATION. Price 1s. each.

On Beauty.
Crown 8vo, cloth, 8s. 6d.

Lyrical Poems.
Crown 8vo, cloth, 7s. 6d.

The New Picture Book.
Pictorial Lessons on Form, Comparison, and Number, for Children under Seven Years of Age. With Explanations by NICHOLAS BOHNY. Fifth Edition 36 oblong folio coloured Illustrations. Price 7s. 6d.

The Home Life of Sir David Brewster.
By his daughter, Mrs. GORDON. 2d Edition. Crown 8vo, price 6s.

"With his own countrymen it is sure of a welcome, and to the *savants* of Europe, and of the New World, it will have a real and special interest of its own. —*Pall Mall Gazette.*

France under Richelieu and Colbert.
By J. H. BRIDGES, M.B Small 8vo, price 8s. 6d.

Works by John Brown, M.D., F.R.S.E.

LOCKE AND SYDENHAM. Extra fcap. 8vo, price 7s. 6d.

HORÆ SUBSECIVÆ. Sixth Edition. Extra fcap. 8vo, price 7s. 6d.

LETTER TO THE REV. JOHN CAIRNS, D.D. Second Edition, crown 8vo, sewed, 2s.

ARTHUR H. HALLAM; Extracted from 'Horæ Subsecivæ.' Fcap. sewed, 2s.; cloth, 2s. 6d.

RAB AND HIS FRIENDS; Extracted from 'Horæ Subsecivæ.' Forty-sixth thousand. Fcap. sewed, 6d.

MARJORIE FLEMING: A Sketch. Fifteenth thousand. Fcap. sewed, 6d.

OUR DOGS; Extracted from 'Horæ Subsecivæ.' Nineteenth thousand. Fcap. sewed, 6d.

RAB AND HIS FRIENDS. With Illustrations by Sir George Harvey, R.S.A., Sir J. Noel Paton, R.S.A., and J. B. New Edition, small quarto, cloth, price 3s. 6d.

"WITH BRAINS, SIR;" Extracted from 'Horæ Subsecivæ.' Fcap. sewed, 6d.

MINCHMOOR. Fcap. sewed, 6d.

JEEMS THE DOORKEEPER: A Lay Sermon. Price 6d.

THE ENTERKIN. Price 6d.

Memoirs of John Brown, D.D.

By the Rev. J. CAIRNS, D.D., Berwick, with Supplementary Chapter by his Son JOHN BROWN, M.D. Fcap. 8vo, cloth, 9s. 6d.

The Biography of Samson

Illustrated and Applied. By the REV. JOHN BRUCE, D.D., Minister of Free St. Andrew's Church, Edinburgh. Second Edition. 18mo, cloth, 2s.

The Life of Gideon.

By Rev. JOHN BRUCE, D.D., Free St. Andrew's Church, Edinburgh. 1 vol. fcap. 8vo, price 5s.

"We commend this able and admirable volume to the cordial acceptance of our readers.—*Daily Review.*

Tragic Dramas from History.

By ROBERT BUCHANAN, M.A., late Professor of Logic and Rhetoric in the University of Glasgow. 2 vols. fcap. 8vo, price 12s.

By the Loch and River Side.

Forty Graphic Illustrations by a New Hand. Oblong folio, handsomely bound, 21s.

The De Oratore of Cicero.

Translated by F. B. CALVERT, M.A. Crown 8vo, price 7s. 6d.

My Indian Journal,

Containing descriptions of the principal Field Sports of India, with Notes on the Natural History and Habits of the Wild Animals of the Country. By COLONEL WALTER CAMPBELL, author of 'The Old Forest Ranger.' 8vo, with Illustrations, price 16s.

Popular Tales of the West Highlands,

Orally Collected, with a translation by J. F. CAMPBELL. 4 vols. extra fcap. cloth, 32s

Inaugural Address at Edinburgh,

April 2, 1866, by THOMAS CARLYLE on being Installed as Rector of the University there. Price 1s.

On the Constitution of Papal Conclaves.

By W. C. CARTWRIGHT, M.P. Fcap. 8vo, price 6s. 6d.

A book which will, we believe, charm careful students of history, while it will dissipate much of the ignorance which in this country surrounds the subject. —*Spectator.*

Gustave Bergenroth. A Memorial Sketch.

By W. C. CARTWRIGHT, M.P. Author of "The Constitution of Papal Conclaves." Crown 8vo, price 7s. 6d.

"To those who knew this accomplished student, Mr. Cartwright's enthusiastic memoirs will be very welcome.—*Standard.*

Life and Works of Rev. Thomas Chalmers, D.D., LL.D.

MEMOIRS OF THE REV. THOMAS CHALMERS. By REV. W. HANNA, D.D., LL.D. 4 vols., 8vo, cloth, £2 : 2s.

—— Cheap Edition, 2 vols., crown 8vo, cloth, 12s.

POSTHUMOUS WORKS, 9 vols., 8vo—

Daily Scripture Readings, 3 vols., £1 : 11 : 6. Sabbath Scripture Readings, 2 vols., £1 : 1s. Sermons, 1 vol., 10s. 6d. Institutes of Theology, 2 vols., £1 : 1s. Prelections on Butler's Analogy, etc., 1 vol., 10s. 6d.

Sabbath Scripture Readings. Cheap Edition, 2 vols., crown 8vo, 10s.

Daily Scripture Readings. Cheap Edition, 2 vols., crown 8vo, 10s.

ASTRONOMICAL DISCOURSES, 1s. COMMERCIAL DISCOURSES, 1s.

SELECT WORKS, in 12 vols., crown 8vo, cloth, per vol., 6s.

Lectures on the Romans, 2 vols. Sermons, 2 vols. Natural Theology, Lectures on Butler's Analogy, etc., 1 vol. Christian Evidences, Lectures on Paley's Evidences, etc., 1 vol. Institutes of Theology, 2 vols. Political Economy; with Cognate Essays, 1 vol. Polity of a Nation, 1 vol. Church and College Establishments, 1 vol. Moral Philosophy, Introductory Essays, Index, etc., 1 vol.

Characteristics of Old Church Architecture, etc.,

In the Mainland and Western Islands of Scotland. 4to, with Illustrations, price 25s.

Dainty Dishes.

Receipts collected by LADY HARRIETT ST. CLAIR. New Edition, with many new Receipts. Crown 8vo. Price 5s.

"Well worth buying, especially by that class of persons who, though their incomes are small, enjoy out-of-the-way and recherché delicacies."—*Times.*

The Constitution Violated.

An Essay by the Author of "The Memoir of John Grey of Dilston," dedicated to the Working Men and Women of Great Britain. Crown 8vo, 3s. 6d.

Sir John Duke Coleridge's

Inaugural Address at Edinburgh Philosophical Institution, Session 1870-71. 8vo, price 1s.

Wild Men and Wild Beasts—Adventures in Camp and

Jungle By LIEUT.-COLONEL GORDON CUMMING. Demy 4to, with Illustrations by Lieut.-Col. BAIGRIE.

Notes on the Natural History of the Strait of Magellan and West Coast of Patagonia, made during the voyage of H.M.S. 'Nassau' in the years 1866, 1867, 1868, and 1869. By ROBERT O. CUNNINGHAM, M.D., F.R.S., Naturalist to the Expedition. With Maps and numerous Illustrations. 8vo, price 15s.

The Annals of the University of Edinburgh.
By ANDREW DALZEL, formerly Professor of Greek in the University of Edinburgh; with a Memoir of the Compiler, and Portrait after Raeburn. 2 vols. demy 8vo, price 21s.

Gisli the Outlaw.
From the Icelandic. By G. W. DASENT, D.C.L. Small 4to, with Illustrations, price 7s. 6d.

The Story of Burnt Njal;
Or, Life in Iceland at the end of the Tenth Century. From the Icelandic of the Njals Saga. By GEORGE WEBBE DASENT, D.C.L. 2 vols. 8vo, with Map and Plans, price 28s.

Select Popular Tales from the Norse.
For the use of Young People. By G. W. DASENT, D.C.L. New Edition, with Illustrations. Crown 8vo, 6s.

Plates and Notes relating to some Special Features in Structures called Pyramids. By ST. JOHN VINCENT DAY, C.E., F.R.SS.A. Royal folio, price 28s.

Papers on the Great Pyramid.
By ST. JOHN VINCENT DAY, C.E., F.R.SS.A. 8vo, price 4s.

The Law of Railways applicable to Scotland, with an Appendix of Statutes and Forms. By FRANCIS DEAS, M.A., L.L.B., Advocate, Demy 8vo.

On the Application of Sulphurous Acid Gas
to the Prevention, Limitation, and Cure of Contagious Diseases. By JAMES DEWAR, M.D. Thirteenth edition, price 1s.

Memoir of Thomas Drummond, R.E., F.R.A.S., Under-Secretary to the Lord-Lieutenant of Ireland, 1835 to 1840. By JOHN F. M'LENNAN, Advocate. 8vo, price 15s.

"A clear, compact, and well-written memoir of the best friend England ever gave to Ireland."—*Examiner.*

A Political Survey.
By MOUNTSTUART E. GRANT DUFF, Member for the Elgin District of Burghs; Author of "Studies in European Politics," "A Glance over Europe," &c. &c. 8vo, price 7s. 6d.

"In following up his 'Studies in European Politics' by the 'Political Survey' here before us, Mr. Grant Duff has given strong evidence of the wisdom of the choice made by the Ministry in appointing him Under-Secretary for India. In the space of about 240 pages, he gives us the cream of the latest information about the internal politics of no less than forty-four different countries under four heads, according to their situation in Europe, Asia, and Africa, Northern and Central America, or South America."—*Pall Mall Gazette.*

By the same Author.

A Glance over Europe. Price 1s.

Inaugural Address to the University of Aberdeen, on his Installation as Rector. Price 1s.

East India Financial Statement, 1869. Price 1s.

Remarks on the Present Political Situation.
A Speech delivered at Elgin, Nov. 15, 1870. Price 1s.

Veterinary Medicines; their Actions and Uses.
By FINLAY DUN. Third Edition, revised and enlarged. 8vo, price 12s.

Social Life in Former Days;
Chiefly in the Province of Moray. Illustrated by letters and family papers. By E. DUNBAR DUNBAR, late Captain 21st Fusiliers. 2 vols. demy 8vo, price 19s. 6d.

Deep-Sea Soundings.
COLLOQUIA PERIPATETICA. By the late JOHN DUNCAN, LL.D., Professor of Hebrew in the New College, Edinburgh; being Conversations in Philosophy, Theology, and Religion. Second Edition. 1 vol. fcap. 8vo. Price 3s. 6d.

"The present volume, if nothing more of Dr. Duncan's wonderful talk than what its pages contain were ever to emerge, would yet be an adequate monument to the deceased, and a gift of the highest value to our speculative literature."—*Daily Review.*

Karl's Legacy.
By the REV. J. W. EBSWORTH. 2 vols. ex. fcap. 8vo. Price 6s. 6d.

Charlie and Ernest; or, Play and Work.
A Story of Hazlehurst School, with Four Illustrations by J. D. By M. BETHAM EDWARDS. Royal 16mo, 3s. 6d.

A Memoir of the Right Honourable Hugh Elliot.
By his Granddaughter, the COUNTESS of MINTO. 8vo, price 12s.

"Lady Minto produced a valuable memoir when she printed the substance of the work before us for private circulation in 1862. It now, in its completed shape, presents a full length and striking portrait of a remarkable member of a remarkable race."—*Quarterly Review.*

The Unconditional Freeness of the Gospel.
New Edition revised. By the late THOMAS ERSKINE of Linlathen. 1 vol. fcap. 8vo. Price 3s. 6d.

By the same Author.

The Purpose of God in the Creation of Man.
Fcap. 8vo, sewed. Price 6d

Good Little Hearts.

By AUNT FANNY. Author of the "Night-Cap Series." 4 vols. in a box, price 6s.

L'Histoire d'Angleterre. Par M. LAMÉ FLEURY. 18mo, cloth, 2s. 6d.

L'Histoire de France. Par M. LAMÉ FLEURY. 18mo, cloth, 2s. 6d.

Christianity viewed in some of its Leading Aspects.

By REV. A. L. R. FOOTE, Author of 'Incidents in the Life of our Saviour.' Fcap., cloth, 3s.

Kalendars of Scottish Saints, with Personal Notices of those of Alba. By ALEXANDER PENROSE FORBES, D.C.L., Bishop of Brechin. 1 vol. 4to. Price to *Subscribers only*, Two Guineas. Large paper copies, Four Guineas.

Frost and Fire;

Natural Engines, Tool-Marks, and Chips, with Sketches drawn at Home and Abroad by a Traveller. Re-issue, containing an additional Chapter. 2 vols. 8vo, with Maps and numerous Illustrations on Wood, price 21s.

"A very Turner among books, in the originality and delicious freshness of its style, and the truth and delicacy of the descriptive portions. For some four-and-twenty years he has traversed half our northern hemisphere by the least frequented paths; and everywhere, with artistic and philosophic eye, has found something to describe—here in tiny trout-stream or fleecy cloud, there in lava-flow or ocean current, or in the works of nature's giant sculptor—ice."—*Reader.*

The Cat's Pilgrimage.

By J. A. FROUDE, M.A., late Fellow of Exeter College, Oxford. With 7 full-page Illustrations by MRS. BLACKBURN (J. B.). 4to, price 6s.

Gifts for Men. By X. H.

1. The Gift of Repentance.
2. The Gift of the Yoke.
3. The Gift of the Holy Ghost.
4. The Promise to the Elect.

Crown 8vo, price 6s.

"Written in a very Christian spirit, and with much skill, originality, and fervour."—*Publisher's Circular.*

Arthurian Localities: their Historical Origin, Chief Country, and Fingalian Relations, with a Map of Arthurian Scotland. By JOHN G. S. STUART GLENNIE, M.A. 8vo, price 7s. 6d.

Works by Margaret Maria Gordon (nee Brewster).

LADY ELINOR MORDAUNT; or, Sunbeams in the Castle. Crown 8vo, cloth, 9s.

WORK; or, Plenty to do and How to do it. Thirty-fifth thousand. Fcap. 8vo, cloth, 2s. 6d.

LITTLE MILLIE AND HER FOUR PLACES. Cheap Edition. Fifty-third thousand. Limp cloth, 1s.

SUNBEAMS IN THE COTTAGE; or, What Women may do. A narrative chiefly addressed to the Working Classes. Cheap Edition. Forty-third thousand. Limp cloth, 1s.

PREVENTION; or, An Appeal to Economy and Common-Sense. 8vo, 6d.

THE WORD AND THE WORLD. Price 2d.

LEAVES OF HEALING FOR THE SICK AND SORROWFUL. Fcap. 4to, cloth, 3s. 6d. Cheap Edition, limp cloth, 2s.

THE MOTHERLESS BOY; with an Illustration by J. NOEL PATON, R.S.A. Cheap Edition, limp cloth, 1s.

"Alike in manner and matter calculated to attract youthful attention, and to attract it by the best of all means—sympathy."—*Scotsman.*

'Christopher North;'

A Memoir of John Wilson, late Professor of Moral Philosophy in the University of Edinburgh. Compiled from Family Papers and other sources, by his daughter, MRS. GORDON. Third Thousand. 2 vols. crown 8vo, price 24s., with Portrait, and graphic Illustrations.

'Mystifications.'

By Miss STIRLING GRAHAM. Fourth Edition. Edited by JOHN BROWN, M.D. With Portrait of Lady Pitlyal. Fcap. 8vo., price 3s. 6d.

Life of Father Lacordaire.

By DORA GREENWELL. Fcap. 8vo. Price 6s.

"She has done a great service in bringing before the English public the career of a great man whose biography they might have refused to read if written by a Roman Catholic."—*Church Times.*

Scenes from the Life of Jesus.

By SAMUEL GREG. Second Edition, enlarged. Ex. fcap. 8vo, price 3s. 6d.

"One of the few theological works which can be heartily commended to all classes."—*Inverness Courier.*

Arboriculture; or A Practical Treatise on Raising and

Managing Forest Trees, and on the Profitable Extension of the Woods and Forests of Great Britain. By JOHN GRIGOR, The Nurseries, Forres. 8vo, price 10s. 6d.

"He is a writer whose authorship has this weighty recommendation, that he can support his theories by facts, and can point to lands, worth less than a shilling an acre when he found them, now covered with ornamental plantations, and yielding through them a revenue equal to that of the finest corn-land in the country. His book has interest both for the adept and the novice, for the large proprietor and him that has but a nook or corner to plant out."—*Saturday Review.*

"Mr. Grigor's practical information on all points on which an intending planter is interested is particularly good. . . . We have placed it on our shelves as a first-class book of reference on all points relating to Arboriculture; and we strongly recommend others to do the same."—*Farmer.*

An Ecclesiastical History of Scotland,

From the Introduction of Christianity to the Present Time. By GEORGE GRUB, A.M. 4 vols. 8vo, 42s. Fine Paper Copies, 52s. 6d.

Chronicle of Gudrun;

A Story of the North Sea. From the mediæval German. By EMMA LETHERBROW. With frontispiece by J. NOEL PATON, R.S.A. New Edition, price 5s.

Notes on the Early History of the Royal Scottish Academy

By Sir GEORGE HARVEY, Kt., P.R.S.A. 8vo, price 3s. 6d.

The Life of our Lord.

By the REV. WILLIAM HANNA, D.D., LL.D. 6 vols., handsomely bound in cloth extra, gilt edges, price 30s.

Separate vols., plain cloth, price 5s. each.

1. THE EARLIER YEARS OF OUR LORD. 8th Thousand.
2. THE MINISTRY IN GALILEE. Second Edition.
3. THE CLOSE OF THE MINISTRY. 6th Thousand.
4. THE PASSION WEEK. 5th Thousand.
5. THE LAST DAY OF OUR LORD'S PASSION. 47th Thousand.
6. THE FORTY DAYS AFTER THE RESURRECTION. 9th Thousand.

Heavenly Love and Earthly Echoes.

By a Glasgow Merchant. 2d Edition. 18mo, price 1s. 6d.

"We have read this volume with unmingled satisfaction. We very cordially recommend it, as one much fitted to commend religion to the young, to cheer and help the tempted and desponding, and indeed to have a wholesome influence on the minds and hearts of all."—*Original Secession Magazine.*

Herminius.

A Romance. By I. E. S. Fcap. 8vo, price 6s.

The Historians of Scotland.

An Annual Payment of £1 will entitle the Subscriber to Two volumes. *Price to Non-Subscribers, 15s. per volume.*

In Preparation.

1. Scoticronicon of John de Fordun, from a contemporary

MS. at the end of the Fourteenth century, preserved in the Library at Wolfenbüttel, in the Duchy of Brunswick; collated with other known MSS. of the original chronicle. Edited by Mr. WILLIAM F. SKENE. In 2 vols. demy 8vo.

2. The Metrical Chronicle of Andrew of Wyntoun, Prior of

St. Serf's Inch in Lochleven, who died about 1426. The work now printed entire for the first time, from the Royal MS. in the British Museum, collated with other MSS. Edited by Mr. DAVID LAING. In demy 8vo.

If the Gospel Narratives are Mythical, what then?

Crown 8vo., price 3s. 6d.

"This intensely interesting treatise."—*The Watchman.*

"Many of the author's remarks are extremely beautiful and suggestive, the result of accurate and earnest thought."—*Freeman.*

Sketches of Early Scotch History.

By COSMO INNES, F.S.A., Professor of History in the University of Edinburgh. 1. The Church; its Old Organisation, Parochial and Monastic. 2. Universities. 3. Family History. 8vo, price 16s.

Concerning some Scotch Surnames.

By COSMO INNES, F.S.A., Professor of History in the University of Edinburgh. Small 4to, cloth antique, 5s.

Instructive Picture Books.

Folio, 7s. 6d. each.

"These Volumes are among the most instructive Picture-books we have seen, and we know of none better calculated to excite and gratify the appetite of the young for the knowledge of nature."—*Times.*

I.

The Instructive Picture Book. A few Attractive Lessons from the Natural History of Animals. By ADAM WHITE, late Assistant, Zoological Department, British Museum. With 54 folio coloured Plates. Seventh Edition, containing many new Illustrations by Mrs. BLACKBURN, J. STEWART, GOURLAY STEELL, and others.

II.

The Instructive Picture Book. Lessons from the Vegetable World. By the Author of 'The Heir of Redclyffe,' 'The Herb of the Field,' etc. Arranged by ROBERT M. STARK, Edinburgh. New Edition, with 64 Plates.

III.

Instructive Picture Book. The Geographical Distribution of Animals, in a Series of Pictures for the use of Schools and Families. By the late Dr. GREVILLE. With descriptive letterpress. New Edition, with 60 Plates.

IV.

Pictures of Animal and Vegetable Life in all Lands. 48 Folio Plates.

The History of Scottish Poetry,

From the Middle Ages to the Close of the Seventeenth Century. By the late DAVID IRVING, LL.D. Edited by JOHN AITKEN CARLYLE, M.D. With a Memoir and Glossary. Demy 8vo, 16s.

Sermons by the Rev. John Ker, D.D., Glasgow.

Eighth Edition. Crown 8vo, price 6s.

"This is a very remarkable volume of sermons. And it is no doubt a most favourable symptom of the healthiness of Christian thought among us, that we are so often able to begin a notice with these words.

"We cannot help wishing that such notice more frequently introduced to our readers a volume of Church of England sermons. Still, looking beyond our pale, we rejoice notwithstanding.

"Mr. Ker has dug boldly and diligently into the vein which Robertson opened; but the result, as compared with that of the first miner, is as the product of skilled machinery set against that of the vigorous unaided arm. There is no roughness, no sense of labour; all comes smoothly and regularly on the page—one thought evoked out of another. As Robertson strikes the rock with his tool, unlooked-for sparkles tempt him on; the workman exults in his discovery; behind each beautiful, strange thought, there is yet another more strange and beautiful still. Whereas, in this work, every beautiful thought has its way prepared, and every strange thought loses its power of starting by the exquisite harmony of its setting. Robertson's is the glitter of the ore on the bank; Ker's is the uniform shining of the wrought metal. We have not seen a volume of sermons for many a day which will so thoroughly repay both purchase and perusal and re-perusal. And not the least merit of these sermons is, that they are eminently suggestive."—*Contemporary Review.*

"The sermons before us are indeed of no common order; among a host of competitors they occupy a high class—we were about to say the highest class—whether viewed in point of composition, or thought, or treatment.

"He has gone down in the diving-bell of a sound Christian philosophy, to the very depth of his theme, and has brought up treasures of the richest and most *recherché* character, practically showing the truth of his own remarks in the preface, 'that there is no department of thought or action which cannot be touched by that gospel which is the manifold wisdom of God.' These subjects he has exhibited in a style corresponding to their brilliancy and profoundness—terse and telling, elegant and captivating, yet totally unlike the tinsel ornaments laid upon the subject by an elaborate process of manipulation—a style which is the outcome of the sentiment and feelings within, shaping itself in appropriate drapery."—*British and Foreign Evangelical Review.*

Readings in Holy Writ.

By Lord KINLOCH. Fcap. 8vo, price 4s. 6d.

Faith's Jewels.

Presented in Verse, with other devout Verses. By Lord KINLOCH. Ex. fcap. 8vo, price 5s.

The Circle of Christian Doctrine;

A Handbook of Faith, framed out of a Layman's experience. By Lord KINLOCH. Third and Cheaper Edition. Fcap. 8vo, 2s. 6d.

Time's Treasure;

Or, Devout Thoughts for every Day of the Year. Expressed in verse. By Lord KINLOCH. Third and Cheaper Edition. Fcap. 8vo, price 3s. 6d.

Devout Moments.

By Lord KINLOCH. Price 6d.

Studies for Sunday Evening.

By Lord KINLOCH. Second Edition. Fcap. 8vo, price 4s. 6d.

Supplemental Descriptive Catalogue of Ancient Scottish Seals.

By HENRY LAING. 4to, profusely illustrated, price £3 : 3s.

The Philosophy of Ethics:

An Analytical Essay. By SIMON S. LAURIE, A.M. Demy 8vo, price 6s.

Notes, Expository and Critical, on certain British Theories

of Morals. By SIMON S. LAURIE. 8vo, price 6s.

The Reform of the Church of Scotland

In Worship, Government, and Doctrine. By ROBERT LEE, D.D., late Professor of Biblical Criticism in the University of Edinburgh, and Minister of Greyfriars. Part I. Worship. Second Edition, fcap. 8vo, price 3s.

Historical Records of the Family of Leslie.

From A.D. 1067 to 1868-69. Collected from Public Records and Authentic Private Sources. By Colonel CHARLES LESLIE, K.H., of Balquhain. 3 vols. demy 8vo, price 36s.

Life in Normandy;
Sketches of French Fishing, Farming, Cooking, Natural History, and Politics, drawn from Nature. By an English Resident. Third Edition, crown 8vo, price 6s.

A Memoir of Lady Anna Mackenzie,
Countess of Balcarres, and afterwards of Argyle, 1621-1706. By ALEXANDER LORD LINDSAY. Fcap. 8vo, price 3s. 6d

"All who love the byways of history, should read this life of a loyal covenanter." —*Atlas.*

Little Ella and the Fire-King,
And other Fairy Tales. By M. W., with Illustrations by Henry Warren. Second Edition. 16mo, cloth, 3s. 6d. Cloth extra, gilt edges, 4s.

Literary Relics of the late A. S. Logan, Advocate, Sheriff of Forfarshire. Extra fcap. 8vo, price 3s. 6d.

Specimens of Ancient Gaelic Poetry.
Collected between the years 1512 and 1529 by the Rev. JAMES M'GREGOR, Dean of Lismore—illustrative of the Language and Literature of the Scottish Highlands prior to the Sixteenth Century. Edited, with a Translation and Notes, by the Rev. Thomas Maclauchlan. The Introduction and additional Notes by William F. Skene. 8vo, price 12s.

Ten Years North of the Orange River.
A Story of Everyday Life and Work among the South African Tribes, from 1859 to 1869. By JOHN MACKENZIE, of the London Missionary Society. With Map and Illustrations. 1 vol. crown 8vo.

Select Writings: Political, Scientific, Topographical, and Miscellaneous, of the late CHARLES MACLAREN, F.R.S.E., F.G.S., Editor of the *Scotsman.* Edited by Robert Cox, F.S.A., Scot., and James Nicol, F.R.S.E., F.G.S., Professor of Natural History in the University of Aberdeen. With a Memoir and Portrait. 2 vols. crown 8vo, 15s.

Memorials of the Life and Ministry of Charles Calder Mackintosh, D.D. of Tain and Dunoon. Edited, with a Sketch of the Religious History of the Northern Highlands of Scotland, by the Rev. William Taylor, M.A., with Portrait. Crown 8vo, price 6s.

The Americans at Home.
Pen and Ink Sketches of American Men, Manners, and Institutions. By DAVID MACRAE. 2 vols. crown 8vo., price 16s.

"A really good work on America, which deserves to be cordially welcomed. It is replete with racy and original anecdotes, and abounds with realistic pictures of American life and character."—*Westminster Review.*

Macvicar's (J. G., D.D.)
The Philosophy of the Beautiful; price 6s. 6d. First Lines of Science Simplified; price 5s. Inquiry into Human Nature; price 7s. 6d.

Mary Stuart and the Casket Letters.

By J. F. N., with an Introduction by HENRY GLASSFORD BELL. Ex. fcap. 8vo, price 4s. 6d.

Max Havalaar;

Or, The Coffee Auctions of the Dutch Trading Company. By MULTATULI; translated from the original MS. by Baron Nahuys. With Maps, price 14s.

Why the Shoe Pinches.

A contribution to Applied Anatomy. By HERMANN MEYER, M.D., Professor of Anatomy in the University of Zurich. Price 6d.

The Herring:

Its Natural History and National Importance. By JOHN M. MITCHELL. With Six Illustrations, 8vo, price 12s.

The Insane in Private Dwellings.

By ARTHUR MITCHELL, A.M., M.D., Deputy Commissioner in Lunacy for Scotland, etc. 8vo, price 4s. 6d.

Creeds and Churches.

By the REV. SIR HENRY WELLWOOD MONCREIFF, Bart., D.D. Demy 8vo. Price 3s. 6d.

Ancient Pillar-Stones of Scotland:

Their Significance and Bearing on Ethnology. By GEORGE MOORE, M.D. 8vo, price 6s. 6d.

Heroes of Discovery.

By SAMUEL MOSSMAN. Crown 8vo, price 5s.

Political Sketches of the State of Europe—from 1814-1867.

Containing Ernest, Count Münster's Despatches to the Prince Regent from the Congress of Vienna and of Paris. By GEORGE HERBERT, Count Münster. Demy 8vo, price 9s.

Biographical Annals of the Parish of Colinton.

By THOMAS MURRAY, LL.D. Crown 8vo, price 3s. 6d.

History Rescued, in Answer to "History Vindicated," being

a recapitulation of "The Case for the Crown," and the Reviewers Reviewed, *in re* the Wigtown Martyrs. By MARK NAPIER. 8vo, price 5s.

Nightcaps:

A Series of Juvenile Books. By "AUNT FANNY." 6 vols. square 16mo, cloth. In case, price 12s., or separately, 2s. each volume.

1. Baby Nightcaps.	3. Big Nightcaps.	5. Old Nightcaps.
2. Little Nightcaps.	4. New Nightcaps.	6. Fairy Nightcaps.

"Neither a single story nor a batch of tales in a single volume, but a box of six pretty little books of choice fiction is Aunt Fanny's contribution to the new supply of literary toys for the next children's season. Imagine the delight of a little girl who, through the munificence of mamma or godmamma, finds herself possessor of Aunt Fanny's tastefully-decorated box. Conceive the exultation with which, on raising the lid, she discovers that it contains six whole and separate volumes, and then say, you grown-up folk, whose pockets are bursting with florins, whether you do not think that a few of your pieces of white money would be well laid out in purchasing such pleasure for the tiny damsels of your acquaintance, who like to be sent to bed with the fancies of a pleasant story-teller clothing their sleepy heads with nightcaps of dreamy contentment. The only objection we can make to the quality and fashion of Aunt Fanny's Nightcaps is, that some of their joyous notions are more calculated to keep infantile wearers awake all night than to dispose them to slumber. As nightcaps for the daytime, however, they are, one and all, excellent.'—*Athenæum.*

ODDS AND ENDS—*Price 6d. Each.*

Vol. I., in Cloth, price 4s. 6d., containing Nos. 1-10.
Vol. II., Do. do. Nos. 11-19.

1. Sketches of Highland Character.
2. Convicts.
3. Wayside Thoughts.
4. The Enterkin.
5. Wayside Thoughts—Part 2.
6. Penitentiaries and Reformatories.
7. Notes from Paris.
8. Essays by an Old Man.
9. Wayside Thoughts—Part 3.
10. The Influence of the Reformation.
11. The Cattle Plague.
12. Rough Night's Quarters.
13. On the Education of Children.
14. The Stormontfield Experiments.
15. A Tract for the Times.
16. Spain in 1866.
17. The Highland Shepherd.
18. Correlation of Forces.
19. 'Bibliomania.'
20. A Tract on Twigs.
21. Notes on Old Edinburgh.
22. Gold-Diggings in Sutherland.
23. Post-Office Telegraphs.

The Bishop's Walk and The Bishop's Times.

By ORWELL. Fcap. 8vo, price 5s.

Man: Where, Whence, and Whither?

Being a glance at Man in his Natural-History Relations. By DAVID PAGE, LL.D. Fcap. 8vo, price 3s. 6d.

"Cautiously and temperately written."—*Spectator.*

The Great Sulphur Cure.

By ROBERT PAIRMAN, Surgeon. Thirteenth Edition, price 1s.

France: Two Lectures.

By M. PREVOST-PARADOL, of the French Academy. 8vo, price 2s. 6d.

"Should be carefully studied by every one who wishes to know anything about contemporary French History."—*Daily Review.*

Suggestions on Academical Organisation,

With Special Reference to Oxford. By MARK PATTISON, B.D., Rector of Lincoln College, Oxford. Crown 8vo, price 7s. 6d.

Practical Water-Farming.

By WM. PEARD, M.D., LL.D. 1 vol. fcap. 8vo, price 5s.

Memoirs of Frederick Perthes;

Or, Literary, Religious, and Political Life in Germany from 1789 to 1843. By C. T. PERTHES, Professor of Law at Bonn. Crown 8vo, cloth, 6s.

On Primary and Technical Education.

Two Lectures delivered to the Philosophical Institution of Edinburgh. By LYON PLAYFAIR, C.B., M.P. 8vo., price 1s.

Popular Genealogists;

Or, The Art of Pedigree-making. Crown 8vo, price 4s.

The Pyramid and the Bible:

The rectitude of the one in accordance with the truth of the other. By a CLERGYMAN. Ex. fcap. 8vo, price 3s. 6d.

Reminiscences of Scottish Life and Character.

By E. B. RAMSAY, M.A., LL.D., F.R.S.E., Dean of Edinburgh. Nineteenth Edition, price 1s. 6d.

"The Dean of Edinburgh has here produced a book for railway reading of the very first class. The persons (and they are many) who can only under such circumstances devote ten minutes of attention to any page, without the certainty of a dizzy or stupid headache, in every page of this volume will find some poignant anecdote or trait which will last them a good half-hour for after-laughter: one of the pleasantest of human sensations."—*Athenæum.*

*** The original Edition in 2 vols. with Introductions, price 12s., and the Sixteenth Edition in 1 vol. cloth antique, price 5s., may be had.

Recess Studies.

Edited by SIR ALEXANDER GRANT, Bart., LL.D. 8vo, price 12s.

Art Rambles in Shetland.

By JOHN T. REID. Handsome 4to, cloth, profusely Illustrated, price 25s.

"This record of Art Rambles may be classed among the most choice and highly-finished of recent publications of this sort."—*Saturday Review.*

Historical Studies.

By E. WILLIAM ROBERTSON, Author of "Scotland under her Early Kings."

CONTENTS.

1. STANDARDS OF THE PAST.
2. LAND.
3. THE KING'S WIFE.
4. THE KING'S KIN.
5. THE CORONATION OF EDGAR.
6. THE POLICY OF DUNSTAN.

ETC. ETC. ETC. In 1 vol. Demy 8vo.

Scotland under her Early Kings.

A History of the Kingdom to the close of the 13th century. By E. WILLIAM ROBERTSON, in 2 vols. 8vo, cloth, 36s.

Doctor Antonio.

A Tale. By JOHN RUFFINI. Cheap Edition, crown 8vo, boards, 2s. 6d.

Lorenzo Benoni;

Or, Passages in the Life of an Italian. By JOHN RUFFINI. With Illustrations. Crown 8vo, cloth gilt, 5s. Cheap Edition, crown 8vo, boards, 2s. 6d.

The Salmon;

Its History, Position, and Prospects. By ALEX. RUSSEL. 8vo, price 7s. 6d.

Druidism Exhumed. Proving that the Stone Circles of Britain were Druidical Temples. By Rev. JAMES RUST. Fcap. 8vo, price 4s. 6d.

Gowodean:

A Pastoral, by JAMES SALMON. 8vo, price 6s.

Natural History and Sport in Moray.

Collected from the Journals and Letters of the late CHARLES ST. JOHN, Author of 'Wild Sports of the Highlands.' With a short Memoir of the Author. Crown 8vo, price 8s. 6d.

A Handbook of the History of Philosophy.

By Dr. ALBERT SCHWEGLER. Second Edition. Translated and Annotated by J. HUTCHISON STIRLING, LL.D., Author of the 'Secret of Hegel.' Crown 8vo, price 6s.

"Schwegler's is the best possible handbook of the history of philosophy, and there could not possibly be a better translator of it than Dr. Stirling."—*Westminster Review.*

The Scottish Poor-Laws: Examination of their Policy, History, and Practical Action. By SCOTUS. 8vo, price 7s. 6d.

"This book is a magazine of interesting facts and acute observations upon this vitally important subject."—*Scotsman.*

The Roman Poets of the Republic.

By W. Y. SELLAR, M.A., Professor of Humanity in the University of Edinburgh, and formerly Fellow of Oriel College, Oxford. 8vo, price 12s.

Gossip about Letters and Letter-Writers.

By GEORGE SETON, Advocate, M.A., Oxon., F.S.A., Scot. Fcap. 8vo, price 5s.

"A very agreeable little *brochure* which anybody may dip into with satisfaction to while away idle hours." —*Echo.*

'Cakes, Leeks, Puddings, and Potatoes.'

A Lecture on the Nationalities of the United Kingdom. By GEORGE SETON, Advocate, M.A., Oxon, etc. Second Edition. Fcap. 8vo, sewed, price 6d.

Culture and Religion.

By J. C. SHAIRP, Principal of the United College of St. Salvator and St. Leonards, St. Andrews. Fcap. 8vo, price 3s. 6d.

"A wise book, and unlike a great many other wise books, has that carefully-shaded thought and expression which fits Professor Shairp to speak for Culture no less than for Religion."—*Spectator.*

John Keble:

An Essay on the Author of the 'Christian Year.' By J. C. SHAIRP, Principal of the United College of St. Salvator and St. Leonards, St. Andrews. Fcap. 8vo, price 3s.

"It is difficult to praise such a book as it deserves without seeming to exaggerate, and still more difficult to give the reader any fair idea of its beauty and power by mere quotation."—*Watchman.*

"The finest essay in this volume, partly because it is upon the greatest and most definite subject, is the first—Wordsworth. . We have said so much upon this essay that we can only say of the three others, that they are fully worthy to stand beside it."—*Spectator.*

Studies in Poetry and Philosophy.

By J. C. SHAIRP, St. Andrews. 1 vol. fcap. 8vo, price 6s.

On Archaic Sculpturings of Cups and Circles upon Stones

and Rocks in Scotland, England, etc. By Sir J. Y. SIMPSON, Bart., M.D., D.C.L., Vice-President of the Society of Antiquaries of Scotland, etc. etc. 1 vol. small 4to, with Illustrations, price 21s.

Proposal to Stamp out Small-pox and other Contagious

Diseases. By Sir J. Y. SIMPSON, Bart., M.D., D.C.L. Price 1s.

The Four Ancient Books of Wales,

Containing the Cymric Poems attributed to the Bards of the Sixth century. By WILLIAM F. SKENE. With Maps and Facsimiles. 2 vols. 8vo, price 36s.

"Mr. Skene's book will, as a matter of course and necessity, find its place on the tables of all Celtic antiquarians and scholars."—*Archæologia Cambrensis.*

The Coronation Stone.

By WILLIAM F. SKENE. Small 4to. With Illustrations in Photography and Zincography. Price 6s.

The Sermon on the Mount.

By the Rev. WALTER C. SMITH, Author of 'The Bishop's Walk, and other Poems, by Orwell,' and 'Hymns of Christ and Christian Life.' Crown 8vo, price 6s.

Disinfectants and Disinfection.

By Dr. ROBERT ANGUS SMITH. 8vo, price 5s.

"By common consent Dr. Angus Smith has become the first authority in Europe on the subject of Disinfectants. To this subject he has devoted a large portion of his scientific life; and now, in a compact volume of only 138 pages, he has condensed the result of twenty years of patient study. To Sanitary officers, to municipal and parochial authorities, and, indeed, to all who are particularly concerned for the public health and life; and who is not? we sincerely commend Dr. Angus Smith's treatise."—*Chemical News.*

Life and Work at the Great Pyramid.

With a Discussion of the Facts Ascertained. By C. PIAZZI SMYTH, F.R.SS.L. and E., Astronomer-Royal for Scotland. 3 vols. demy 8vo, price 56s.

On the Antiquity of Intellectual Man from a Practical and

Astronomical Point of View. By C. PIAZZI SMYTH, F.R.SS.L. and E., Astronomer-Royal for Scotland. Crown 8vo, price 9s.

An Equal-Surface Projection for Maps of the World, and

its Application to certain Anthropological Questions. By C. PIAZZI SMYTH, F.R.SS.L. & E. Astronomer-Royal for Scotland. 8vo, price 3s.

History Vindicated in the Case of the Wigtown Martyrs.

By the Rev. ARCHIBALD STEWART. Second Edition. 8vo, price 3s. 6d.

Dugald Stewart's Collected Works.

Edited by Sir WILLIAM HAMILTON, Bart. Vols. I. to X. 8vo, cloth, each 12s.

Vol. I.—Dissertation. Vols. II. III. and IV.—Elements of the Philosophy of the Human Mind. Vol. V.—Philosophical Essays. Vols. VI. and VII.—Philosophy of the Active and Moral Powers of Man. Vols. VIII. and IX.—Lectures on Political Economy. Vol. X.—Biographical Memoirs of Adam Smith, LL.D., William Robertson, D.D., and Thomas Reid, D.D.; to which is prefixed a Memoir of Dugald Stewart, with Selections from his Correspondence, by John Veitch, M.A. Supplementary Vol.—Translations of the Passages in Foreign Languages contained in the Collected Works; with General Index.

Jerrold, Tennyson, Macaulay, and other Critical Essays.

By JAMES HUTCHISON STIRLING, LL.D., Author of 'The Secret of Hegel.' 1 vol. fcap. 8vo, price 5s.

"The author of 'The Secret of Hegel' here gives us his opinions of the lives and works of those three great representative Englishmen whose names appear on the title-page of the work before us. Dr. Stirling's opinions are entitled to be heard, and carry great weight with them. He is a lucid and agreeable writer, a profound metaphysician, and by his able translations from the German has proved his grasp of mind and wide acquaintance with philosophical speculation."—*Examiner.*

Christ the Consoler;

Or Scriptures, Hymns, and Prayers for Times of Trouble and Sorrow. Selected and arranged by the Rev. ROBERT HERBERT STORY, Minister of Roseneath. Fcap. 8vo, price 3s. 6d.

Outlines of Scottish Archæology.

By Rev. G. SUTHERLAND. 12mo, sewed, profusely Illustrated, price 1s.

Works by Professor James Syme.

OBSERVATIONS IN CLINICAL SURGERY. Second Edition. 8vo, price 8s. 6d.

STRICTURE OF THE URETHRA, AND FISTULA IN PERINEO. 8vo, 4s. 6d.

TREATISE ON THE EXCISION OF DISEASED JOINTS. 8vo, 5s.

ON DISEASES OF THE RECTUM. 8vo, 4s. 6d.

EXCISION OF THE SCAPULA. 8vo, price 2s. 6d.

The History of English Literature.

By M. H. TAINE. Translated from the French by HENRI VON LAUN. 2 Vols. demy 8vo.

Thermodynamics

By P. G. TAIT, Professor of Natural Philosophy in the University of Edinburgh 1 vol. 8vo, price 5s.

Day-Dreams of a Schoolmaster.
By D'ARCY W. THOMPSON. Second Edition. Fcap. 8vo, price 5s.

Sales Attici:
Or, The Maxims, Witty and Wise, of Athenian Tragic Drama. By D'ARCY WENTWORTH THOMPSON, Professor of Greek in Queen's College, Galway. Fcap. 8vo, price 9s.

Memoir and Correspondence of Mr. Thomson of Banchory.
Edited by Professor SMEATON. Demy 8vo, price 9s.

From Pesth to Brindisi; being Notes of a Tour in the Autumn of 1869 from Pesth to Belgrade, Constantinople, Athens, Corfu, Brindisi, and Naples. By Sir CHARLES TREVELYAN. 8vo, sewed, price 1s.

Twelve Years in China:
By a British Resident. With coloured Illustrations. Second Edition. Crown 8vo, cloth, price 10s. 6d.

Travels by Umbra.
8vo., price 10s. 6d.

Hotch-Pot.
By UMBRA. An Old Dish with New Materials. Fcap. 8vo, price 3s. 6d.

The Merchant's Sermon and other Stories.
By L. B. WALFORD. 18mo, price 1s. 6d.

Memoirs of Alexandra, late Empress of Russia, and Wife of Nicholas I. By M. DE GRIMM. Translated by LADY WALLACE. 2 vols. c own 8vo., price 21s.

Tiny Tales for Little Tots.
With Six Illustrations by WARWICK BROOKES. Square 18mo, price 1s.

What is Sabbath-Breaking?
8vo, price 2s.

Dante's—The Inferno.
Translated line for line by W. P. WILKIE, Advocate. Fcap. 8vo, price 5s.

Life of Dr. John Reid,
Late Chandos Professor of Anatomy and Medicine in the University of St. Andrews. By the late GEORGE WILSON, M.D. Fcap. 8vo, cloth, price 3s.

Researches on Colour-Blindness.
With a Supplement on the danger attending the present system of Railway and Marine Coloured Signals. By the late GEORGE WILSON, M.D. 8vo, 5s.

An Historical Sketch of the French Bar from its Origin to the Present Day. By ARCHIBALD YOUNG, Advocate. Demy 8vo. Price 7s. 6d.

"A useful contribution to our knowledge of the leading French politicians of the present day."—*Saturday Review.*

www.ingramcontent.com/pod-product-compliance
Lightning Source LLC
Chambersburg PA
CBHW021119270326
41929CB00009B/954

* 9 7 8 3 7 4 1 1 0 3 0 9 4 *